Financing Real Estate Investments For Dummies®

Cheat Sheet

Loan Application Checklist

Don't walk into your next application meeting with a loan officer or a lender empty-handed. Make sure you have the following information and documents:

- Your net worth: Assets – Liabilities
- Your debt ratio: Total Monthly Payments ÷ Total Monthly Income
- Previous two months' bank statements
- Previous 30 days' pay stubs
- Previous two years' federal income tax returns with schedules
- Previous two years' W-2s
- Property appraisal or comparative market analysis
- Projected costs of repairs and renovations
- Estimated time to repair and renovate the property to sell or rent it out
- Projected property sales price (for buy-and-sell investments) or cash flow (for buy-and-hold properties): Cash Flow = Monthly Income – Monthly Expenses
- LTV (Loan-to-Value) ratio for the property: Loan Amount ÷ Property's Current Market Value
- Zoning information and information on any plans to rezone
- County and city records related to the property

Pre-Closing Checklist

Every real estate investor has at least one horror story about a closing gone bad. To steer clear of trouble, prepare in advance:

- Obtain and review a copy of the appraisal.
- Review the title commitment.
- Review all closing documents, including the legal description.
- Review a copy of the HUD-1 closing statement.
- Insure the property — get a policy, not just a commitment
- Do a final walk-through on the property.
- Obtain utility final readings and schedule the transfer.
- Review the updated tenant rent roll (rental property only).
- Have your certified funds or wire transfer ready to go.
- Confirm the date, time, and location of closing.

For Dummies: Bestselling Book Ser

D1231352

BESTSELLING
BOOK SERIES

Financing Real Estate Investments For Dummies®

Cheat Sheet

Seller Financing Do's and Don'ts

Even when banks and private lenders turn you down for a loan, you may still be able to obtain financing through the seller by way of a land contract or lease option agreement. To protect yourself, keep the following do's and don'ts in mind:

- **Don't** sign a land contract or lease option agreement without having your attorney examine it first and making sure you understand it fully.

- **Do** beware of the *forfeiture clause* that enables the seller to repossess the property if you fail to honor the terms of the contract.

- **Do** inspect the title carefully to make sure the owner/seller is the rightful (and sole) owner of the property and has no undisclosed liens against the property.

- **Do** obtain a title insurance policy prior to signing any agreement.

- **Do** make sure to record the contract at the county's register of deeds office after you and the seller sign it.

- **Don't** try to hide the transaction from the seller's bank to avoid the due on sale clause; doing so may backfire on you.

- **Do** confirm (before signing) whether any lease option agreement allows you to sublet the property and/or reassign your option to buy it if these are strategies you may want to explore.

Comparing Loan Costs

When choosing between two or more loans, take the following steps to compare costs over the expected life of the loan:

1. **Start with the amount the bank charges you up front in loan origination fees, *discount points* (interest you pay upfront — typically a percentage of the loan — to lower the interest rate), and other fees.**

2. **Multiply the monthly payment times the number of months you plan to pay on the loan.**

3. **Add the two amounts to determine your total payment.**

4. **Total the amount of each payment that goes toward paying the principal of the loan.**

   Your lender can tell you how much of each payment goes toward principal.

5. **Subtract the total you determined in Step 4 from the total in Step 3.**

   The result is the total amount you can expect to pay for the loan over the life of the loan. Check out Chapter 6 for an example.

Wiley, the Wiley Publishing logo, For Dummies, the Dummies Man logo, the For Dummies Bestselling Book Series logo and all related trade dress are trademarks or registered trademarks of John Wiley & Sons, Inc. and/or its affiliates. All other trademarks are property of their respective owners.

Copyright © 2009 Wiley Publishing, Inc. All rights reserved. Item 2233-5.

For more information about Wiley Publishing, call 1-800-762-2974.

For Dummies: Bestselling Book Series for Beginners

Financing Real Estate Investments

FOR DUMMIES®

by Ralph R. Roberts and
Chip Cummings with Joe Kraynak

WILEY

Wiley Publishing, Inc.

Financing Real Estate Investments For Dummies®

Published by
Wiley Publishing, Inc.
111 River St.
Hoboken, NJ 07030-5774
www.wiley.com

WILEY

About the Authors

Ralph R. Roberts, CRS, GRI, is a seasoned professional in all areas of real estate, including buying and selling homes, investing in real estate, and building and managing real estate agent teams. He has been profiled by the Associated Press, CNN, and *Time* magazine, and has done hundreds of radio interviews. He has authored and coauthored several successful titles, including *Flipping Houses For Dummies, Foreclosure Investing For Dummies, Foreclosure Self-Defense For Dummies, Mortgage Myths: 77 Secrets That Will Save You Thousands on Home Financing,* and *Foreclosure Myths: 77 Secrets to Saving Thousands on Distressed Properties!* (John Wiley & Sons); *Protect Yourself Against Real Estate and Mortgage Fraud: Preserving the American Dream of Homeownership* (Kaplan); and *REAL WEALTH by Investing in REAL ESTATE* (Prentice Hall).

To find out more about Ralph Roberts and what he can offer you and your organization as a speaker and coach, visit AboutRalph.com. For details on how to protect yourself and your home from real estate and mortgage fraud, check out Ralph's blog at Flipping Frenzy.com. And don't miss the latest addition to Ralph's family of Web sites and blogs, GetFlipping.com, where Ralph offers additional information and tips on the art of flipping houses and investing in foreclosures and pre-foreclosures. You can contact Ralph by emailing him at RalphRoberts@RalphRoberts.com or calling 586-751-0000.

Chip Cummings, CMC, is a recognized expert in the areas of real estate lending and e-Marketing, and is a Certified Mortgage Consultant with more than 25 years in the mortgage industry and more than a billion dollars in sales volume.

Chip has written hundreds of articles and appeared numerous times on radio, television, and in various magazines including *Entrepreneur, Mortgage Originator, Real Estate Banker/Broker,* and *The Mortgage Press.* He is an experienced professional in all areas of real estate financing, including residential and commercial mortgages, government lending, regulatory and compliance issues. He is past president of the MMBA (Michigan Mortgage Brokers Association), and is a licensed mortgage broker and lender in Michigan.

As an international speaker, he has addressed groups and organizations of all types, and trains thousands of mortgage professionals from around the country every year. Chip is a certified national trainer for continuing education in more than 40 states, and has served as an expert witness in state and federal courts. He is also the author of *ABC's of FHA Lending* and *Stop Selling and Start Listening! – Marketing Strategies That Create Top Producers* (Northwind), *Mortgage Myths: 77 Secrets That Will Save You Thousands on Home Financing, Foreclosure Myths: 77 Secrets to Saving Thousands on Distressed Properties!* and *Cashing In on Pre-foreclosures and Short Sales* (John Wiley & Sons).

Chip lives in Rockford, Michigan with his wife Lisa and three children, Katelyn, CJ, and Joe.

To learn more about Chip Cummings, his many successful products or how he can help your organization as a speaker or business consultant, visit www.ChipCummings.com. To receive a complimentary subscription to his multimedia e-newsletter and online events, check out www.eCoachingClub.com. You can also reach Chip by emailing him at info@ChipCummings.com or by calling 616-977-7900.

Joe Kraynak (joekraynak.com) is a freelance author who has written and coauthored numerous books on topics ranging from slam poetry to computer basics. Joe teamed up with Dr. Candida Fink to write his first book in the *For Dummies* series, *Bipolar Disorder For Dummies,* where he showcased his talent for translating the complexities of a topic into plain-spoken practical advice. He then teamed up with Roberts to write the ultimate guide to flipping houses — *Flipping Houses For Dummies* and delivered encore performances in *Foreclosure Investing For Dummies, Advanced Selling For Dummies*, and *Foreclosure Self-Defense For Dummies.* In *Financing Real Estate Investments For Dummies,* Joe assists Chip and Ralph in delivering the ultimate guide to scoring some cash to fuel your investments in real estate.

Dedication

From Ralph: To real estate investors and professionals who are dedicated to supporting and promoting the American dream of homeownership.

From Chip: To my assistant Debbie Forth who has managed to keep me organized for the last 14 years, and to my wife Lisa who puts up with all the crazy hours and remains my #1 fan.

Authors' Acknowledgments

Thanks to acquisitions editor Lindsay Lefevere, who chose us to author this book and guided us through the tough part of getting started and to our agent, Neil Salkind of StudioB (www.StudioB.com), who ironed out all the preliminary details to make this book possible. Chad Sievers, our project editor, deserves a loud cheer for acting as a very patient collaborator and gifted editor — shuffling chapters back and forth, shepherding the text through production, making sure any technical issues were properly resolved, and serving as the unofficial quality control manager. Megan Knoll, our copy editor, earns an editor of the year award for ferreting out our typos, misspellings, grammatical errors, and other language faux pas-es, in addition to assisting Chad as reader advocate — asking the questions we should have asked ourselves. And, we tip our hats to the production crew for doing such an outstanding job of transforming a loose collection of text and illustrations into such an attractive bound book.

We also wish to express our appreciation to the National Association of Mortgage Brokers, National Association of Realtors®, the Mortgage Bankers Association of America, and the Michigan Mortgage Brokers Association for their support and assistance.

We owe special thanks to our technical editor, Patrick Lecomte, for flagging technical errors in the manuscript, helping guide its content, and offering his own tips, tricks, and insights from the world of real estate financing.

Publisher's Acknowledgments

We're proud of this book; please send us your comments through our Dummies online registration form located at http://dummies.custhelp.com. For other comments, please contact our Customer Care Department within the U.S. at 877-762-2974, outside the U.S. at 317-572-3993, or fax 317-572-4002.

Some of the people who helped bring this book to market include the following:

Acquisitions, Editorial, and Media Development

Project Editor: Chad R. Sievers

Acquisitions Editor: Lindsay Lefevere

Copy Editor: Megan Knoll

Assistant Editor: Erin Calligan Mooney

Editorial Program Coordinator: Joe Niesen

Technical Editor: Patrick Lecomte, MA, MBA

Editorial Manager: Michelle Hacker

Editorial Assistant: Jennette ElNaggar

Cover Photos: © Comstock Images

Cartoons: Rich Tennant
(www.the5thwave.com)

Composition Services

Project Coordinator: Patrick Redmond

Layout and Graphics: Melanee Habig, Melissa K. Jester, Christine Williams

Proofreader: ConText Editorial Services, Inc.

Indexer: Potomac Indexing, LLC

Publishing and Editorial for Consumer Dummies

> **Diane Graves Steele,** Vice President and Publisher, Consumer Dummies
>
> **Kristin Ferguson-Wagstaffe,** Product Development Director, Consumer Dummies
>
> **Ensley Eikenburg,** Associate Publisher, Travel
>
> **Kelly Regan,** Editorial Director, Travel

Publishing for Technology Dummies

> **Andy Cummings,** Vice President and Publisher, Dummies Technology/General User

Composition Services

> **Gerry Fahey,** Vice President of Production Services
>
> **Debbie Stailey,** Director of Composition Services

Contents at a Glance

Table of Contents

Introduction

● ●

*R*eal estate investing is an expensive habit. You need money to finance the purchase, renovate your fixer-upper, and cover the holding costs while you prepare to sell or rent the property. The good news is that it doesn't all have to be *your* money. In fact, the less of your own money you can use and the more you can borrow, the bigger the return on your investment. Add the potential credit and market woes like the first decade of the 2000s, and investing in real estate also becomes a bit more of an adventure.

Lining up financial resources well in advance of scouring the neighborhood for investment opportunities enables you to pounce on a bargain and gives you leverage in negotiating the price you ultimately pay for a property. When you place an offer on a house and other bids come in, the seller may accept your offer of thousands of dollars less simply because you have the financing in place to quickly close the deal. Ready cash also frees you to plan and begin rehabbing the property immediately instead of waiting around for sluggish loan approvals and credit checks.

If you're thinking that you can't possibly get your mitts on enough cash to finance your venture, *Financing Real Estate Investments For Dummies* is the book for you. Here you discover the best sources for investment capital and how to go about tapping into these sources to fuel your next venture.

About This Book

This book isn't a get-rich-quick guide to investing in real estate or a guide or a tutorial on how to buy property with no money down (although we do cover that topic). *Financing Real Estate Investments For Dummies* delivers what the title promises — a treasure map that shows you where to find sources of real estate investment capital and guidance on how to dig it up.

Ralph and Chip are both seasoned investors. We've each built wealth through investing in real estate — buying and selling fixer-uppers and buying and renting out both residential and commercial property. Although we have used our own money on occasion to finance our purchases and renovations, we've primarily succeeded with the use of other people's money (OPM). Our grandmothers were our first financial backers, but we've expanded our options since then.

We have more than 50 years' worth of combined experience in buying and selling real estate and securing the financing to do it. In this book, we share what we know with you, showing you how to tap into loans from banks; mortgage companies; private lenders; federal, state, and local government programs; and more. In the process we cover financing for both residential and commercial properties.

Conventions Used in This Book

Compared to other books on financing real estate investments, *Financing Real Estate Investments For Dummies* is anything but conventional, but we do use some conventions to call your attention to certain items. For example:

- *Italics* highlight new, somewhat technical terms, such as *hard money,* and emphasize words when we're driving home a point.

- **Boldface** text indicates key words in bulleted and numbered lists.

- Monofont highlights Web addresses.

Financing the purchase and renovation of residential properties, such as homes, is quite different from financing the purchase and renovation of commercial properties. You deal with different lenders who use different methods for evaluating your loan application and the property you're planning to buy.

In this book, we cover both types of financing, but you should know up front the differences between residential and commercial property:

- **Residential:** One- to four-family dwellings classify as residential properties, which qualify for residential financing.

- **Commercial:** Properties used to conduct business and any rental properties designed to house more than four families qualify as commercial real estate. Loan approval for these properties hinges more on the property's potential for generating sufficient income to make the payments than on the borrower's financial strength.

In addition, even though you see three author names on the cover of this book — Chip, Ralph, and Joe — the "we" is usually Chip and Ralph talking. Joe is the wordsmith — the guy responsible for keeping you engaged and entertained and making sure *we* explain everything as clearly and thoroughly as possible.

What You're Not to Read

Although we encourage you to read this book from cover to cover to maximize the return on your investment, we realize that in today's busy world you may have time to read only the information pertinent to your situation. If so, you can safely skip anything you see in a gray shaded box. We stuck this material in a box for the same reason that most people stick stuff in boxes — to get it out of the way, so you wouldn't trip over it. However, you may find the stories and brief asides uproariously funny and perhaps even mildly informative (or vice versa).

Foolish Assumptions

We assume you already mastered the basics of investing in real estate. If you haven't, we encourage you to pick up a copy of either (or both) *Real Estate Investing For Dummies,* 2nd Edition, by Eric Tyson and Robert S. Griswold, or *Commercial Real Estate Investing For Dummies* by Peter Conti and Peter Harris (Wiley).

If you're interested in flipping houses or focusing on foreclosure properties, check out *Flipping Houses For Dummies* or *Foreclosure Investing For Dummies* by Ralph R. Roberts with Joe Kraynak. If you're thinking of becoming a landlord, we strongly encourage you to first read *Property Management For Dummies* by Robert S. Griswold. Not everyone has the right stuff to be a landlord, but if you know what you're getting into before you take on the role, you can significantly improve your survival odds.

How This Book Is Organized

Financing Real Estate Investments For Dummies facilitates a skip-and-dip approach. It presents the information in easily digestible chunks, so you can skip to the chapter or section that grabs your attention or meets your current needs, master it, and then skip to another section or simply set the book aside for later reference.

To help you navigate, we took the 17 chapters that make up the book and divvied them up into five parts. Here, we provide a quick overview of what we cover in each part.

Part I: Gearing Up for Financing Your Real Estate Investments

When you become a real estate investor, you're essentially building a business; you should build it on a strong foundation. In this part, we cover the basics, providing you with definitions of standard terminology and concepts you're likely to encounter, introducing you to the various sources of investment capital, showing you how to protect yourself against potential risks, and leading you through the process of gathering all the documents and other information you need to apply for financing.

In the process, we reveal the power of using OPM to gain leverage and expose your own money and other assets to less risk.

Part II: Financing the Purchase of Residential Properties

In this part, we explore the many residential loan programs currently available, show you how to compare different loan packages to find the one that costs the least overall, and lead you through the loan application process from filling out the forms to closing.

By the end of this part, you should have the financing you need to start hunting for residential real estate investment opportunities.

Part III: Financing the Purchase of Commercial Properties

In this part, we introduce you to the most common commercial property types, so you can choose the type best suited to your investment goals and evaluate the properties based on their potential for generating a positive cash flow. We take you on a tour of some of the unique sources of financing available for commercial ventures. Finally, we step you through the process of applying for commercial real estate loans from application to closing.

Part IV: Sampling More Creative Financing Strategies

In this part, you discover the pros and cons of *hard money* — cash that's generally easier but more expensive to borrow for purchasing investment properties. We also show you how to finance the purchase through the seller by purchasing properties on contract, how to partner with an investor who's cash heavy, and how to track down no-money-down deals.

These options aren't for everybody, but when you're in the market for investment properties and can't get your hands on conventional financing, these unconventional sources can be a deal saver.

Part V: The Part of Tens

The Part of Tens is the highlight of every *For Dummies* title, offering quick strategies, tips, and insights on whatever subject the book covers. The chapters in this Part of Tens reveal how to avoid the ten most common mistakes when financing real estate investments, which questions you should ask prospective lenders, ten steps to take to prepare for your next closing, and ten strategies for surviving a credit crunch.

Icons Used in This Book

Throughout this book, we sprinkle icons in the margins to cue you in on different types of information that call out for your attention. Here are the icons you'll see and a brief description of each.

We want you to remember everything you read in this book, but if you can't quite do that, be sure to remember the important points flagged with this icon.

Tips provide insider insight from behind the scenes. When you're looking for a better, faster, cheaper way to do something, check out these tips.

"Whoa!" This icon appears when you need to be extra vigilant or seek professional help before moving forward.

Where to Go From Here

Financing Real Estate Investments For Dummies is sort of like an information kiosk. You can start with the chapters in Part I to master the basics and then skip to Part II if you're planning on financing the purchase of residential property or Part III if your focus is more on commercial properties.

For a quick primer on financing the purchase of real estate investments, check out Chapter 1. Chapter 4 is a great place to start if you're not sure where to start looking for lenders — this chapter touches on everything from banks and mortgage companies to private lenders and partnering with others who have cash.

We do consider Chapter 6 required reading. All too often investors get burned because they focus too much on interest rates and not on other factors contributing to the overall cost of borrowing money. This chapter offers a quick way to compare two loans side-by-side to determine which one costs less over the life of the loan.

If you're planning to invest in commercial properties, Chapter 8 is also required reading. In this chapter, we show you how to evaluate different types of properties the way lenders do it when you apply for a loan.

If you're looking for information on a very specific topic, flip to the back of the book, where you can find a comprehensive index of key topics.

Part I

Gearing Up for Financing Your Real Estate Investments

The 5th Wave   By Rich Tennant

"Robert wants to use a traditional method of financing our real estate investments known as OPM — Other People-in-laws' Money."

In this part . . .

The key to scoring affordable financing and keeping a bigger chunk of your after-tax profits from real estate investments is preparation. By understanding the leverage you can gain using other people's money (OPM) to finance your investments and having all your financial records in place, you increase your odds of securing financing with attractive terms and interest rates.

By understanding tax laws and loopholes before you get started, you can lay the groundwork necessary to maximize your tax deductions and exclusions and keep more profit for yourself. And by understanding the differences between different types of lenders, you gain access to additional sources of investment capital you may never have considered.

In this part, we help you build your real estate investment venture on a firm foundation so you have ready access to cash while minimizing your exposure to risk.

Chapter 1

Taking a Crash Course in Real Estate Investment Financing

*A*re you eager to set out on the road to building wealth through real estate? Although we hate to hold you back, we do discourage you from moving forward without the proper preparation. Our advice doesn't necessarily mean, however, that you need to read the entire book from cover to cover before you purchase your first investment property.

Here, we provide a quick primer on real estate financing along with what you need to do to secure financing for your real estate investments. We also provide a generous supply of references to other chapters in the book where you can find more detailed information on specific topics. So without further ado, let the real estate financing primer begin.

Don't let negative economic and credit information dampen your desire to invest in real estate. The best time to purchase real estate is when prices are low. You can still find and secure financing; you just may need to look and work a little harder and smarter to get it.

Pumping Up Your Purchasing Power with Borrowed Money

If you have any reservations about borrowing money to buy real estate, you need to overcome those reservations by developing a better understanding of leverage — using borrowed money to buy more and better properties, thus improving your chances of earning bigger profits.

In the following sections, we show you why the goal of owning a property free and clear isn't such a smart move, reveal the secret of leveraging the power of borrowed money, and explain how you can offer "cash" for properties even when financing the purchase.

Although we encourage investors to borrow money to increase their leverage, keep in mind that borrowing money can carry significant risks. As an investor, you can take action to minimize the risks — by carefully evaluating your real estate market and properties under consideration, overestimating costs, underestimating profits, developing realistic backup plans, and so on; however you can never completely eliminate the risk. You have to decide for yourself what an acceptable level of risk is.

Minimizing your potential by owning property free and clear

For many Americans, paying off their mortgage early and owning their home free and clear is the real American dream. Life would be so much better if they didn't have to deal with a house payment.

For real estate investors, however, owning property free and clear means that valuable equity is locked up in those properties — equity they can use to finance the purchase of other revenue-generating real estate. Don't get caught in the trap of thinking that paying off a mortgage loan is a smart move — it may be a noble goal, but it's rarely a savvy strategy.

Maximizing your potential with other people's money

Other people's money (or *OPM* for short) is money that you borrow from other people to finance your investments. OPM isn't much of a secret. Assuming you own a home, you probably used OPM to buy it. You may have put down 5 to 10 percent of your own money as a down payment and then borrowed the rest.

Dealing with a major credit crunch

The mortgage meltdown, foreclosure epidemic, and global financial crisis that all came to a head in 2008 led many real estate investors to believe that credit had all but dried up. Banks were failing left and right, and the United States was forced to step in with more than $1 trillion in economic rescue funds to keep cash flowing to individuals and businesses that needed credit. Surely, real estate investors would be the last on the list for cheap and easy credit.

Actually, the credit crunch didn't put real estate investors out of business. In fact, in many cases, it made conditions better for investors:

✔ When the bubble burst, properties became much more affordable. Investors could buy better properties for less money.

✔ As millions of people worked through foreclosure, demand for rental properties soared.

✔ Financial institutions, eager to rid their books of empty, expensive, cash-sucking foreclosures, became more willing to offer great deals. I (Chip) just had a client pay $82,000 for a brand new property with a market value of about $275,000. The bank had taken it back from a builder, was more than glad to just get it off the books, and was willing to finance it with a 15-year loan.

A credit crunch doesn't mean that financing disappears — it just means that you probably need to look for it in some unusual places. Even FHA has investor financing with 25 percent down — and a lot of foreclosures they're willing to deal on. Throughout this book, we show you how to tap into these markets — credit crunch and all.

In most cases, OPM helps you earn a profit. When you calculate in the appreciation of the home, the tax savings it represents, inflation, and other factors, you're likely to earn more money off the home than you pay out in interest over the life of the loan — barring a major housing meltdown.

The same applies to your real estate investments. The more OPM you can put to work for you, the more you stand to earn — as long as your earnings from it exceed the cost of borrowing it. For more info about OPM, check out Chapter 5.

Paying cash with borrowed money

In the world of real estate, cash is king. The buyer who shows up with cash is in a significantly stronger position to purchase a property and negotiate an attractive price and terms than a buyer who shows up needing financing.

When we say cash is king, however, we're not advising you to show up with a suitcase full of money. We're telling you to show up with preapproved financing — a financial backer who can deliver the cash on closing day. In other words, although you're financing the purchase as explained throughout this book, you're still placing yourself in a position to offer cash.

Brushing Up on Basic Real Estate Financing Lingo

Throughout this book, we toss around some jargon common in the real estate and mortgage lending industries. To the average consumer, these terms may sound Greek, but we assure you that they're part of the English language. In the following sections, we define the most common and often misunderstood of these terms.

Identifying types of lenders

The moneymen and -women you deal with when securing financing for purchasing investment property play various roles in the process. You need to know whom you're working with:

- **Commercial lenders:** They're financial institutions rather than individuals. They include banks, credit unions, mutual savings banks, savings and loan associations, and stock savings banks. (Chapter 9 discusses commercial lenders in greater detail.)

- **Private lenders:** A private lender is any individual who loans money outside the channels of institutional lending. This person can be a friend or relative, such as your Aunt Mabel, or an investor. Real estate investors often rely on private lenders for access to investment capital when banks and other financial institutions turn them down. (For more about private lenders, check out Chapter 11.)

- **Mortgage banker:** Mortgage bankers are financial institutions that directly fund home loans and either service those loans themselves (arranging and collecting monthly payments and managing any escrow accounts) or sell the mortgages to investors and contract out the servicing of the loans.

- **Servicer:** The servicer is the institution contracted or appointed to collect the monthly payments from the borrower. They have to account for all payments and disbursements and provide yearly statements showing all transactions within a mortgage account to the borrower.

✔ **Mortgage broker:** Mortgage brokers are licensed by the state to assist borrowers in finding mortgage lenders, comparing loan programs, applying for mortgage loans, and securing financing for purchasing real estate. They act as the eyes and ears for many different mortgage lenders.

✔ **Loan officer:** Loan officers work for mortgage bankers or brokers to assist clients in securing financing for purchasing real estate. They essentially do the same thing brokers do, but they have to work for a licensed broker or lender.

✔ **Loan originator:** Another name for a mortgage broker or loan officer.

See Chapter 4 for more on these types of lenders.

Grasping different loan types

Throughout this book, we introduce you to various types of loans for financing the purchase of real estate, including conforming and nonconforming loans, jumbo loans, and hard money loans. In the following list, we define the most common loan types and toss in some additional information that you may find useful.

✔ **Conforming loan:** A *conforming loan* is one that meets the criteria set forth by Fannie Mae or Freddie Mac — the organizations that purchase the loans and then package them up to sell on Wall Street. In general, to qualify for a conforming loan, the borrower must

  • Show sufficient income to cover monthly payments.

  • Have enough cash for a down payment and reserves.

  • Have a good credit history.

For additional details about conforming loans and current criteria, visit the Fannie Mae Web site at `www.efanniemae.com`.

✔ **Nonconforming loans:** These include everything else outside the Fannie/Freddie box. Sometimes referred to in the market as *subprime* or even *exotic* loans, they're bought by other financial companies or investment banks and packaged to be sold to Wall Street investors. When the subprime market suffers, as it did starting in 2008, far fewer of these types of securities make it to market.

✔ **Conventional loans:** These loans are outside the sphere of the government. In other words, they're not FHA- or VA-secured loans and aren't underwritten by any government agency.

✔ **Jumbo loans:** As its name suggests, a *jumbo loan* represents a lot of money — specifically, more money than you can borrow under the limits of a conforming loan.

✔ **Hard money loans:** Also referred to as *bridge loans*, they're typically short-term, high-interest loans that enable investors to get their mitts on some cash in a hurry. You can expect to pay several points upfront (a *point* is equivalent to one percent of the total loan amount) plus up to double the going interest rate. (For more about hard money and strategies for using it to your advantage, check out Chapter 11.)

✔ **Government loan programs:** The government isn't really in the business of loaning money to homeowners and investors, but it facilitates the process for lenders by insuring the loans — if the borrower defaults on the loan, the government steps in to cover any losses for the lender.

The two most common government loan programs are Federal Housing Authority (FHA) and Veterans Administration (VA) loans. But federal, state, and local governments also provide loan programs to encourage investment in disaster areas and neighborhoods that they're seeking to develop. Within the FHA and VA programs are some great hidden opportunities for investors. (See Chapter 4 for more about specific government loan programs.)

Brushing up on important legal lingo

Even though real estate deals are generally classified as financial, they involve plenty of legalities, especially in relation to who owns the property or has a stake in it. Although real estate–related legal terms can fill an entire dictionary, you should have a working knowledge of the following three:

✔ **Deed:** A *deed* is a legal document that grants rights to a property. Whenever you purchase a property, whoever is handling the closing must file the deed with the county's register of deeds to make the transfer of ownership official. As the official owner, you have the right to borrow against the property and transfer your rights of ownership.

Be careful signing any deed, especially a *quitclaim deed* (the deed that allows a property's owner to relinquish all rights to the property). Real estate con artists often use the quitclaim deed to hijack property from unwary owners. They may hide a single page quitclaim deed in a stack of papers, fooling the owner into signing the document without knowing what they're signing. Then, they run down to the register of deeds and file the deed, making themselves the new owners, so they can take out bogus loans against the property.

Who gets first dibs?

In the event of a foreclosure, certain liens take *precedence* over others, meaning that when the property is sold at auction, certain lien holders are paid off first:

✔ **Tax lien:** The proceeds from the foreclosure sale pay off any unpaid property taxes first.

✔ **First mortgage:** If any money from the proceeds of the sale remain, it pays off the first mortgage or as much of the first mortgage as possible. This is also referred to as a *senior lien*.

✔ **Second mortgage:** If the homeowner took out a second mortgage, any remaining proceeds from the sale go toward paying it off. Any second (or third or fourth) mortgages are also referred to as *junior liens*.

✔ **Construction liens:** If money still remains, it goes to the next lien holders in order of precedence.

✔ **Homeowners:** After all the lien holders receive their cuts, the foreclosed-upon homeowners get the remaining crumbs, which can actually be quite a chunk of change if they had a lot of equity in the property.

✔ **Lien:** A *lien* is a legal claim that a creditor holds against a property in lieu of payment. Several parties can place a lien on a property, including the lender who holds any first or second mortgage, the county tax assessor (for unpaid taxes), and contractors (if they financed the repairs or renovations).

As an investor, knowing who (if anyone) has a lien against a property you're purchasing and the monetary value of that lien is important. All lien holders need to be paid in full upon sale of the property. If the property has a lien against it that the seller fails to disclose, you may become liable for paying it when you take ownership of the property.

✔ **Promissory note:** Whenever you borrow money, you have to sign a promissory note pledging to pay back the loan in full according to terms of the loan, which always specifies a deadline for full payment. Think of a promissory note as an IOU (as in "I owe you" this amount of money).

The promissory note is your pledge to pay back the loan. The mortgage or deed of trust names the property as collateral in the event that you default on the loan.

Pointing out mortgage concepts

When you take out a loan, the lender requires something of value (*collateral*) to make sure it has something valuable to sell and recoup its investment if you default on the loan. This collateral is officially presented in the form of a mortgage or deed of trust depending on the jurisdiction:

- ✔ **Mortgage:** A *mortgage* is a contract between the lender and borrower that gives the lender the right to foreclose on the property in the event that the borrower defaults on the loan.

- ✔ **Deed of trust:** A *deed of trust* is a mortgage contract that places control of the deed in the hands of a third party — a trustee. The trustee has the power to foreclose on the property in the event that the borrower defaults on the loan.

The mortgage market is large and complex, but it consists of two main divisions: a *primary* and a *secondary* mortgage market.

- ✔ **Primary:** This is the market in which you do business. It consists of financial institutions that lend you money.

- ✔ **Secondary:** This is the market where institutional lenders and Wall Street investors converge. The primary lenders who actually loan money to homeowners and investors turn around and sell the mortgages or deeds of trust to investors. This gives the lenders more money to make available to borrowers.

Examining equity

Equity is the amount of money you'd have if you sold the property today and paid off the balance due on the loan. More importantly, as an investor, you can pull equity out of a property by borrowing against it. This power enables you to put that equity to work for you in other investments.

 Thanks to the credit crisis in 2008 and 2009, the equity requirements to obtain financing are growing. Lenders are taking a closer look at market values, especially in what they call *declining areas* — areas showing a pattern of recently declining housing values. As an investor, you should be doing the same thing. Be cautious when calculating equity positions and profit margins.

 Although we encourage investors to tap the power of equity, keeping some equity in a property (especially the home you own) is a good idea. Having equity to borrow against in the event of a financial setback may save you from foreclosure and bankruptcy.

Looking at loan-to-value (LTV)

The *loan-to-value* (LTV) is the ratio of the total loan amount to the value of the property. If you're buying a $200,000 home with $40,000 down and applying for a $160,000 loan, the LTV would be

$160,000 ÷ $200,000 = 80 percent

 Generally speaking, lenders want to see lower LTVs for investment properties than for homes because a lower LTV provides more of a buffer to cover the increased risks inherent in investment properties. Check out Chapter 3 for more about calculating the LTV and how lenders use this number to evaluate risk.

Distinguishing Investment and Home Financing

Your first real estate investment should be your own home. In fact, if you don't own your home, we advise you to put down this book and pick up a copy of *Home Buying For Dummies* by Eric Tyson and Ray Brown (Wiley) first. Owning your own home carries the least risk and the most potential tax benefits while bringing you up to speed on the basics of real estate investing and ownership.

After you've purchased a home, you should have a fairly good understanding of the mortgage loan application and approval process. (We provide a refresher course in Chapter 7.) However, real estate financing differs quite a bit when you take on the role of investor rather than homeowner. You and the lender take on more risk. As a result, you can expect to pay more for the privilege of borrowing money. In addition, your borrowing strategy is likely to change. In the following sections, we cover these differences in greater detail, so you know what to expect before diving in.

Paying a premium for riskier investment loans

When you invest in your own home, you literally have a vested interest in making payments — if you don't, you lose the roof over your head. On the flip side, if you lose an investment property, it may be painful, but it's never *that* serious, and lenders are well aware of the difference. For them, investment loans are riskier propositions. To mitigate the risk, they generally

- ✔ Require a larger down payment.

- ✔ Demand a larger loan-to-value ratio. (See "Looking at loan to value (LTV)" earlier in this chapter.)

- ✔ Charge more interest upfront in the form of points.

- ✔ Charge a higher interest rate.

- ✔ Require proof that you have *reserves* or liquid assets available in case things don't go as planned.

The actions that lenders take to mitigate the risks and the interest rates and fees they charge vary greatly depending on the borrower and the deal that's on the table. Just make sure you have all the documentation and figures ready when you meet with your lender for the first time, as explained in Chapter 3.

Using quick cash to snag bargain prices

When you're shopping for a mortgage to buy a home for your family, you're usually looking for a low-interest package, no or very few points, and attractive terms. With investment properties, *cash flow* trumps interest rate. In other words, access to cash is often more important than the cost of the loan. To find out more about the relative importance of cash flow and how to shop for loans with the lowest interest rates and fees, see Chapter 6.

If the numbers work, what you pay in interest doesn't matter. Interest is just another expense. If you subtract all your expenses and can still earn the profit you want, paying thousands of dollars in interest over a relatively short period is acceptable.

Accounting for taxes on your capital gains (or losses)

When buying and selling a primary residence, you don't have to think too much about the tax ramifications of the transactions. In the United States, a huge chunk of any profit you earn from the sale is usually tax exempt — up to $250,000 if you own the home yourself or double that if you and your spouse sell the home.

However, when you're selling investment real estate, any profits are subject to capital gains taxes. During the writing of this book, profits from real estate investments were taxed as follows:

✔ **Long-term capital gains:** 15 percent if you hold the property for at least a year and a day.

✔ **Short-term capital gains:** 35 percent if you sell the property in fewer than 12 months from the date you purchased it.

✔ **Income tax:** If profits from investing in real estate are your sole income, the IRS may consider it your job and tax your profits as income, complete with an additional 15 percent in self-employment tax.

We're not tax experts. Consult a CPA who has experience dealing with real estate investors for details on how the government is going to tax your profits and for suggestions on how to reduce your tax burden. Your measure of success isn't how much you gross but how much you net. By reducing your tax bill, you can significantly increase your net gain.

Protecting your personal assets

Just like most things worth doing, real estate investing exposes you to risk. Perhaps the biggest risk is that you're working with borrowed money from lenders who expect you to pay it back. If you make a lousy investment decision or an investment goes belly-up despite your best efforts, lenders are going to do everything legally possible to collect their money.

You also face the ever-present risk of litigation — having a disagreement with a buyer, seller, tenant, contractor, or someone else that eventually leads to a costly lawsuit.

Eliminating risk isn't possible, but you can take several measures to lessen the risk, including operating through an LLC, transferring personal assets to someone else, or having a qualified attorney cover your back. Check out Chapter 2 for more details.

Exploring Common Sources of Investment Capital

You probably picked up this book because you want to start investing in real estate, but you don't know where to dig up the cash to do your first deal. In the following sections, we show you where to start digging.

Tapping your own cash reserves

If you're single, or you and your significant other are on the same page about this real estate investing thing, cracking into your nest egg to finance your investments may be the quickest way to get your fingers on some investment capital.

It's also the riskiest option, because if anything goes wrong — you get laid off or fired, become too ill to work, or encounter unexpected expenses — you have fewer reserves to keep you afloat. In addition, limiting yourself to your own resources also limits your purchase power — you have to buy houses in a lower price range and may not have sufficient cash to properly renovate the property.

A great way to ruin a relationship is to bet the farm on big profits without the knowledge and complete agreement of your spouse or significant other. If your investment doesn't pan out (and even if it does), the other person may take offense at not being consulted.

Even with these caveats, many beginning investors have gotten their start by financing their own ventures — partially or in full. And you want to know about these resources if you need some quick cash in a pinch.

Clearing out your bank accounts

Having a few thousand dollars socked away in a savings account is always a good idea, just in case you run into a cash flow problem. If that house you bought and fixed up is taking a few months longer than expected to sell, your little nest egg can help cover the payments until you find a buyer.

Use your savings as a reserve, not as your main mode of financing. Having some cash to fall back on can save you in a pinch.

Borrowing against the equity in your home

As your home's value rises and you pay down the principal, you build equity. You can often borrow against this equity by taking out a home equity loan or line of credit and then use the money for whatever you want, including purchasing other real estate. The recent credit crisis has made it harder to find these loans, but they're still out there for well-qualified borrowers.

We don't recommend that you cash out all the equity in your home, but if you have a substantial amount of equity, cashing out a portion of it can help you come up with a down payment or cover the cost of repairs and renovations. (For more about home equity loans and lines of credit, skip to Chapter 11.)

Financing investments through a self-directed IRA

More and more investors are choosing to set up *self-directed IRAs* and other types of retirement accounts that enable them to invest in real estate rather than in stocks and bonds. The reasoning: Real estate often provides a better and sometimes even more secure return on your investment.

With a self-directed IRA, you can buy and sell properties out of your retirement account. Setting up a self-directed IRA, however, is no simple matter. Typically, a trust company manages the money and properties in the account, and all profits and losses from your investments must stay in that account. Withdrawing money from the account results in the same IRS penalties you have to pay if you withdraw money from any type of retirement account.

Consult your financial advisor and accountant for details about using a self-directed IRA to finance your real estate investments. If a self-directed IRA isn't an option, you may be able to borrow money against your retirement account. Keep in mind, however, that borrowing against your retirement savings places those savings at risk, as does any other investment.

Charging expenses on your credit cards

Maxing out your credit cards to purchase a car, clothes, electronics, groceries, and other items that provide no return on your investment is never a good idea. Using your credit cards to purchase investment properties that offer a solid, relatively quick return on your investment, however, can be a savvy (though risky) financial move.

Consider credit cards a last resort to cover the costs of repairs and renovations if financing is tight near the end of a project. With this strategy, your investment activities can directly affect your personal finances, which increases your exposure to risk. For more about this option, check out Chapter 11.

Borrowing from commercial lenders

One of the best ways to finance the purchase of investment properties is to meet with a qualified mortgage broker who can help you find and evaluate various loan programs. These plans are often your best deals — costing the least in upfront fees and interest.

For more about finding commercial lenders, check out Chapter 4. If you're investing in residential property, Chapter 5 reveals the various residential loan programs to choose from. If you're buying commercial property, turn to Chapter 9 for guidance on choosing the right loan program.

Don't confuse "commercial property" with "commercial lender." A *commercial property* is any property that isn't a one- to four-family residential dwelling. A *commercial lender* is an institution (as opposed to an individual) that loans money. In other words, you can use a commercial lender to finance the purchase of residential investment property.

Obtaining a hard money loan

When banks and other financial institutions turn down your requests for investment capital (or you don't have the time to convince them that a deal is pure gold), consider borrowing money from a hard money lender, as explained in Chapter 11.

One of the main advantages of a hard money lender is that the person is likely to accept the property you're buying as all the collateral needed to secure the loan, so you don't have to place your home at risk.

Financing your purchase through the seller

Property owners who are eager to sell and don't need all the cash at once are often willing to finance the purchase themselves. This tactic enables them to profit in two ways — by selling you the property for more than they paid for it and collecting interest from you. Seller financing take either of the following forms:

- ✔ **Land contract:** A *land contract* is like a mortgage, except the seller acts as the bank.

- ✔ **Lease option agreement:** A *lease option agreement* is like a rent-to-own deal — you lease the property for a specified period, at the end of which time you have the option to buy it.

For more about seller financing, check out Chapter 12.

Taking on a partner

Whenever you don't have something (like money, skills, time, or talent) to accomplish a particular goal, you can acquire those skills, buy or hire them, or create a partnership with someone who already has what you need. If you have something someone else needs and they have what you need, you have what it takes to form a mutually beneficial relationship. For details on how to partner with someone who has the cash you need, check out Chapter 13.

Choose a partner as carefully as you choose a spouse. Partnerships often end when one person scams the other or disagreements arise over who's putting more into the projects and who's getting more out of them. Have your attorney write up a contract, complete with a prenuptial type agreement stating how all the assets will be divvied up in the event that you part company.

Prepping to Meet with a Lender

Walk into a bank empty-handed and explain to the loan officer that you need a loan to start investing in real estate, and we can almost guarantee that you'll be laughed out the door. Before you even think about meeting with a prospective lender, get all your ducks in a row. Copy all the financial documents lenders are going to ask for and construct a fairly detailed plan on how you're going to profit by investing in real estate. This section gives you an overview of what you need to do before visiting your lender. Chapter 4 provides complete in-depth info.

Gathering paperwork and other info

Before approving your request for a loan, lenders want to know whether you're good for the money — how likely you are to make the monthly payments and pay back the loan in full. For investors, this means two things:

- ✔ You're in pretty good financial shape right now and have a fairly clean credit history.
- ✔ The property you're planning to buy is more than worth the money you're borrowing to pay for it, and (if you're going to be renting out the property) it will generate sufficient income to more than cover all your expenses along with the monthly payments.

To verify your creditworthiness for yourself and be sure you have all the documents and other information your lender requires, stuff a folder full of a copy of each of the following items:

- ✔ Credit reports from all three credit reporting agencies
- ✔ A net worth statement (assets – liabilities = net worth)
- ✔ A debt ratio statement (ratio of what you owe to what you own)
- ✔ Last two months' bank statements
- ✔ Last 30 days' pay stubs

✔ Last two years' federal tax returns and schedules

✔ Statements of any business income

✔ Appraisal or comparative market analysis for the property

✔ Cash flow analysis of the property

✔ Loan-to-value ratio of the property

✔ Zoning information for the property's location

✔ City and county records for the property

Crafting a business plan

Real estate investors often scoff at the idea of creating a *business plan* — a detailed presentation that shows how an investor plans to purchase a specific property and earn a profit from it. Investors often just want to buy and sell and rent out property and make a lot of money — that's the plan. They don't like to think of themselves as pencil-necked pencil pushers. If they feel in their gut that a property is a solid investment, that's good enough for them.

At least that's the false image that many people have of investors. The most successful investors, however, do the math. They crunch the numbers. And if the numbers don't work, they don't do the deal.

Do your homework. Do a comparative market analysis of the property to make sure it's worth what you think it's worth. If you're buying rental property, check the rental history of the property — the owner's tax records showing income and expenses. Craft a business plan showing exactly how this property is going to be a revenue generator.

Chapter 2

Shielding Your Personal Assets from Investment Risks

*F*unny thing about lenders — when you borrow money from them, they expect you to pay it back. To ensure repayment of a loan, the lender usually requires that you sign a promissory note and a mortgage or deed of trust. The *promissory note* is your personal promise to repay the loan in full. The *mortgage* or *deed of trust* names certain property as collateral for the loan.

If you happen to *default* on the loan (fail to make payments as stipulated), the lender has the right to *foreclose* (sell your property to the highest bidder). If the lender can't sell the property for at least as much as you owe on it, it may be able to sue you for the difference *(deficiency)* in jurisdictions that allow deficiency judgments.

As an investor, you want to limit the assets that the lender has the right to seize in lieu of payment. If you fail to make payments on a loan you took out to purchase an investment property, for example, you want to make sure that the bank can't take possession of the home you live in, other businesses you own, or other assets, such as your car. To prevent the lender from going after personal assets and other business assets as payment, you need to *shield* those assets — keep them legally and financially separate from your investment properties. In this chapter, you discover various strategies for doing just that.

It's a jungle out there. Fraud is more common in the real estate industry than most professionals are willing to admit, so in this chapter, we also show you how to protect yourself against becoming a victim or unwitting accomplice to real estate and mortgage fraud.

Understanding Why You Need to Protect Your Personal Assets

As an investor, you're a small-business owner, but you're also an individual who may have a spouse and a family to support. You probably have a home, a car, one or more personal bank accounts, a retirement account, and other valuables that you've worked very hard for a long time to accumulate. You want to build even more wealth by investing in real estate, and you're willing to take some risks, but can you live with losing everything you now own?

The correct answer is (or should be) "no." No, you shouldn't risk everything you now own to invest in real estate. Why? We can think of two very good reasons:

- ✔ You don't want to or have to risk everything. You can protect some or all your assets from risk by following the advice we offer in this chapter.

- ✔ If your investment goes belly up, you can recover much more quickly and perhaps even pursue future investments by holding on to more of your current assets.

In any investment, you should try to limit your exposure (both financially and emotionally) to the individual deal. You're investing your time and talent and perhaps a little of your own money. In addition, you're the one who's taking on the burden of managing the project, dealing with hassles, and worrying about whether your investment is going to eventually turn a profit. All the lender is doing is putting up the money, so let the lender step up to the plate and take the *financial* risk. That's the price it pays for being able to do business with you.

Limiting Your Personal Liability by Forming an LLC

Businesses form corporations for any number of reasons, but one of the primary reasons is to establish the business as a separate entity. If, for example, you do business in your own name, you become personally liable for anything that happens in the course of doing business. If someone decides to sue you over something related to your business, all your personal belongings are at stake.

By setting up a corporation, you essentially create a fall guy who takes the blame if something terrible happens. A customer can sue your corporation to the point of bankruptcy, and in most cases, you can simply walk away with your home, your car, and your personal savings and belongings all intact.

One of the best and most popular corporate entities for real estate investors is the *limited liability company* or *LLC*. By forming an LLC, you limit your exposure to risk to the company, so it can fold without negatively affecting your personal finances.

In the following sections, we provide guidelines on setting up an LLC and managing your investments through it. For details about creating and managing an LLC, check out *Limited Liability Companies For Dummies* by Jennifer Reuting (Wiley).

Understanding the pros and cons

On its surface, an LLC appears to be the best of all possible business entities, and in some ways it really is, but prior to taking the plunge, consider its potential advantages and disadvantages.

An LLC offers the following benefits:

- ✔ **Generally requires less paperwork and fewer hassles:** Small business owners who form S-corps often get frustrated pretending that they're some huge corporation — filing all sorts of forms, holding or pretending to hold corporate meetings, and keeping a record of each meeting's minutes. With an LLC, you avoid most of that nonsense — at least the meetings and the minutes.

- ✔ **Provides greater protection:** Operating as a sole proprietorship leaves you completely vulnerable to lawsuits and other legal claims against your personal assets. An LLC provides the same sort of protection you can expect under the corporate umbrella.

- ✔ **Allows you to dodge the passive income bullet:** If too much of your income from real estate holdings is classified as *passive*, the IRS could convert your Sub-S into a C-corp (a regular corporation), exposing you to double taxation. With an LLC, you can do a *pass-through*, in which your real estate earnings pass through the company and are treated as personal income so that the company isn't taxed separately, as well.

Although an LLC offers the protection of limited liability, it does have a couple of its own limitations, as well:

- ✔ If a member of the LLC dies or goes bankrupt, the LLC is dissolved, whereas a corporation can continue to exist as long as it has shareholders.

- ✔ All properties within the LLC are exposed to risks associated with the other properties held in the same LLC. In other words, someone trying to collect money for one of the LLC's properties can go after the other properties to collect payment. For this reason, limiting the number of properties held in any one LLC is a good idea.

Setting up an LLC

Anyone with a free weekend, a computer, and an Internet connection can set up an LLC (although we recommend that you use an attorney). You download the forms, fill them out, and submit them to your state commerce department, secretary of state, or bureau of corporations. Although each state has slightly different procedures to follow and forms to complete, you should be able to find all the instructions and documents you need on your state's Web site.

Go to your favorite online search engine and type in "corporation" followed by the name of your state — for example, "corporation Arizona" (without the quotation marks). This search should bring up a link to the department in your state that handles LLCs and corporations.

You can set up most LLCs on your own for very little expense and paperwork, but we encourage you to consult with an attorney. A savvy attorney can ensure you've set up your corporate shield in a way that makes it less vulnerable to being pierced. You may also want to hire an accountant to manage the finances for the company and ensure that any taxes that come due are paid on time.

The choice of which state you form your corporation in is of utmost importance, especially in terms of how you're taxed. Delaware, for example, is very corporation-friendly, which is why you see so many financial institutions, especially credit card companies, centered in Delaware. Discuss the options with your accountant and attorney.

Taking and securing title to real estate

When you have an LLC in place, perform all business transactions in the name of the LLC rather than in your own name. Whether you're taking out a loan, signing a purchase agreement, or putting your John Hancock on closing papers, make sure your LLC is listed as the responsible party and that you're signing as a representative of the company.

Accomplishing this task is fairly easy on your part because other people are usually in charge of drawing up the paperwork. All you need to do is instruct the person (real estate agent, closing agent, loan officer, or whoever is handling the paperwork) to prepare it in the name of the LLC.

Unfortunately, on conventional loans with conventional lenders for typical one- to four-family dwellings, getting a loan in the name of the LLC is nearly impossible, but you can still have the LLC *hold* the property, providing some protection from personal liability. You have an easier time taking loans out in the name of the LLC when purchasing larger properties (5+ units) and commercial deals.

If you can't take title in the name of your LLC, move the property into the LLC as soon as practical. You can do this by using a *quit-claim deed* — typically a one-page legal document that enables you to deed the property to another individual or business entity. You simply sign the quitclaim deed, specifying that the LLC is the new deed holder, and then file the quitclaim deed with your county's register of deeds. Your attorney can supply you with a quitclaim deed that's valid in your county.

Follow your attorney's advice carefully, because this strategy can trigger a *due-on-sale clause,* in which case you would need to pay back the loan in full immediately. The IRS allows investors to transfer real estate for estate-planning purposes, so you're in the clear as long as you follow the rules.

Some LLCs choose to perform certain transactions under an *assumed name* — a name that differs from that of the company. We strongly discourage the use of assumed names in real estate transactions, because they provide little, if any, protection for you. Always transact your investment business under the LLC's name.

Eyeing Sub-S corporations and partnerships

Although we recommend LLCs for most investors, a Subchapter S corporation (or Sub-S for short) is a viable alternative. A Sub-S is an actual *corporation* (as opposed to a *company*) that chooses not to pay taxes on earnings but instead have those earnings pass through to the shareholders so they pay taxes on them. It's another way of dodging the double-taxation bullet (taxing the corporation as well as the individual shareholders).

A Sub-S can also provide you with a great measure of protection and allow for other deductions and a wider variety of activities than are possible under an LLC. For example, a Sub-S allows you to partner with other business entities in addition to individuals.

If you plan on partnering up with another investor, you need to formalize the relationship by forming a partnership, as we discuss in Chapter 13. A *partnership* is simply a business entity in which the members agree to work toward a common goal. You need to have a written agreement in place that stipulates how the partnership functions, who's responsible for what, and how assets are to be divided should the partnership dissolve. The partnership itself, however, provides you with little or no protection. You still need to set up a corporation or an LLC for protecting your personal assets and those of your partner(s).

Transferring Personal Assets via Trusts

As an investor, you're a business owner, and most responsible business owners keep their business and personal finances separate. You can be sued by anyone at any time, and you want to protect your family and personal assets as best as possible. An excellent way to accomplish this is to place your personal assets under someone else's name or into a separate entity — a *trust.* Consider the following options:

- ✔ Transfer personal assets to your spouse, one of your children, another relative, or a designated third-party administrator such as an attorney or financial planner.

- ✔ Shift your assets into a *trust* — a legal device you as an individual place your assets in for the benefit of others, such as your family.

Investors often spend a great deal of time and effort building wealth only to see the fruits of their efforts chipped away by unjustified lawsuits and taxes. By holding your assets in an estate or trust, you not only protect them against legal claims, but you can also reap substantial tax benefits. Sophisticated investors often use multiple business entities (including LLCs and other corporate structures) to manage their assets and protect them from a variety of risks. As you acquire more properties, consider employing a similar strategy. For more about estate planning, check out *Estate Planning For Dummies* by Jordan Simon and Brian Caverly (Wiley).

In the following sections, we address the advantages and disadvantages of placing your assets in someone else's name and assist you in deciding which option is best for you.

Weighing the pros and cons of owning property in another's name

Investors and business owners often protect assets by placing them in the name of a spouse or other relative. Before you make this move, however, you need to have a firm grasp of the pros and cons to protect the property.

Some investors hold some investments in their own names, and some in the name of their spouses. This strategy increases the number of properties you can finance (by getting around Fannie Mae and Freddie Mac limits on the number of residential properties/mortgages you can hold) and also enables you to diversify your assets and limit liabilities.

A real estate investor, for example, may choose to have her spouse listed as the sole owner of their home, car, and other big-ticket assets and then take out loans and the title to investment properties in her own name only. If she defaults on a loan, she can lose the investment property, but the family home and car are safe.

So, what's the catch? Placing assets in someone else's name can increase your exposure to several risks:

- ✔ **You lose some control over those assets.** If all your personal assets are listed in your husband's name only, for example, a divorce may leave you at a severe disadvantage.

- ✔ **You may affect your kids' future financial aid.** If you own property in the name of your children, the value of that property can influence the financial aid calculations should your children decide to attend college and require financial assistance.

- ✔ **You may encounter tax consequences.** Putting assets in the names of your children may also trigger gift tax requirements or estate tax issues.

- ✔ **You're at the mercy of that person's legal issues.** If the holder of your assets becomes disabled or runs into his own liability issues, your assets can get tied up for a long time in the legal wrangling. Bankruptcy, insolvency, or even death (and the subsequent probate) can turn the best of plans into a financial fiasco.

Placing assets in someone else's name can be a bit of a hassle, but it usually doesn't cost all that much. For example, you can head down to the bureau of motor vehicles and change the name on the title for any vehicles you own for a small fee. Likewise, you can use a quitclaim deed to assign ownership of a property for a small recording fee. Before you do, however, consult your attorney or accountant to find out about all the ramifications of transferring ownership of your properties because the laws and procedures vary from state to state.

Gaining asset and tax protection with an irrevocable trust

Trusts are the most versatile tool for transferring title of assets without tax implications or increased risk, but they have some limitations. We encourage you to discuss your situation with a qualified estate planner who can assist you in weighing the potential benefits and drawbacks of different options and then set up the trust for you.

Trusts come in two flavors — revocable and irrevocable. A *revocable* trust is one you can change or terminate during your lifetime. An *irrevocable* trust is one that you can't change or dissolve — as *grantor* (creator of the trust), you no longer own the assets held in trust. The trust does. An irrevocable trust benefits you in two important ways:

- ✔ Because you no longer own the assets, they're protected against any legal actions taken against you.

- ✔ The property and its appreciation are outside of your taxable estate, allowing you to avoid paying estate taxes on the value of your holdings.

Both revocable and irrevocable trusts protect assets from probate, but only irrevocable trusts can eliminate estate taxes.

The ultimate way to protect assets is to hold them in an offshore asset protection trust, but we're not advising that you do that. The next best thing is to have your assets owned by a Sub-S or LLC and then have the shares of the corporation owned by an irrevocable trust — this is the fortress of U.S. asset protection. The IRS frowns upon any sort of tax optimization scheme, particularly the offshore variety, so before employing any such scheme, consult a tax attorney.

Considering real estate investment trusts (REITs)

Real estate investment trusts (or REITs for short) give small investors a way to pool their assets and own investment real estate as a group. REITs offer investors three significant benefits:

- ✔ **Investors can diversify their real estate holdings by owning pieces of multiple properties.** Instead of purchasing a $200,000 property, for example, a small investor can own a $10,000 share in 20 properties, spreading the risk.

- ✔ **Small investors can afford to buy into higher-end real estate.** REITs allow minor league investors to play a smaller role in the major leagues, because it costs less to buy in.

- ✔ **REITs simplify the transfer of ownership to different investors.** Instead of selling the property, you simply transfer shares.

If you have an LLC with 100 or more investors, consult your attorney for assistance in setting up a REIT, to ensure that it meets all the requirements, including the following:

- ✔ Your REIT must have at least 100 shareholders. Why 100? That's just one of the rules.

- ✔ You must distribute at least 90 percent of your REIT's taxable income. In other words, at least 90 percent of the profits earned by the assets in the REIT must flow through to shareholders.

- ✔ Ninety five percent of your REIT's income must come from financial investments (including real estate, securities, and annuities), with 75 percent of that total coming from real estate (net profit from sale of assets, rent/lease payments, and so on).

Staying Away from Promissory Notes with Recourse Clauses

Promissory note is a fancy term for an IOU. Whenever you borrow money, the lender almost always requires that you sign a promissory note promising to pay back the money under a set of specific conditions, including the *term* (amount of time you have to pay the loan in full), interest rate, *principal* (total amount you borrowed), and payment amount of each scheduled payment.

Promissory notes usually include a *recourse clause* stipulating that the person signing for the loan is pledging individual assets as additional collateral to secure the loan. If the loan goes bad, the lender can then come after the borrower's personal assets to recoup any losses.

In the following sections, we explain nonrecourse loans (the most desirable option), discuss what you need to do if your contract has a recourse clause, and point out the risks involved in *cross-collateralized loans* — loans that enable the lender to lay claim to property other than the property the loan was used to purchase.

Opting for a nonrecourse loan

If you're trying to borrow money for a potentially lucrative investment, a recourse loan may be your only option, but in most cases, you want a loan that places only the property you're financing at risk — a *nonrecourse loan.*

Nonrecourse means that the property stands on its own. Fail to make your payments, and all you stand to lose is the property you borrowed the money to buy . . . and your pride. Borrowers typically use nonrecourse loans for financing the purchase of larger commercial-type properties, where the lender understands that the real value is in the property and the income it generates. If a $15 million loan on a hotel goes bad, the lender knows he can't shake enough quarters and nickels out of you to pay it back. Instead, he can get the money out of the property.

In some cases, lenders allow you to buy into a nonrecourse clause by paying a higher interest rate or agreeing to other terms that are more favorable to the lender. It never hurts to ask, but on smaller properties, you can usually count on having to agree to some sort of recourse clause. (See the next section for more on how to negotiate this recourse clause.)

 Any type of fraud, misrepresentation, or misappropriation of funds in respect to the loan or the property — such as claiming that the building generates more rental income than it really does — can void the nonrecourse clause and give the lender the right to come after your personal assets.

Negotiating the recourse clause

Although we suggest you go the nonrecourse route as often as possible, some contracts require a recourse clause. Fortunately, this clause is usually negotiable. A lender typically doesn't remove it entirely, but you may be able to negotiate a recourse clause that limits your liability. Ask your loan officer or broker whether any options are available. Following are some areas that may be open for negotiation:

✔ **Property limitations:** You may limit the recourse, for example, to other real estate holdings in your LLC, thus protecting your personal residence and other assets.

✔ **Time limitations:** You may be able to place a time limitation on your liability; for example, if you make payments on time for five years, your personal liability is released.

✔ **Partial recourse:** This provision limits your liability to a certain percentage of the loan or a certain amount (less than the full amount). Partial recourse can also limit the lender's ability to collect only under certain conditions.

 Almost every residential loan (for one- to four-family investment property) requires personal recourse. Just make sure you understand the limitations and options. When signing a promissory note, make sure that the recourse clause is limited to the assets you're willing to put at risk.

Avoiding cross-collateralization

To protect their money, lenders like to know that you have plenty of *collateral* — anything of value that they can take from you and sell to get their money back in the event you're unable or unwilling to pay back the loan. When the housing market is thriving and property values are on the rise, lenders tend to accept the property you're financing as collateral on the loan. If you don't make your payments, they can foreclose, sell the property, and get back all or nearly all their money.

Your recourse to recourse loans

I (Chip) once had 16 doctors who went in together on a commercial building as an investment. The bank wanted a full recourse loan on each of them, which would have given them a total of 1600 percent coverage on the loan. We negotiated for a 10 percent personal recourse on each investor, which still provided the lender with 160 percent coverage. We were also able to eliminate personal liability after five years of satisfactory payments.

The moral of this story is this: Don't accept what the lender offers as a final offer. As long as you're a serious investor with a solid plan in place, you can usually negotiate more attractive terms with the lender.

Cross-collateralization nightmare

Several years ago, I (Chip) had a friend who had a great idea for a retail clothing store. Couldn't lose, or so he thought. Unfortunately, his overconfidence led him to be careless in borrowing money for his new venture. He allowed the loan he secured to buy the building to be cross-collateralized with the store's inventory and many of his personal assets.

A sharp downturn in the market transformed his dreams to dust in a mere 18 months, but the worst was yet to come: The lender not only foreclosed on the building and took his inventory but also went after his home, car, boat, and retirement fund. The financial strain eventually ended his marriage.

Any investment that's worth pursuing usually involves some risk, but going all in when you don't really have to is folly. By avoiding the cross-collateralization trap, you limit your risk to the new investment.

No investment is a sure thing. Protect yourself from unforeseen and unfortunate circumstances as much as possible.

On riskier investments — when property values are declining or the property's value is close to the amount being borrowed or a large loan is being taken out to purchase multiple properties — the lender may want to *cross-collateralize* the loan. With cross-collateralization, two or more properties act as collateral for a single loan. If you fail to make payments on the loan, the lender can foreclose on other properties to collect the amount due.

For the investor, cross-collateralization exposes other properties to the liabilities of one. Stay away from these types of loans if at all possible. You can't always avoid cross-collateralization, but we encourage you to at least try. Otherwise, you may lose a good income property just because one of your other properties is a dog.

Steering Clear of Real Estate and Mortgage Fraud

Wherever you find money, you find crooks — con artists determined to score some quick cash. As a real estate investor, you're vulnerable to real estate and mortgage fraud in any or all of the following three ways: as a target, as a perpetrator, or as an unwitting accomplice. And all these roles can ultimately undermine your long-term success, not to mention your reputation.

Refusing to play a role in fraud for housing

Fraud for housing used to be the most common type of real estate and mortgage fraud and the most "harmless" (although still illegal). It consists of lying on a loan application so you can purchase a home to live in – as opposed to "fraud for profit," in which you're committing fraud to obtain money.

When you're acting as an investor, you're at a pretty low risk of becoming a perpetrator of fraud for housing because you're not buying the property to live in it. However, you may be at risk for becoming an accomplice if you're trying to sell a property to buyers who are having trouble qualifying for a mortgage loan.

If prospective buyers are having trouble qualifying for a loan to buy the property you're selling, they may just not be able to afford the payments. Don't try to "help" them by encouraging them to lie on their loan application or by referring them to a loan officer who's known for bending the rules.

In the following sections, we describe the main types of real estate and mortgage fraud, to empower you to steer clear of scams and schemes that can get you into trouble.

Ignorance of the law is no excuse for breaking it. Unfortunately, ignorance is as rampant as fraud in the real estate industry. Many real estate professionals may try to convince you that something illegal is okay because everybody does it or because these are "victimless crimes." However, as we've seen from the mortgage meltdown beginning in 2008, homeowners and investors ultimately pay the price. For more about real estate and mortgage fraud, check out *Protect Yourself from Real Estate and Mortgage Fraud: Preserving the American Dream of Homeownership* by Ralph R. Roberts and Rachel Dollar (Kaplan Publishing).

Telling the truth on your application

A huge percentage of real estate and mortgage fraud could be eliminated if everyone in the industry, including investors, would work together to ensure that all the information on loan applications is complete and accurate.

Buyers and those who assist them often think that accuracy is optional, but the loan application, the 1003 (commonly referred to as a ten-oh-three, or officially as the Uniform Residential Loan Application), clearly states, just above the space for your signature, the following:

I/We fully understand that it is a federal crime punishable by fine or imprisonment, or both, to knowingly make any false statements concerning any of the above facts as applicable under the provisions of Title 18, United States Code, Section 1001, et seq.

What constitutes a *false statement?* Here's a list of what may be considered false:

- ✔ Stating or providing false records that you're employed somewhere you're not.

- ✔ Stating or providing false records of income.

- ✔ Providing false identification.

- ✔ Boosting your credit score by piggybacking on someone else's better credit.

- ✔ Falsifying ownership of assets, either by stating that you own items you don't or by renting assets. (Some disreputable companies allow you to rent assets, so you appear to own more assets than you really do.)

- ✔ Failing to disclose a silent second. A *silent second* is a separate mortgage typically taken out to cover the down payment. As we discuss in Chapter 14, taking out a second mortgage to finance the down payment is okay, but not disclosing it is illegal. It creates the false impression that you're more financially secure than you really are.

Dodging predatory lenders

Although lenders are often the victims of mortgage fraud, they may also be guilty of committing fraud and are even more frequently guilty of lending practices that prey on uninformed borrowers. Whenever you're applying for a loan, keep one hand on your wallet and one eye out for the following questionable and perhaps illegal lending practices:

- ✔ Charging you higher-than-normal loan origination fees (including points).

- ✔ Encouraging you to bend the truth on a loan application, so you can qualify for a loan you would otherwise not qualify for.

- ✔ Having you sign a blank loan application and then filling in the details for you later.

- ✔ Refinancing your mortgage repeatedly within a short period of time.

- ✔ Selling you a high-cost, high-interest loan when you would qualify for a low-cost, low-interest loan.

✔ Adding products or services such as credit life insurance to a loan without adequately informing you about the need or cost of these products or services. Watch out for hidden (undisclosed) fees.

✔ Selling you products or services that are nonexistent or offer no benefit.

✔ Convincing you to borrow more than you can reasonably afford to pay back.

✔ Pressuring you to accept high-risk loans, such as balloon-payment loans, interest-only mortgages, subprime or adjustable rate mortgages (ARMs), and loans with high prepayment penalties.

✔ Selling high-interest loans based on ethnicity or nationality rather than your credit history and financial situation.

Always obtain three or more quotes from different companies before choosing a loan and compare the quotes carefully (see Chapter 6 for details). Doing so enables you to see any hidden loan costs more clearly. When applying for and closing on a loan, read the documents carefully to make sure the information is accurate and complete.

Saying "no" to inflated appraisals

One of the main instruments that real estate con artists use to ply their trade is the *inflated appraisal* — a document showing that a property is worth significantly more than its true market value. By obtaining an inflated appraisal (forging one or paying off a crooked appraiser), the con artist can create equity in a property where none exists.

As an investor, never try to sway the opinion of an appraiser or allow a loan officer, real estate agent, or anyone else to convince you to go along with a deal that involves an inflated appraisal.

Also, be careful about overpaying for a property whose value has been artificially boosted by inflated appraisals. You can protect yourself by ordering your own independent appraisal before purchasing a property. Find an appraiser in the area who has a solid gold reputation and plenty of experience in the market you're buying into. Don't let the seller or seller's agent recommend an appraiser. You pay a few hundred dollars for your own appraisal, but it can save you from making a mistake costing tens or even hundreds of thousands of dollars.

We also recommend against using online appraisals or computerized valuation models. You want a real live person, a qualified appraiser who knows the local market, to physically inspect the property and provide you with an educated estimate of its market value. There's really no substitute.

Turning your back on cash-back-at-closing schemes

One of the most prevalent forms of fraud, particularly when the market is down, consists of providing the buyer with *cash back at closing*. The buyer agrees to pay more for the property than it's worth and obtains an inflated appraisal showing that the property is actually worth the purchase price. The seller agrees to raise the asking price and kick back the excess money to the buyer at closing. Many people think these arrangements are okay, but don't be fooled — cash back at closing is illegal. Protect yourself:

✔ Don't offer buyers cash back at closing or any other "perks" that the lender is actually financing, including "free" furniture, a cruise, upgrades, and so on.

✔ Don't accept cash back at closing, even if it comes in some other form, such as "free" furniture, upgrades, rebates, refunds, or anything else that's actually being paid out of the loan amount.

Avoiding illegal flipping

Flipping houses, as described in *Flipping Houses For Dummies*, is perfectly legal. You buy a house below market value, fix it up, and then sell it for a profit. However, another type of flipping is clearly illegal. It consists of buying a property, typically a dilapidated house, at well below market value, doing a few cosmetic repairs to make it look nice, and then selling it for much more than its true market value.

As an investor, avoid illegal flipping. In addition to breaking the law, this type of flipping ruins your long-term success. Illegal flippers may score some quick cash, but they quickly ruin their reputations and often end up in legal trouble. It's not worth it.

 To avoid becoming the victim of an illegal flip, always check the recent sales prices of similar homes in the same neighborhood to make sure the asking price of the property you're about to purchase is realistic. Make sure you're the one choosing the home inspector and the appraiser. If the seller offers to handle this for you, politely decline the offer.

Defending yourself against chunking schemes

Real estate investors often become the targets of con artists through what is commonly referred to as a *chunking scheme*. The con artist dangles a quick-cash, no-hassle investment opportunity in front of the eager investor and offers to take care of all the details. The investor only has to put up the cash or sign the papers for the loan that to finance the deal.

The organizer promises to place renters, collect the rent, make the mortgage payments, and so on, and tells the investor that the rental payments will cover the mortgage and maybe even earn a little extra cash each month. The investor can sell the property at any time and profit from it because the property is sure to appreciate.

The truth behind the deal is that the properties are usually over-valued, the renters don't exist, and the con artist never intends to make the mortgage payments. Investors are left with dilapidated homes, unpaid mortgages, and destroyed credit.

The best way to avoid getting sucked in by a chunking scheme is to plug your ears when you hear someone pitching a no-risk, no-hassle way to earning riches in real estate. Quite frankly, such deals don't exist. Do your homework. Visit the property and inspect it with your own two eyes. Oversee the management of the property. Don't let someone else "handle all the details" because they probably intend to handle you out of your money.

Refusing a builder bailout

Builders who become overextended may try to dig themselves out of a financial hole by selling homes (or whatever they're building) before completion to unsuspecting buyers. In some cases, the builder eventually completes the project. In other cases, he may take the cash and leave the buyer with an unfinished building or even a vacant lot.

When banks finance new construction (see Chapter 9), they don't give the builder all the money at once. They set up an account that the builder draws from during the building process. The bank wants to make sure the project is completed, so it ties the cash draws to success and to certain milestones. When those mile-stones are completed, the bank can then free up the money to pay for the supplies and services. For example, if the rough lumber needed for a project costs $28,000, the bank would give the builder a draw for $28,000, which would then flow to the lumber company *after* the framing was complete. The lumber company would then sign a waiver of lien, acknowledging payment and freeing up its claim to the property.

When a builder becomes strapped for cash, he may try to get the money sooner by employing any of the following strategies:

- ✔ Falsifying inspection reports
- ✔ Submitting fake certifications of work performed
- ✔ Fooling the inspectors by removing items from some buildings and installing them in others to make it appear as though progress is being made
- ✔ Selling an incomplete property to the buyer

The best way to avoid builder bailout scams is to choose a reputable builder and refuse to close on the deal until you have the building thoroughly inspected by a professional inspector of your choosing.

Acting with integrity: The golden rule

Far too many investors succumb to the temptation to commit fraud because they're in a hurry to make a quick buck. All these "investors" eventually fail because they tarnish their own reputations and damage the very industry that puts money in their pockets.

The best way to achieve long-term success as a real estate investor is to make a commitment to follow the golden rule — treat others as you would want to be treated. You can still earn a handsome profit in real estate by purchasing properties legitimately and setting a fair price when you sell. You don't have to break or bend the laws to be successful. You just need to do your homework.

Chapter 3

Gathering Essential Documents, Facts, and Figures

*L*enders aren't exactly tripping over themselves to lend money, especially in the recent credit debacles of the mid-2000s. They want to know who they're lending it to, for what, and how and when they're going to get paid back. They usually operate conservatively, weighing the risks before quoting you a price. If they see your venture as too risky, they may reject your loan application outright. If they believe you're in a strong position to pay back the loan in full, they may offer you financing at lower interest rates to win your business. If they see you as a moderate risk, you may receive financing at higher rates.

In any event, the lender wants to see how you look on paper — the value of what you own, how much you owe, how much you earn, your credit history, and so on. Before you even think about applying for a loan, gather all the documents and information that lenders are likely to request. This chapter leads you through the process.

Examining Your Credit Reports

Good credit is gold. Without it, you have access to your money only. With it, you can put other people's money to work for you. Whenever you apply for a loan, the lending institution performs a *credit check* — a background check to make sure that you're not up to your gills in debt, that your income covers expenses, and that you pay your bills on time. They examine your credit history (documented by the three major credit reporting agencies), bank statements, pay stubs, W-2s, tax forms, and other financial records.

To ensure success at obtaining loans, become proactive in ensuring your credit history remains unblemished. Check your credit report every three months or so, correct any errors, and take steps to improve your credit rating, as instructed in the following sections. No irregularity is too small to correct. (Checking your own credit report doesn't negatively affect your credit score as can too many *credit inquiries* from prospective creditors. Check your credit history regularly, but keep loan and credit card applications to a minimum.)

The following sections show you how to obtain, review, and correct your credit report. We also offer suggestions on how to improve your credit score.

Obtaining free copies of your reports

As of September 1, 2005, the Federal Trade Commission (FTC) mandated each of the three major credit reporting companies provide you with a free credit report once every 12 months (a total of three free credit reports per year). These three major national credit reporting bureaus contain slightly different information about your credit history, or what's called a *credit report* or *credit profile*.

To obtain your free credit report, do one of the following:

- ✔ Submit your request online at www.annualcreditreport.com.

- ✔ Phone in your request by calling toll-free 877-322-8228.

- ✔ Download the Annual Credit Report Request Form from www.annualcreditreport.com (click the link to request your report through the mail), fill it out, and mail it to Annual Credit Report Request Service, P.O. Box 105281, Atlanta, GA 30348-5281.

Some banks offer free credit reports, so consider checking with your bank or credit union, too.

If you already obtained your three free credit reports this year and want something more recent, you can order a credit report for less than ten bucks from any of the following three credit report agencies:

Credit score stats

Credit reporting agencies rely on one or more statistical models to determine your credit score. One of the most popular models is the Fair Isaac Company (FICO) rating system. The credit company assigns numerical values to particular pieces of data in your credit history, such as the length of your credit history and the various types of interest you're paying. They then plug these numbers into the statistical model, which spits out your credit score. It's basically a numbers game that weighs the data on your credit report in the following manner:

✔ 35 percent of the score is based on payment history

✔ 30 percent is based on outstanding debt or how much you currently owe

✔ 15 percent is based on the length of your credit history or how long you've been borrowing

✔ 10 percent is based on recent inquiries on your report (whenever a lending institution requests a report)

✔ 10 percent is based on the types of credit, such as mortgage or credit card interest

---

✔ **Equifax:** 800-685-1111 or online at www.equifax.com.

✔ **Experian:** 888-397-3742 or online at www.experian.com.

✔ **TransUnion:** 800-916-8800 or online at www.transunion.com.

Financial institutions may not file reports with all three agencies. To obtain a complete credit history, order a three-in-one report that contains data from all three agencies. All three agencies offer these three-in-one reports.

Checking your credit score

To give your credit rating an air of objectivity, credit reporting agencies often assign you a *credit score* that ranges roughly between 300 (you never paid a bill in your life) and 900 (you borrow often, always pay your bills on time, and don't carry any huge balances on your credit cards). A "good" credit score is 700 or above. A "great" credit score is anything higher than 780.

Your credit score determines not only whether you qualify for a loan but also how much you're qualified to borrow and at what interest rate. A high credit score enables you to borrow more and pay less interest on it. A high score can also lower your home and auto insurance rates so keeping a close eye on your score is important.

Although the law requires each credit agency to supply you with one report annually, it doesn't require them to provide your credit score. When you're getting your free report, you can choose to pay extra to include your credit score.

Inspecting your report for problems

When you receive your credit report, inspect it carefully for the following red flags:

- ✔ Names that are the same as or similar to yours, but aren't you.

- ✔ Relative with the same name; for example, a father (Senior) if you're Junior.

- ✔ Addresses of places you've never lived.

- ✔ Aliases you've never used, which may indicate that someone else is using your Social Security Number or the credit reporting agency has mixed someone else's data into yours.

- ✔ Multiple Social Security Numbers, flagging the possibility that information for someone with the same name has made it into your credit report.

- ✔ Wrong date of birth (DOB).

- ✔ Credit cards you don't have.

- ✔ Loans you haven't taken out.

- ✔ Records of unpaid bills that you either know you paid or have good reason for not paying.

- ✔ Records of delinquent payments that weren't delinquent or you have a good excuse for not paying on time.

- ✔ Inquiries from companies with whom you've never done business. (When you apply for a loan, the lender typically runs an *inquiry* on your credit report, and that shows up on the report.)

An address of a place you've never lived or records of accounts, loans, and credit cards you never had may be a sign that somebody has stolen your identity. Yikes! Contact the credit reporting company immediately and request that a fraud alert be placed on your credit report. For tips on protecting yourself against identity theft and recovering from it, check out *Preventing Identity Theft For Dummies* by Michael J. Arata, Jr. (Wiley).

Repairing your credit and boosting your score

If you have a credit score of 700 or higher, pat yourself on the back. You're above average and certainly qualified to borrow big bucks at the lowest available rates. Anything below about 680 sounds the warning sirens that you need to dispute errors on your report or repair your credit as quickly as possible. This number is the point at which lending institutions get out their magnifying glasses and begin raising rates and denying credit.

If your credit rating dips below 700, take steps to improve it, such as the following:

- ✓ **Dispute any erroneous items on your credit report.** Disputing a claim doesn't always result in a correction, but you can add a paragraph to your report explaining your side of the story.

- ✓ **Apply for fewer loans and credit cards.** When you apply for a loan or credit card, the lending institution typically orders an inquiry that shows up on your credit report. Evidence that you're applying for several loans or credit cards in a short period of time can make you appear financially desperate.

- ✓ **Pay off your credit card balances, if possible, or at least enough so the balance is 50 percent or below your available credit limit.** Doing so shows that your credit isn't maxed out.

Paying off high-interest credit card balances is always a good idea, but don't start consolidating loans and closing out accounts. Having four open accounts with a balance of $1,000 each on a $5,000 credit limit looks better than one account with a credit limit of $5,000 and a $4,000 balance. Why? Because of something called *credit utilization* — your total debt relative to the amount of credit available to you. Keeping your credit utilization below 80 percent (preferably below 60 percent) improves your score.

Avoid credit enhancement companies on the Web that claim to provide seasoned credit within 90 days. Law enforcement authorities are shutting down these sites on a regular basis. Legitimate credit counselors can help you repair your damaged credit, but it takes some work and a little belt-tightening. Quick fixes are typically fraudulent fixes. For additional tips on boosting your credit score, check out *Credit Repair Kit For Dummies,* 2nd Edition, by Steve Bucci (Wiley).

Avoiding mistakes that can sabotage your loan approval

After you apply for a loan, resist the urge to make any life-changing decisions that negatively affect your current financial status. Major changes can undermine your efforts to secure a loan, so follow these sage do's and don'ts:

- ✔ **Do stay married:** Divorce drains your emotions, energy, and finances. It cuts your assets in half and increases your liabilities, obliterating your chances of securing a loan.

- ✔ **Don't apply for other loans or credit cards:** Any last-minute inquiries that pop up on your credit report can be a red flag that cautions prospective lenders.

- ✔ **Do avoid buying big-ticket items:** Buying an expensive vehicle can sink a deal. If you must have the vehicle, buy, fix, and sell the investment property first, and then purchase the vehicle with your profit.

- ✔ **Don't make any major purchases on credit:** This advice goes for a car, furniture, health club membership, big-screen TV, and any other purchase that can throw off your debt-to-income ratio (see "Calculating your debt ratio" later in this chapter).

- ✔ **Don't cosign for any loans:** No matter what your relationship with the borrower is (or how badly your son, daughter, or long-lost uncle needs the money), don't cosign a loan. Doing so exposes your credit history to potential blemishes when others fail to make their payments.

- ✔ **Don't withdraw or move substantial amounts of cash:** If a prospective lender looks at an account expecting to see $10,000, and it shows a $50 balance, you have some explaining to do.

- ✔ **Do pay your bills on time:** Records of unpaid bills and delinquent payments can get back to prospective lenders. If you have a stack of unpaid bills, pay them now. If a bill is due on the 1st and you pay it on the 15th, you can avoid the late fee. Paying it before the 30th typically keeps the late payment off your credit report. But any bill payment after the due date is considered late and qualifies as *slow pay,* which lenders can figure into their formula assuming they know about it.

If your financial situation changes between the application and the time of closing, you're legally obligated to inform the loan officer and lender of the change.

Chasing Down Vital Paperwork

You can approach a loan application in one of two ways: Either show up with all the paperwork, facts, and figures in hand or consult with a lender first and find out what she needs. The first approach is best, because it demonstrates to lenders that you're well organized and are committed to providing them with everything they need to do their job.

However, in order to come prepared to your lender, you must know which paperwork you need for the meeting. In the following sections, we reveal the information and documentation most lenders are going to require to process your loan application.

Delving into your personal financial information

Unless you plan to borrow money solely against business assets, lenders are going to want to know everything about your personal finances — the value of everything you own, the total you already owe on other loans and credit cards, your monthly and annual income, monthly bills, and so on. And they'll want documentation to back up all those figures.

The following sections show you how to calculate some of these important figures, including your net worth and debt ratio, and list the documentation required to prove the amount of cash you have and the monthly and annual income you earn.

Calculating your net worth

Most people in real estate and banking know their own net worth. Asking folks in these circles, "What's your net worth?" is about as natural as asking them their name. When we ask most consumers to estimate their net worth, however, they look puzzled, as if we had asked them for the square root of pi. They simply have better things to entertain themselves.

Net worth is simply whatever money you would have if you sold all your stuff and then paid off all your debts, including your taxes. Officially, the equation goes like this:

Net Worth = Assets – Liabilities

A strong positive net worth indicates that you

✔ Own more than you owe

✔ Don't borrow more than you can afford to pay back

✔ Can pay off a loan by liquidating assets, if needed

✔ Pay your taxes on time

✔ Probably know more about net worth than you realize

To prove to a lender that you're net worthy, follow these simple steps to calculate your net worth:

1. **Jot down a list of your assets and liabilities.**

   The tough part is identifying assets and liabilities. Following these steps are lists of common assets and liabilities, which can help you identify yours.

2. **Total your assets.**

3. **Subtract your liabilities.**

   The next time someone asks, "What's your net worth?" you're prepared to answer.

The following lists of items may stimulate your brain cells and help you identify different examples of assets and liabilities.

✔ **Home:** If you sold your home today, what could you get for it? If you recently had an appraisal, use that number, assuming the appraiser assigned it an honest value.

✔ **Other real estate:** If you have a vacation home or other real estate, consider how much you could get for it if you sold it today.

✔ **Car:** The blue book value (current value), not what you paid for it.

✔ **Savings account:** Whether you have $5 or $50,000, it counts.

✔ **Checking account:** The current balance as recorded in your check register. No cheating. If you just wrote five checks that haven't cleared yet, you don't really have that money.

✔ **Retirement savings:** 401(k), IRA, SEP, or other account that you don't dip into for your daily living expenses.

✔ **Investments:** Stocks, bonds, and mutual funds that aren't part of a retirement account.

✔ **Jewelry, antiques, and artwork:** If you're not sure what this stuff is worth, have it professionally appraised. People often think that their stuff is worth much more than it really is.

✔ **Furniture:** If you sold all your furniture at an auction or garage sale, what could you get for it?

✔ **Cash value of life insurance:** If you have term life insurance, it's worth $0. If you use a life insurance policy as an investment, how much is it worth today?

If you don't have it, don't count it. The money you stand to inherit when Aunt Millie kicks the bucket doesn't count.

Now for the painful part — liabilities. These are items such as the following:

✔ **Mortgage principal:** The amount you owe on your house today and on any other loans you've taken out on the house.

✔ **Car loan:** How much would paying off your car loan today cost? Write it down.

✔ **Student loans:** If you're paying off any student loans from your old college days or are named as a cosigner on any of your kids' student loans, record the amounts as liabilities.

✔ **Credit card debt:** Dig out your credit card bills and tally up the total you currently owe on them.

✔ **Taxes owed:** Do you owe any back taxes or property taxes? Total the amount.

✔ **Personal loans:** Did you borrow $5 from the neighbor to buy candy from the neighborhood kids? Write it down.

You may be able to obtain most of the liability information you need from your credit report, as discussed earlier in this chapter in the section "Examining Your Credit Reports." However, if you know that you have a debt that doesn't appear on the credit report, be sure to include it in your calculations.

Calculating your debt ratio

Almost every lender examines your debt ratio, so you should know what it is before the topic ever comes up. Your *debt ratio* is how much you pay out in monthly bills compared to your gross monthly income. Generally speaking, you can estimate your debt ratio by dividing your total monthly payments (on loans and credit cards) by your total monthly income:

Debt Ratio = Total Monthly Payments ÷ Total Monthly Income

Your total monthly payments apply only to payments on loans and credit card balances, not for other expenses like groceries, gas, or clothing. They include payments on long-term debts, such as a car loan or student loan payments, alimony, child support, or a balance you carry on one or more credit cards. Debt ratios come in two flavors:

✓ **Back-end debt ratio:** The *back-end ratio* consists of your total debt payments (including your house payment with homeowner's insurance and property taxes) divided by your monthly income. According to the Federal Housing Authority (FHA), your back-end debt ratio should not exceed 43 percent.

✓ **Front-end debt ratio:** The *front-end debt ratio* (also called the *housing ratio*) consists of your house payment alone (including property taxes and insurance) divided by your total monthly income. According to the FHA, your front-end debt ratio should not exceed 31 percent. If your total gross household income is $6,000 per month, for example, your house payment alone should not exceed $1,860.

Gathering bank statements

Almost all lenders are going to ask for copies of the most recent two months' bank statements, so they can see how much cash you have in savings and checking, determine whether you have a healthy cash flow, and check for any activity that looks out of the ordinary (such as large deposits or withdrawals that can't be explained by other documentation). Make a copy of your two most recent bank statements — whether you receive statements monthly or quarterly.

On the copies, take a black magic marker and mark out the account numbers to prevent others from gaining unauthorized access to your accounts.

Tracking down your pay stubs and W-2s

If you work a regular job, you probably get a paycheck every week or two that shows your gross pay, your deductions (state and federal income tax, Social Security, and so on), and what's left — your *net pay.* Most lenders want a full month (30 days' worth) of consecutive paycheck stubs — not one from last week and another from two months ago; they need to be the most recent and consecutive. They should also show your year-to-date (YTD) earnings.

Most lenders also want to see proof of previous years' income. Of course, they can obtain this evidence by looking at your previous two years of federal income tax returns, but many lenders also like to see your W-2 forms, so be sure to make copies of these as well.

If you don't have a regular job, skip ahead to the section "Accounting for business income" to find out which records you need to supply to prove your business income.

Gathering tax returns and schedules

Every lender requires you to submit along with your loan application your federal income tax returns. Make sure you provide copies of your two most recent federal income tax returns. Copy the complete federal tax return, including all schedules and attachments, not just the first two pages of the return. Include *everything* — don't leave something out just because you don't think it's relevant.

You don't need to supply your state income tax returns unless state grants or subsidies are involved in the transaction or financing.

Pulling up other useful documents

If you follow the instructions in the previous sections, you now have all the major facts, figures, and documentation you need related to your personal finances. However, additional documentation may also be useful (and necessary) in determining whether you qualify for a particular loan. Your lender or broker may need the following:

- ✔ Any documents that support your income, such as employment contracts with step increases; union benefit agreements; notes receivable; real estate earnings; earnings from trusts, estates, or settlements; or documentation showing major lottery winnings.

- ✔ Property income, including GAI (Gross Annual Income) from rents; storage fees; fees for facilities, such as clubhouse, pools, satellite TV, cable, laundry, or Internet; parking or carport fees; pet income; income from signage; a percentage of tenant sales (for retail commercial properties); and so on.

- ✔ Documentation of any unusual liabilities (or the exclusion of them), such as major reimbursed business expenses, personally guaranteed business loans (appearing on your credit report), or old loans that you've paid off but that haven't cleared from your report.

Create copies of any documentation that supports your claims of assets, liabilities, and income. Prospective lenders may request specific documents, but gathering everything you have available in advance makes your job that much easier later on.

Accounting for business income

If you don't have a regular job or you have income (or losses) from a business, you need to supply proof of your income or loss:

✔ Some of this documentation may already be included in your federal income tax returns. Be sure to include *all* schedules (C's E's, K-1's, and so on) so that the lender has an accurate picture of each of your investments and business holdings.

✔ If you own 25 percent or more of any company, corporation, or LLC, provide copies of each entity's federal returns for the past two years.

✔ To provide more recent data, produce a report showing YTD income and expenses for the business. You can produce such reports fairly easily by using a business or personal finance program, such as Quicken or QuickBooks. If you have an accountant, ask the accountant to produce a report for you.

Documenting the property you plan to purchase

Your gut feeling that a particular property is a great investment may be enough to convince you to sign a purchase agreement, but it's rarely enough to convince lenders to finance the purchase. You need to have a plan in place for how you're going to profit from the investment, complete with fairly realistic estimates concerning the costs and revenue potential.

Many novice investors view the loan application process as a big hassle that just gets in the way of their vision and profits. However, by forcing you to think ahead, the process actually protects you from making bad investment decisions. As an investor, you should only purchase a property to make money or create future wealth, and you should be able to show how an investment will further those goals before you ever sign a purchase agreement.

In the following sections, we show you how to estimate and document the profit potential for investment properties.

Obtaining an appraisal or comparative market analysis

As a real estate investor, your goal is to discover properties that are likely to generate profits. Basically you don't want to pay more for the property than it's worth. To help in your calculations, get your hands on a *comparative market analysis* or appraisal. Your real estate agent can provide you with a comparative market analysis that shows the probable value of the property in relation to similar properties that have sold recently or are currently on the market.

You want to keep your eyes open for property that's likely to make you profits in one or both of the following two ways:

✔ **Income from sale:** You're looking to buy low and sell high or legally "flip" the property. For more about flipping properties, check out *Flipping Houses For Dummies.*

✔ **Rental income:** You're planning a *buy-and-hold* strategy, in which your rental income covers (or more than covers) your expenses until you decide to sell the property (hopefully for more than you paid for it).

If you want something more formal and more detailed, you may consider hiring an appraiser. A qualified appraiser can evaluate the market value of the property (to assist in estimating your potential income from selling it) or evaluate the income of the property by using a Net Operating Income (NOI) formula (see Chapter 8).

When you're just checking out some properties, bringing in an appraiser may be premature (and an unnecessary expense). Most investors rely on their own market knowledge and perhaps their agents' insight to estimate the property's value. The appraiser enters the picture just prior to closing to confirm that the property is worth the price you're paying. However, if you're seriously considering a property and are questioning your instincts, you may want to hire an appraiser for a second opinion before moving forward.

The seller whose property you're thinking of buying may already have had an appraisal done, in which case, you may be able to review it just by asking. (Don't place blind faith in the seller's appraisal — use it only to confirm or question your own evaluation.)

Looking ahead to potential resale value and repair costs

When you obtain an appraisal, the appraiser usually takes into account the property's current condition. If you plan to flip the property for a quick profit, estimate the market value of the property after repairs. What's a realistic price you think you can get for the property after fixing it up? Your real estate agent should be able to help you come up with a realistic value.

You also need to estimate your total costs for the project, including the cost of repairs and renovations, holding costs for the duration of the project (the total you plan to spend on loan interest, property taxes, loan interest, and utilities), and the cost of selling the property (any real estate agent commissions and closing fees).

Overestimate costs and underestimate the final sale price, so you have a bit of a buffer. For details about making well-calculated investments when flipping properties, check out *Flipping Houses For Dummies* by none other than Ralph and Joe, two of your esteemed authors (Wiley).

If you're planning on holding the property for several years rather than doing a quick flip, you still need to consider the potential future value of the property. For example, if you're buying into a neighborhood where home values are on the rise, then paying close to the appraised value of the property may make sense. The question you need to answer is this: How likely is it that I will more than recoup my investment when I finally decide to sell the property?

Performing a quick cash flow analysis

One of the best ways to build wealth in real estate is to purchase property and hold it indefinitely. During the time you hold the property, you profit in three ways:

- ✔ The property appreciates, gaining in value.

- ✔ Renters pay down your *principal* (the amount you owe on the property).

- ✔ You get a tax write-off for any expenses you incur relating to the rental property.

Of course, your profit hinges on the assumption that you earn more in rent than the property costs you in expenses (including taxes, insurance, landlord-paid utilities, repairs, and improvements). In short, you (and your lenders) want to make sure that that your investment delivers a positive cash flow so you're not losing money.

The formulas for calculating cash flow (or NOI) are fairly basic:

GAI – VAC = EGI

EGI – TOE = NOI

If those formulas look like Greek to you, read on:

- ✔ **GAI** is your Gross Annual Income; simply calculate your yearly income from all possible sources (rent, carport, laundry, storage, parking, and so on).

- ✔ **VAC** is a vacancy allowance; use a minimum of 5 percent of the GAI to allow for vacancy (periods when you have no renters).

- ✔ **EGI** is your Effective Gross Income — the total workable revenue you see from the property. Another way of looking at it is that this is the amount of money you have on hand to cover your property's expenses.

- ✔ **TOE** represents your Total Operating Expenses; this figure includes all the costs to operate the property, except the loan payments. It includes maintenance, taxes, insurance, management, landscaping, landlord-paid utilities, office expenses, and so on.

✔ **NOI** is your Net Operating Income; this number represents your profit on a yearly basis, assuming you pay *cash* for the property.

This formula works for *all* buy-and-hold properties. It shows you and your lenders how much you can afford to pay monthly for the financing. We look at calculating those numbers in Chapter 8.

Calculating the loan-to-value (LTV) ratio

The *loan-to-value (LTV) ratio* is a mathematic representation of how much you owe on your home compared to its appraised value. Banks use LTVs to justify lending money to high-risk borrowers. Even if you have a low credit score and a history of paying your bills a little late, a bank may be willing to cut you some slack and approve your loan if your LTV ratio is low. In other words, the more equity you have in your home, the more likely the bank will approve your loan.

For example, if your home appraises for $250,000 and you owe $200,000 on it, the LTV is $200,000 ÷ $250,000, or 80 percent. Anything below 80 percent is considered great and often qualifies you to borrow more money at a lower interest rate.

Be realistic and know how much you can really afford to borrow. Don't cause yourself stress and future problems by trying to stretch your finances too thin. If after you do your calculations it looks as though you can't afford to borrow more money, don't. Check out some of your other options instead, as we explain in Part IV.

Obtaining zoning information

Most counties or cities zone properties for specific uses, usually to keep businesses out of residential districts or vice versa. Before you purchase a property, find out how it's zoned so you know about anything that could restrict the way you use the property. Check with the local city or county assessment or building inspection office regarding the following:

✔ How the property is currently zoned

✔ Any plans to change the zoning for this area

✔ Whether your intended use of the property fits the current and any new zoning restrictions

✔ Whether the property is subject to changes in zoning require-ments; some properties have "grandfather" clauses that allow them to operate without being subject to changes in the zoning requirements, but these clauses may expire when ownership of a property changes

Pulling city and county records

When you're investing in real estate, knowledge is power; the more you know about a property before you buy it, the less likely you are to encounter nasty surprises later. The info you gather may also improve your chances of obtaining financing to purchase and restore the property. One way to obtain additional information is to research the public records.

Call the city or county assessor's office or the County Real Estate Mapping Division (every county has one) and find out how to access the parcel maps, aerial maps, tax records, building records, zoning or building appeals, violations, and ownership records. The county has to make all these documents available to the public. Many cities and townships post their records and even property histories online.

If you notice any red flags in the property records, such as a building code violation, address them before you purchase the property and they become *your* headache. In many cases, liabilities for violations and/or discrepancies (such as boundary lines, easements, *riparian rights* [relating to a body of water], natural resource claims, and so on) reach back to only a certain number of previous owners. You don't want to get stuck on the hook for someone else's problem from long ago.

Zoning fiasco

If you think that zoning restrictions are something you can deal with later, think again — they may just deal with you later. Several years ago, I (Chip) bought a property without thinking too much about zoning restrictions and grandfather clauses. I planned to use the property pretty much the same way the owner before me used it. Because no grandfather clause was in place that would expire when I took ownership, I figured I was safe.

Unfortunately, a different type of grandfather clause was in place — one I hadn't considered. The clause stated that if the property burned down, *nothing* could be built in its place. The lot would have to remain vacant regardless of how it was zoned!

Fortunately, the building didn't burn down when I owned it, but getting insurance was tough, and I was severely limited in what I could do with the property. It was zoned for multifamily, but I had to convert it back to single family to get the Certificate of Occupancy that's required before you can lease the property.

The "cleaner" the package, and more documentation you have, the more valuable the property becomes — and the easier to sell later on. Get your ducks in a row early on so that problems don't cause expensive delays later.

Show Me the Money: Identifying Sources of Ready Cash

When you're applying for a loan, the lender will ask you to do one important thing: "Show me the money!" Where will you get the necessary cash for the down payment, the closing costs, the pre-paid items, any repairs or inspections, any third-party fees, or commissions? Do you have sufficient cash reserves to cover unexpected expenses or income shortfalls?

You need to be able explain and document those sources of available cash, as we discuss in the following sections.

Sources of cash for down payments, closing costs, and prepaid items

Although you can usually count on financing the major portion of the purchase price, you probably need to pay some closing costs and other expenses out of pocket. Your lender wants to know up front where the money's going to come from. The money can come from just about any source, as long as you have documentation to prove the money exists:

- ✔ Checking and savings accounts
- ✔ Retirement accounts
- ✔ Money from the sale of other properties
- ✔ Refinancing or selling other assets
- ✔ Commissions
- ✔ Bonuses
- ✔ Gifts
- ✔ New loans

Documentation can include bank or other financial statements, sales receipts, HUD-1's from the sale/refinance of real estate, loan agreements, and credit card statements.

Rainy day funds: Cash reserves

On most transactions, lenders want to know you have *reserves* — cash set aside to cover the cost of unpleasant surprises. Simple transactions may require two to three months' cash reserves of the monthly payment or principal, interest, taxes, and insurance (PITI). More-complex transactions may require reserves for construction allowances, credit losses, tenant improvements, and replacement reserves (for example, for new refrigerators or stoves in apartment units). The lender establishes the reserve requirements, and different lenders have different guidelines for calculating minimum reserves.

The more reserves you have, the better. Even shaky loans get approved based on a borrower having strong reserves.

Getting Prequalified or Preapproved

You're always in a stronger position to purchase a property at an attractive price if you have cash or financing in place when making your offer. Cash is king. Financing is queen. Having to secure financing is about a *2*. Because you're reading a book on financing, we can safely assume that, like most investors, you don't have enough cash on hand to purchase investment properties. The next best option is to prequalify or obtain preapproval for a loan:

- ✔ **Prequalification:** *Prequalification* means a lender or broker has reviewed your financial records and determined that you would probably qualify for a particular loan. The lender performs some basic calculations to determine whether your front-end and back-end debt ratios meet the FHA qualification requirements.

- ✔ **Preapproval:** *Preapproval* is a more formal, final step in which the lender obtains all the borrower's documentation and underwrites the loan — without a property. With preapproval, the lender agrees to finance the purchase of an investment property up to a certain amount. As long as the property complies with the lender's standards, the loan is a done deal.

Gaining preapproval puts you in a much stronger position to negotiate. To the seller, it's almost as good as cash. Preapproval is also much better for you as a borrower because it insulates you from changing market conditions. You can move quickly on a property and lock in an approval even if credit tightens and interest rates rise. (Chapter 7 leads you through the loan process so you can do everything necessary to obtain preapproval.)

Chapter 4

Scoping Out Prospective Lenders

*T*o pursue your dream of owning some investment property, you need some start-up cash. Sure, you can shake all the money out of your piggy bank and cookie jar, but that probably won't score you enough cash to finance your first major acquisition. You need serious cash — probably at least 100 grand — and you don't want to have to go through the neighborhood loan shark to get it.

If you haven't shopped for money before, you may have the misconception that the answer is simple — just head down to the bank. But as we reveal in this chapter, you have many more options from which to choose. If the bank won't loan you the money or offer you a decent deal, maybe someone else will.

In this chapter, we introduce you to the money lenders, including bankers, brokers, and some less-conventional sorts. You may be surprised at the variety available. In later chapters, we get into the nitty-gritty of actually asking for the money.

Borrowing Directly from Banks

You don't need a treasure map to locate huge stores of cash. At just about every major intersection in every town or city, you can find a bank chock-full of greenbacks. Unfortunately, depending on market conditions, your friendly neighborhood bank may not be as eager as you might expect to give you the combination to the vault.

But is a bank the best place to go for a loan? Maybe, maybe not. In the following sections, we weigh the pros and cons of financing through a bank and examine the types of loans banks typically offer. After reading through these sections, you should have a pretty clear idea of what banks can and can't do for you as an investor.

Weighing the pros and cons

Financing your investments through a bank, particularly the bank you use to manage your personal finances, may seem like the perfect solution, at first. It's probably convenient, you already know some of the people, and you feel comfortable doing business with them.

 Don't dismiss any source of financing without first exploring it. Before you head down to your bank to apply for a loan, however, weigh the pros and cons of borrowing from a bank. You may discover that a bank is the perfect solution for your financing needs or that the perfect solution isn't so ideal after all.

Pros

Financing your real estate investments through a bank, especially a local bank, offers several perks, including the following:

- ✔ **Security and reliability:** Federally insured banks are generally dependable institutions, although even the most solid institutions are vulnerable to bankruptcy.

- ✔ **Convenience:** Banks typically have many branches, which can give you access to convenient locations when you need assistance or a quick draw from a line of credit to act on an investment opportunity.

- ✔ **Portfolio lending:** Smaller financial institutions, including banks and credit unions, may be more open to holding loans in their own portfolios rather than selling them to bigger banks or mortgage companies. This allows them to be more flexible on interest and terms. However, portfolio lending is usually available only for short-term (less than three years) loans.

- ✔ **Community Reinvestment Act (CRA) goals:** Banks may be required by federal law to lend money for certain projects (including residential and commercial properties) within their immediate geographical area. A lucrative rehabilitation investment project can get the green light just because of the bank's CRA requirements. (For more about the CRA option, check out Chapter 9.)

✔ **Insights and guidance:** Local banks understand the local real estate market. They're aware of trends and market conditions, and can provide a great deal of insight into the viability of an investment property in a specific area. Your banker may just develop into your own personal real estate investment advisor.

✔ **Preferential treatment:** Although the world may seem to be becoming more impersonal, relationships still count, especially when dealing with money. As you develop a relationship with people at the bank, especially loan officers and executives, you place yourself in a stronger position to negotiate more affordable loans.

✔ **Improved access to REO properties:** When a bank forecloses on a mortgage, it often takes possession of the foreclosure property and transfers it to its Real Estate Owned (REO) department, which then tries to sell the property. If everyone at the bank knows you as a trustworthy investor, you may have a better chance of obtaining good deals on these properties.

During economic slowdowns, when credit usually tightens, REO (or bank-owned) properties become more available. In addition, because banks get stuck holding so many of these properties, they're often willing to finance purchases. Through careful negotiations, you can not only buy properties at great prices but also have the bank finance them. For more about this strategy, check out Chapter 17.

Cons

Although banks offer a host of valuable benefits, they also come with a few drawbacks, including the following:

✔ **Limited financing options:** Unlike brokers, banks don't help you shop for loans. They can offer you the loan programs from their own menu only. They may not even offer certain loans (such as government loans) for particular types of properties. A *mortgage broker* can provide more options by working with dozens of banks. Check out "Dealing with a Middleman (or Woman): Brokers" later in this chapter.

✔ **Possible complications:** Many banks *broker* their loans out (sell them to other lenders or institutions), so you end up dealing with another lender anyway without reaping any of the benefits of working through a broker, such as a faster, hassle-free closing.

✔ **Possible loan processing delays:** Many banks rely on hourly employees to handle loan transactions. As a result, they have no financial incentive to wrap things up quickly. Mortgage brokers, on the other hand, are paid only when the loan closes. They're typically paid on a straight commission for producing the loan, so they have an added incentive to see that it closes quickly.

Mortgage broker or loan officer?

You're likely to hear plenty of industry lingo bandied about, but the first two terms you need to sort out are "mortgage broker" and "loan officer." A *mortgage broker* is a licensed company or professional who assists clients in finding and arranging financing through lenders. Brokers are regulated by the state. A *loan officer* may simply be an individual who works on behalf of a licensed lender or mortgage broker to facilitate the process. Some states license the individual loan officers as brokers.

For all practical purposes, a loan officer offers the same services as a mortgage broker but is required by law to work for the licensed broker or lender. It's sort of like going into your doctor's office and seeing a nurse practitioner — sometimes the practitioner offers better advice than the doctor even though the practitioner isn't licensed to practice medicine.

Of course, you're usually better off working directly with an experienced broker, but if you find a great loan officer, you may do just as well or better.

Conventional loans

Banks typically deal in loans that are considered *conventional* or *conforming* — meaning the loan conforms to all the requirements of Fannie Mae and Freddie Mac (see the nearby sidebar).

Conventional loans are the bread and butter of residential real estate financing, particularly for homeowners but also for investors. With conventional loans, you can always be sure that

- ✔ Capital is available.
- ✔ Loan costs and interest rates are generally attractive.
- ✔ Interest rates among lenders vary only slightly because the money is coming from Wall Street through Fannie and Freddie.

Because conventional loans are primarily intended for consumers borrowing money to purchase a home, plenty of information is available on how to find the best deals on conventional mortgages. For more information, we recommend *Mortgages For Dummies,* 3rd Edition, by Eric Tyson and Ray Brown (Wiley). To separate mortgage fact from fiction, check out our book *Mortgage Myths: 77 Secrets That Will Save You Thousands on Home Financing* (Wiley).

Conventional loans are also available for investors, although they tend to cost more and be more restrictive — with a loan-to-value) usually no higher than 75 percent and 1 to 1.5 points. (For more about LTV, see Chapter 3. For information about points, refer to

Chapter 6.) As an investor, keep in mind that having access to cash is often more important than the cost of gaining access.

Subprime (nonconforming) loans

Subprime loans (also known as *nonconforming loans*), are the bad boys of the mortgage lending industry. At least that's what many people were led to believe during the great mortgage meltdown in the late 2000s. Due to some irresponsible underwriting by lenders and irresponsible borrowing on the part of consumers, subprime loans did contribute to the mortgage meltdown, but that doesn't make them all bad. They do serve a useful purpose when used appropriately.

Subprime loans are everything that Fannie Mae and Freddie Mac aren't. Although some subprime loans known as Alt-A loans can go through Fannie and Freddie, most don't. (An *Alt-A loan* or *alternative A-paper* loan is one for which the approval is based primarily on the borrower's lower credit score, or other situations such as self-employment, that increase the risk of repayment.) Instead, subprime loans are usually available through other institutional investors, pension funds, insurance companies, various large and small mortgage banking firms, and even individuals.

Fannie and Freddie who?

The question is more like "Fannie and Freddie what?" Fannie Mae is actually a nickname for the FNMA, or Federal National Mortgage Association. Freddie Mac is a nickname for FHLMC, or Federal Home Loan Mortgage Corporation.

Both organizations do pretty much the same thing — they purchase residential mortgages and then convert the mortgages into securities for sale to Wall Street investors, indirectly financing the purchase of homes. In other words, they sort of act as the middlemen between banks and Wall Street investors. The end result is that they make money readily available for the purchase of homes and other real estate.

Although both institutions began as government-chartered, private companies, they're now controlled by the government as a result of the problems they ran into during the mortgage meltdown that started in 2008. While we were writing this book, it was still too early to tell whether the end result would be a consolidation, merger, or something else entirely, but whatever happens, Fannie and Freddie should essentially function the same way but with more restrictions.

Instead of Fannie and Freddie setting the qualifications for these loans, the market and individual investors lay down the rules and decide what's available and to whom. As a result, they can offer a much greater variety of loan packages that appeal to niche markets and address specific needs, such as the following:

- ✔ Limited-documentation loans make it easier for investors who don't have the necessary financial documents (tax returns, pay check stubs, and W-2s) to qualify for loans.

- ✔ Hybrid adjustable rate loans can help investors with short-term financing and cash flow by providing flexibility in interest rates.

- ✔ Rehabilitation programs can open doors to investors by funding special projects or development in certain areas.

Subprime loans have some drawbacks, particularly if the borrower doesn't fully understand the terms, which can be complicated. When shopping for any loan, make sure you're working with a qualified and trustworthy professional who can clearly explain your options and the ramifications of choosing a particular option. In short, know what you're getting into before signing on the dotted line.

One of the main drawbacks of subprime mortgages is that certain programs can disappear overnight as the appetites of Wall Street investors and consumers change. Numerous creative subprime loan packages emerged leading up to the mortgage meltdown, and many of these options disappeared as soon as loan defaults shot up.

Dealing with a Middleman (or Woman): Mortgage Brokers

A *mortgage broker* is sort of like a real estate agent, but instead of helping you find the right house, the broker helps you find the right loan. Ideally, a broker sits down with you to determine what you're planning on using the money for and then assists you in selecting the lender and loan package that best meets your needs. Through a broker, you gain access to dozens of financing options as opposed to the limited few you may find with a local bank.

In the following sections, we discuss the pros and cons of working through a broker and then show you how to find brokers and research their credentials and references.

Weighing the pros and cons

As you probably already guessed, we think that most investors can benefit by shopping for loans through a broker — a good broker, that is. In the following sections, we list the reasons why. To give a balanced perspective, we also list a couple of reasons why you may not want to use a broker. Furthermore we give you clues to uncovering a good broker and what you can do to verify the broker is reputable and the right choice for you.

Pros

Mortgage brokers offer a host of benefits for fueling your real estate purchases and development, including the following:

- ✔ **Better selection:** A broker has access to many different lenders, each of whom may offer several different loan packages, so you're more likely to find a loan that meets your unique needs.

- ✔ **Bargaining power:** Mortgage brokers can negotiate fees and terms with large lenders and play one off the other to negotiate the best deal on your behalf.

- ✔ **Marketplace knowledge:** Brokers are more in tune with new and creative financing programs and options. When new programs become available, they're often the first to know.

 Although mortgage brokers specialize in the mortgage lending industry, many are also very knowledgeable about the real estate market in their area. In addition, a well-established broker is likely to have connections with other investors, local bankers, real estate attorneys, and so forth. Take full advantage of what your broker has to offer.

Cons

Mortgage brokers are sort of like doctors and lawyers — if you find the right one, you have no reason not to use a broker. However, finding and keeping a qualified broker who's dedicated to serving your needs can be quite a challenge. Watch out for the following:

- ✔ **Lack of experience:** Many brokers may not be experienced enough or large enough to deal with the right lenders. You can spend a lot of time researching and checking credentials and references before you find a great broker.

- ✔ **High turnover:** Brokers can disappear overnight. Becoming a broker doesn't require a huge capital investment, so brokers often come and go. After a long search, you may find a top-notch broker only to discover that several months later the person is no longer in business. You may end up losing time, money, and a valuable resource.

Shaking the branches for a broker

Although you can certainly flip through the "Mortgages" section of the phone-book ads or search the Internet for "mortgage brokers any town, your state USA" to find brokers in your area, these methods don't focus in on the highest quality prospects. The best way to find qualified, experienced mortgage brokers is to search through the people who actually borrow money to finance their real estate investments — real estate investors.

Obtain referrals from investors in your area, so you know the broker has experience working with investors and has provided satisfactory service to at least one person. Most investors will also tell you which brokers to avoid.

If you don't know other real estate investors in your area, you have some work to do. Join a reputable real estate investment club such as the Rental Property Owners Association (RPOA) and start networking. (Search the Web for "rental property owners association" followed by your state.) You can pick up plenty of market knowledge just by attending meetings and talking with people who've been there and done that.

Checking a broker's credentials

Ideally, a mortgage broker works on your behalf to find you the best deal. Unfortunately, brokers don't have a *fiduciary* (legal financial) responsibility to you as the borrower. As a result, some brokers may try to sell you on a loan that brings them a higher commission rather than provide you with a better deal. This is why finding a trustworthy broker who has a stellar reputation is so important.

In the following sections, we show you how to do your own background check on mortgage brokers, verify their credentials, and interview the top three candidates.

Doing a background check

After you have a list of possible candidates, start trimming that list to three finalists by doing a background check on each candidate:

> ✔ **Check the National Association of Mortgage Brokers (NAMB) Web site at www.namb.org to make sure the broker is a member.** NAMB members follow a strict code of ethics, tend to be more dedicated to the profession, and are required to take continuing education courses.

✔ **Search the Internet for the company's or individual's name.** If the candidate has a bad reputation, dissatisfied clients are likely to post something about it on the Web.

✔ **If the company or individual has a Web site or blog, visit the site and explore.** Make sure the broker deals in both conventional and subprime loans. The more established brokers also offer government loans, including Federal Housing Authority (FHA) and Veteran's Administration (VA) loans. (Check out the section "Borrowing from Uncle Sam: Government Loan Programs" later in this chapter for these types of loans.)

✔ **Visit your state's Web site and verify that the broker is licensed in your state.** If you can't find your state's Web site, call the licensing board in your state capital. All 50 states have licensing requirements for mortgage lenders. Some states have licensing for individuals as well. Check for any administrative actions or sanctions, or complaints (many complaints aren't public unless the department of licensing takes action). You may also want to check your state attorney general's Web site.

✔ **Check the Better Business Bureau (BBB) for any complaints.** Start at the national Web site's home page at (www.bbb.org), which can direct you to the Web site for your local branch.

✔ **Contact your local chamber of commerce to determine whether the broker is a member in good standing.** Being an established member of the local business community is always a big plus.

✔ **Contact each broker who's made the first cut and obtain three references from investors and three references from real estate agents the broker has worked with.** (Make sure the real estate agents are well-established in the community, not just part-timers.) Call the references and ask about their experience working with the broker.

Don't just go with the broker who has the largest ad in the phone book or the local newspaper. Check their credentials with the state licensing board, the BBB, and the state attorney general's office for complaints and/or regulatory actions or sanctions.

Interviewing the top candidates

After you've chopped your list of candidates down to three, call to set up an interview with each of them. During the interview, be sure to ask the following questions:

✔ **How long have you been in business?** You're looking for someone who's been a broker for at least a couple of years.

✔ **How many transactions do you process in a year?** Good brokers average at least 40 to 50 transactions per year. Someone who processes way fewer than average may lack motivation. A broker who processes way more may not be careful enough.

✔ **What percentage of your transactions are conventional, non-conventional, and government loans?** Brokers generally deal with far more conventional loans, but look for a broker who has experience with all three types.

✔ **What percentage of your transactions are investor loans?** Brokers who do a substantial percentage of their business with investors are usually a better choice than those who exclusively serve consumers/homeowners.

✔ **How many lenders do you work with?** Generally speaking, the more the merrier. The more lenders the broker has access to, the wider the selection of loan packages.

✔ **What's your specialty?** Just as real estate agents specialize in certain types of homes, mortgage brokers specialize in certain types of loans (such as government loans, first-time home buyers, construction loans, and so on). Choose a broker who specializes in the types of loans that best fit your investment strategy. (See Chapters 5 and 9 for descriptions of different residential and commercial loan types.)

✔ **What are your application fee requirements?** Determine how much money the mortgage broker charges upfront at the time of application and what those fees are applied toward. Compare costs among the brokers and make sure they're applying any fees to real services rather than pocketing them as extra money.

✔ **What's your policy on locking in interest rates?** Does locking in a rate cost extra? How long does the rate remain locked? How soon before closing does the rate have to be locked?

✔ **What's your refund policy for cancelled loan applications?** Some brokers actually charge upfront fees up to $1,000 or more if you cancel a loan application. You're better off knowing about it now than when you need to cancel an application.

 During the interview, make sure you get along with the broker and that your personalities match up pretty well. If this is a good fit, you'll be working together for some time. You want somebody you can get along with.

Taking the Hard-Money Route through Private Lenders

Hard money is called "hard" for a reason — it's hard to get, hard to pay, and generally costs more than your average loan. Hard money comes from individuals or small groups of private investors who like to obtain a high return on their money and are willing to take some additional risk in order to get it.

Because hard money costs more, you may wonder why anyone on earth would even consider it. Just like any other type of investment method, hard money has its upsides and downsides. Hard money offers several benefits:

- ✓ **More financing options:** You gain access to cash you may not be able to get through a conventional lender. Hard money loans typically cost more in points upfront and interest, but the terms can be more flexible than with conventional loans.

- ✓ **More collateral options:** Hard-money lenders often accept the *future value* (after renovations) of a property as collateral, so you don't have to borrow against other assets, like your home.

- ✓ **More flexibility:** You can often close the transaction faster, with less paperwork, and even set up a separate escrow account with a hard money lender to pay for repairs and renovations.

- ✓ **Less intrusion into your business:** Banks tend to be more intrusive, wanting more information about the business operation than a hard money investor does. The hard-money lender sets a lower LTV requirement, so you have less equity risk from the start. Even so, hard-money lenders do want to know the plan for repayment and see a business plan if it's contingent on a business tenancy arrangement.

On the flipside, hard money does have a few significant drawbacks:

- ✓ **Higher cost:** Sometimes gaining access to cash, whatever the cost, is good investment decision — as long as you account for that cost in your calculations and can still turn the profit you want.

- ✓ **Lower ratios:** Another disadvantage of hard-money loans is that the LTV's (loan-to-value ratios) are typically lower. For example, instead of being able to borrow 80 to 90 percent of the value of the property, you may only be able to borrow 65 to 75 percent. However, hard-money lenders are often willing to make the calculations on the future value of the property. For more about using hard money to finance your real estate investments, check out Chapter 11.

Hard-money lenders may be more willing to negotiate with investors, especially investors who have a solid track record. Some lenders, for instance, may charge three or four points upfront to reduce their exposure to the risk of an early default but then agree to refund one or two points when you've paid off the loan.

Borrowing from Uncle Sam: Government Loan Programs

The housing market plays an important role in driving the economy, so the U.S. government does what it can to support this key industry. One of the primary support mechanisms are government (or government-secured) loans made available to first-time home buyers. If you're like most Americans, you probably used an FHA (Federal Housing Administration) or VA (Veterans Administration) loan to purchase your first home.

Through the FHA, the U.S. Department of Housing and Urban Development (HUD) also offers loans to homeowners and investors to assist in rehabilitating properties. Government loans are designed to help the marketplace in areas where the private sector can't. After Hurricane Katrina, for example, several government programs came to the rescue, encouraging investors to assist in rebuilding the damaged areas. Special grants and state and federal loan programs gave investors access to cash that the banks and private sector wouldn't or couldn't offer.

 In most cases, the government steers clear of lending money directly to homeowners and investors. Instead, the government *secures* the loans. If the borrower fails to pay back the loan, the government steps in, picks up the tab, takes the property, and tries to sell it to recoup its loss. Additionally, most government programs are limited to owner-occupied properties.

As a homeowner, you're already aware of some of the benefits that government-secured loans offer homeowners, but government loans can also benefit investors in two important ways:

✔ Understanding government loans can enable you to flip the property to a buyer down the road. For example, the *Good Neighbor Next Door loan* (GNND) enables qualified buyers (including teachers, law-enforcement professionals, and firefighters) to purchase certain HUD homes with only a $100 down payment, or even some HUD repo's at half price; *203(k) loans* help an owner rehabilitate a property, pay for additions, and even purchase new appliances. Using the GNND loan and a 203k loan, a qualified investor can actually buy a home for half its market value with a $100 down payment and then sell it several years down the road to earn a handsome profit.

✔ You may be able to purchase government-owned properties directly (usually those foreclosed on due to nonpayment of an FHA or VA loan) and finance the purchase through the government agency.

For more about using specific government-sponsored loan programs to finance real estate purchases and rehabilitation, see
Chapter 5.

Financing through the Seller

Before most homeowners can pack up and move, they have to sell
their homes and pay off their current mortgages so they can afford
to buy their new homes. Homeowners who've paid off their mortgages or have sufficient cash available, however, don't need the full
purchase price upfront. They can sell you the home and *finance*
the purchase. In other words, the seller becomes the bank.

If a seller is willing and able, you can often purchase the property
on contract through a lease option agreement or a land contract.
The contract takes the place of the mortgage document that most
buyers sign when they close on a house. In the following sections,
we explain how these contracts work. For more about the pros and
cons of financing through the seller and the nitty gritty of how to
harness the power of seller financing, check out Chapter 12.

Lease options

A *lease option agreement* is sort of a rent-to-own deal. You rent the
property from the owner for a fixed period (usually no more than a
few years), at the end of which time you have the option to buy the
property. Normally, the seller requires some sort of down payment
(often less than a typical mortgage lender requires), which should
be applied to the purchase price, along with monthly rent equivalent to about 1 percent of the purchase price.

A lease option agreement can be a great way to finance the purchase of an investment property, assuming you're working with a
seller who deals aboveboard, and you have a great plan in place
for obtaining cash or alternative financing by the time your option
to buy the property rolls around.

So how does a lease option work? The monthly payment consists
of rent plus some additional money that's applied to the purchase
price. In other words, if the going rate for rent on the property is
$1,000 per month, you may have a monthly payment of, say, $1,500
with the extra $500 being added to your down payment. This
ensures that you're building equity in the property during the lease
part of the agreement, and it provides the seller/lender with some
security in the event that you back out of the deal.

Make sure that the lease option agreement is *very specific* regarding the application of payments and terms of exercising your option. Otherwise, you may lose a lot of money in rent that you assumed was being applied to the purchase price or lose your option to buy on some minor technicality. Have a qualified real estate attorney look over the agreement before you sign it, and make sure you understand it completely.

Land contracts

With a *land contract* (also called a *contract for deed*), the seller essentially functions as a bank, so you're cutting out the middleman. In most cases, you handle the transaction through a reputable escrow company. The deed is held in escrow, and you make payments to the escrow company. When you've finally paid the loan in full, the escrow company releases the deed to you.

Land contracts are often win-win situations, benefiting both the seller and the investor:

- ✔ The seller profits not only from the sale of the property but also from the interest the buyer is paying. They earn investment income generated by an asset they know and love — their own real estate.

- ✔ The investor benefits by not having to pay a lot in closing costs and being able to obtain a loan without having to jump through hoops for a bank or mortgage company. With the increased cash flow, an investor can obtain more properties by using this strategy.

Make absolutely sure that payments are handled by a servicing company — *not* by the seller — and that the deed is placed into escrow. The last thing you want is to make payments for seven years, only to find out that the underlying mortgage wasn't paid, the property has a tax lien against it, and the seller is nowhere to be found to sign off on the deed! Been there, done that, not going back for seconds.

Teaming Up with a Cash-Heavy Partner

Successful partnerships begin with individuals whose needs and offerings complement one another — in other words, when one partner has what the other needs, and vice versa. People who have plenty of cash often don't have plenty of time, talent, and motivation to purchase, renovate, and manage real estate, and they really don't have to — they can hire someone else to do it for them. This is where you come in as an investor. You have (or should have) the know-how. All you need is the money.

In the following sections, we introduce you to various ways to structure a partnership that typically work well in real estate. In Chapter 13, we go a little deeper to show you how to partner with the right individual(s).

Opting for a limited partnership

A *limited partnership* is called "limited" for a very good reason — the liability protection (none) and tax benefits (insignificant) of a partnership are very limited. Legal actions against one partner can lead to actions against all partners, and each partner can be held personally liable for actions of the partnership as a group. In other words, if you're going to partner up with someone, you really need to form the partnership inside the protective bubble of a corporation, as discussed in the following section.

Limited partnerships do offer a few benefits. They're

✔ Easy to set up

✔ Inexpensive

✔ Simple to manage for the few involved parties

You can set up a limited partnership with two or more people (including yourself) on a per-property basis or to invest in multiple properties. Just make sure you have all the terms of the partnership *in writing*. The agreement should address the following three areas:

✔ **Partner responsibilities:** Spell out what each partner is responsible for — supplying capital, finding and buying real estate, making repairs and renovations, marketing and selling the property, and so on.

✔ **Profit sharing:** Specify how profits from the real estate ventures are going to be split.

✔ **Dissolution:** Stipulate how you're going to divide any cash and other assets if you decide to dissolve the partnership later. Yeah, we know — when forming a partnership, the last thing you want to think about is the possibility that it will end, but it's better to come to an agreement now when you're friends than later when you're at each others' throats (hopefully, that doesn't happen).

Have an attorney draw up the partnership agreement and explain the terms to everyone involved. Each partner should have his own legal representation to ensure that his interests are protected.

If you're forming a corporation, a partnership agreement is still very useful in clarifying each partner's responsibilities. If you decide not to use a written agreement, at least make sure that your corporation papers clearly explain how distributions will be applied — usually determined by shareholder percentage of ownership and disclosed on the K-1 (the tax schedule showing the total annual payments, deductions, and credits to the shareholder).

Going the corporation route

Even if you happen to form a partnership with one or more other individuals, managing your partnership as a *corporation* offers additional benefits in terms of taxes and liability protection. You have three options here:

- **LLC:** A limited liability corporation (LLC) limits your exposure to risk. If someone takes legal action against the corporation, your personal assets are protected. For most investors, we recommend forming an LLC, as discussed in Chapter 2.

- **Sub-S corp:** A Sub-S corp (short for Subchapter S corporation) also limits your exposure to risks and allows for pass-through taxation (unlike a C-corp). With *pass-through taxation,* the corporation's profits pass through to your individual income tax return, avoiding *double-taxation* (in which both you and your corporation are taxed). Only individuals, not other business entities, can own a Sub-S corp, and the corporation can have a maximum of 75 shareholders. With a Sub-S, you run the risk of the IRS forcing it into C-corp status (described in the following bullet) if the corporation shows as having too much *passive income* (income you don't really do anything to earn, such as rental income, that's taxed at a lower rate than *earned income*).

- **C-corp:** A C-corp (short for Chapter C corporation) also limits your personal liability, but we don't recommend going the C-corp route for most real estate investors. First, you need to have at least 75 shareholders or establish a real estate investment trust (REIT), as discussed in Chapter 2. A C-corp also exposes you to double-taxation, which can really take a bite out of your profits.

A Sub-S corporation is simple to establish and file for, but make sure to file for the Sub-S election with the IRS right away after forming the corporation. For more about forming and managing a corporation, check out *Incorporating Your Business For Dummies* by The Company Corporation (Wiley).

Part II

Financing the Purchase of Residential Properties

The 5th Wave   By Rich Tennant

"We got a hybrid loan. It starts out as a fixed rate loan, converts into an ARM, and if the lender's not satisfied with his return, we host his in-laws every other summer in the basement."

In this part . . .

When most folks buy a home, they're usually best off to look for a 30-year fixed-rate mortgage that keeps their payments low and steady and allows them to pay off the loan in a reasonable amount of time. When you're financing real estate investments, however, cash flow becomes much more important. You usually want to use as little of your own money as possible, so you have cash on hand to cover other investments and unexpected expenses.

This part gives you the tools to secure the financing you need to start hunting for residential real estate investment opportunities. In this part, we explore the many residential loan programs currently available, show you how to compare different loan packages to find the one that costs the least overall, and lead you through the loan application from filling out the forms to closing.

Chapter 5

Finding the Residential Loan Program That's Right for You

In This Chapter

▶ Understanding why choosing the right loan is so crucial

▶ Focusing more on cash flow than on loan costs and interest

▶ Checking out what your government can do for you

▶ Dodging prepayment penalties

Consumers have hundreds of different residential loan programs to choose from, including zero-down-payment programs, 40- and 50-year terms, interest-only loans, and complicated adjustable-rate mortgages that can double your payment overnight! In addition, investors may have access to government financing through rehabilitation loans, renaissance loans, and even grants for redevelopment. With so many types of loans and other financing to choose from, how do you pick the type that's best for you as an investor?

This chapter introduces you to the most common residential loan types, explains how each program works, and guides you in choosing the right type of loan for your investment needs.

The market is in constant flux, so new mortgage programs are constantly being introduced while obsolete programs are being phased out. In writing this chapter, we've tried our best to provide information that's detailed enough to be useful, but general enough to accommodate market changes.

Understanding Why Finding the Right Residential Loan Is Key

You're not the only one who wants to earn a buck off real estate. Lenders want to earn their keep, too, so they charge all sorts of interest, fees, and penalties. As an investor working through one of these lenders, you have two primary goals:

- ✔ **Gain access to cash.** You need cash to do deals. Check out the following section, "Choosing a Loan Type to Maximize Your Cash Flow" for more information.

- ✔ **Pay as little as possible for access to that cash.** After all, the more you pay in interest, fees, and penalties, the less money you walk away with at the end of the day.

In order to meet these two goals, you want to locate the right residential loan. To help you know what's available, throughout this chapter we roll out a veritable smorgasbord of loan types so you can home in on the type that sounds best for a particular deal. Another key to locating the right loan is to examine *all* the pros and cons of each available loan before making a selection. We cover this important step in Chapter 6.

When searching for the right residential loan, you also need to know the difference between residential and commercial loans. *Residential* mortgage loans finance the purchase of properties that people live in — single-family homes, multifamily dwellings, apartment buildings, condos, and co-ops. *Commercial* loans finance the purchase of properties that house businesses. With residential loans, lenders typically examine the ability of the *borrower* to make payments and eventually pay back the loan. With commercial properties, lenders give more weight to the *building's* ability to produce sufficient income. (See Part III for more about financing the purchase of commercial properties.)

Choosing a Loan Type to Maximize Your Cash Flow

When most folks buy a home to live in, the main ingredients they're looking at in a mortgage loan are interest rate, *term* (number of years to pay off the loan), and monthly payment. They want a monthly mortgage payment they can afford without paying an exorbitant amount of interest over the life of the loan.

As an investor, your needs are different. Your primary goal is to gain access to cash, even if you have to pay more to gain that access. The interest rate, terms, and payment matter only as they relate to your all-important cash flow. As a result, the criteria you use for comparing loans are likely to differ a great deal from the criteria you use to select a mortgage for a primary residence.

We toss the term *cash flow* around quite a bit and even use it as a verb, as in "Wow, this property really cash flows!" So what is cash flow, exactly? *Cash flow* simply means that the property is bringing in more cash than is going out each month. If your property is losing money, it has a negative cash flow . . . and you have problems.

When you're more focused on gaining access to financing than worrying about the cost of financing, your options suddenly multiply. You can begin to consider loans that you would otherwise dismiss outright as costing too much. In addition, you can begin to explore a host of options that aren't available to the average homeowner, such as rehabilitation loans.

In the following sections, we show you how cash flow enables you to leverage the power of using other people's money to finance your investments and introduce you to a few types of loans that can maximize the cash you have available for investments.

The power of OPM (other people's money)

One of the secrets to maximizing your investment profits is to use as little of your own money and as much of other people's money (OPM) as possible. By using OPM, you stretch your investment dollar — you can buy more and better properties and increase your profit potential as a result.

Whenever you finance the purchase of a property, rather than paying cash with your own money, you're using OPM. Throughout this book, we reveal various sources of OPM, including bank loans, government-secured loans, hard-money lenders, small-business loans, and so on. We introduce the concept of OPM here, so you have a better understanding of why you want to borrow money (rather than using all your own money) to purchase real estate. After you grasp the concept of OPM and understand the leverage it gives you, you're better prepared to begin evaluating the sources of OPM.

The magic of using OPM is in the numbers, as the following examples reveal:

- ✔ You invest $100,000 cash to buy, renovate, and sell a house for $120,000. You just made a 20 percent profit ($20,000 profit divided by your investment of $100,000 equals 20 percent).

- ✔ You invest $20,000, borrowing the other $80,000 to buy, renovate, and sell a house for $120,000. You just made a 100 percent profit ($20,000 profit divided by your investment of $20,000 equals 100 percent).

Did I overpay for that loan?

Several years ago, I (Chip) obtained a mortgage for a two-family duplex at 9.50 percent interest, and paid 3 points to get it. The market rate for mortgages was about 6 percent at the time, and qualified home buyers were usually able to secure a mortgage without paying any points. Most people would have thought I was crazy.

Was I?

Crazy like a fox, maybe. I needed a loan to purchase an investment property, and because the property had been severely neglected and in disrepair, the type of loan I needed wasn't readily available in the marketplace. Without cash, I couldn't do the deal, so I was willing to pay a premium to gain access to the cash I needed. It was just a short-term solution until I could make some repairs to the point that the property became eligible for more-conventional (and less-expensive) financing. But the cash flow made it very attractive (and profitable) — even at the higher interest rate.

When financing real estate investments, you have to remember to stop thinking like an average homeowner and start thinking like an investor. Put your investor cap on when examining the terms and make sure the cash flow works for the property you're planning on buying.

In these examples, you earn five times more profit percentage-wise by using other people's money, even though you earn the same profit in terms of dollar amount. You may argue that you still end up with $20,000 in your pocket either way. But say you have $100,000 to invest, as in the first example. Instead of buying one property with $100,000, you can divvy it up into $20,000 chunks to buy five $100,000 properties (borrowing $80,000 for each). You now control $1,000,000 worth of real estate and when you sell the properties, you earn $20,000 each for a total profit of $100,000!

 Borrowing money is always risky, but you have to take some risk. Throughout this book, we show you ways to reduce the risk, but unforeseen events can undermine the best-laid plans. As a real estate investor, you need to decide for yourself whether the potential benefits outweigh the risks.

The following sections reveal some loan types that can free up more of your own money and maximize the use of OPM.

Interest-only mortgages

An *interest-only loan* is just what it sounds like; if you take out an interest-only loan for $100,000, in two years, after making 24 interest-only payments, you still owe $100,000. Sound like a bum deal?

It may be, if you plan on living in your home for 15 years and the value of the home doesn't appreciate significantly. But if you're using the loan for a quick flip, it may be perfect. You pay off the loan in full right after you sell the house. In the meantime, you have more investment capital to put toward renovations or other properties.

The key to using interest-only loans wisely is in making sure the property provides a positive cash flow — enough revenue to more than cover all your costs, including the monthly interest you're paying, and the value of the property is stable or rising. When considering interest-only loans, be aware of the following:

✔ Most interest-only loans are adjustable rate mortgages (ARMs), so carefully check the adjustment period, index, margin, and cap. (For more about ARMs, check out the following section.)

✔ Rarely is an interest-only loan interest-only for the life of the loan. Read the fine print to determine when and how you must pay the principle. Some loans require a lump-sum payment three to five years down the road. They suck you in with low monthly payments early and then sock you with huge bills later. This fake-out may be devastating to the average homeowner, but if you know about it and plan for it, an interest-only loan can be your ticket to a profitable investment property.

Nobody can judge a loan type as good or bad without considering how the investor uses the loan to finance the investment. If a no-interest loan frees up some cash so you can complete the repairs and renovations on a property more quickly, the fact that your entire payment was going only toward interest matters very little.

Grabbing a hold of ARMs

Adjustable rate mortgages (ARMs) have interest rates that fluctuate. You may take out a loan for 5 percent and find yourself paying 8 percent the following year. Even so, ARMs can play a valuable role in your investment strategy. They're often easier to qualify for, and if you can sell the property or refinance the loan before the rate jumps, you may be able to avoid any huge increases in interest and payments.

As was revealed during the great foreclosure crisis that began in 2008, ARMs are risky business for most homeowners. Tight credit can undermine your plans to sell or refinance. In the meantime, your monthly payment increases could make the property unaffordable. Realize that when you take out an ARM, you're taking a gamble. To minimize your exposure to risk, figure out the worst-case scenario and plan accordingly.

When shopping for ARMs, examine the following factors to determine the worst-case scenario:

- ✔ **Initial interest rate:** The interest rate when you sign for the loan. This is usually a *teaser* rate to make the initial payments more attractive.

- ✔ **Adjustment period:** The frequency at which the rate can go up or down. This is typically one, three, or five years but can also be months rather than years.

- ✔ **Index:** ARMs are tied to an *index* that typically rises or falls based on government lending rates. Ask which index the lender uses, how often it changes, and how it has performed in the past. Several indexes are considered standard, including the Treasury index, the London InterBank Offered Rate (LIBOR), the Cost of Funds Index (COFI), the Prime Rate, various T-Bills, and the Fed Funds Rate.

The Treasury index is always a little safer and secure and is the most common. Take some time to look up whatever index your lender uses, and make sure you can find it in *The Wall Street Journal* (the financial rates section) or a similar publication.

- ✔ **Margin:** The percentage above the index that the lender charges — think of it as a markup. For example, if the index is at 3 percent and the margin is 2 percent, you pay 5 percent interest. If the index rises two percentage points to 5 percent, you pay 7 percent interest. The margin remains the same throughout the life of the mortgage.

- ✔ **Cap:** The highest interest rate the lender can charge, no matter how high the index rises. So if the lender sets the cap at 9 percent, you never pay more than 9 percent interest, no matter how high the index goes. The lender likely will quote a yearly cap and a lifetime cap as, for example, "2/6", which means the rate can go up 2 percent per year (or per adjustment), and 6 percent over the life of the loan.

Make sure you understand all the possible adjustments that can take place and calculate the payments under a worst-case scenario. Plug this number into your *pro forma* calculations (your projections) to make sure that your property will still cash flow under the worst of circumstances. We can't stress enough the need to do your homework, and possibly consult your highly qualified and trusted mortgage broker before selecting an ARM.

Hybrids

A *hybrid loan* is a combination of an ARM and a fixed-rate loan. With a hybrid term, the interest rate remains fixed for a certain number of years, after which time the rate is adjustable. For example, with a 3/1 hybrid, the interest rate remains fixed for 3 years and then becomes an adjustable-rate loan in which the rate can be adjusted every year. A 2/28 hybrid has a fixed interest rate for the first 2 years and then adjusts each year for the next 28 years.

These types of loans are better suited for situations in which you plan on holding the property for at least a couple of years before selling it and you're fairly certain that interest rates won't drop over the next couple years. If you're planning on selling the property quickly, an adjustable rate mortgage with a low introductory interest rate may be a better choice. (See the previous section for more on adjustable rate mortgages.) On the other hand, if you plan on holding the property for longer than a couple of years, a fixed-rate mortgage may be more appealing.

The main advantage of a hybrid over a straight ARM is that it provides, at least for a time, a guaranteed fixed interest rate, which can help you establish more reliable cash flow projections for the duration of the fixed-interest term. You still need to be careful, however; hybrid loans can turn into time bombs if your projections are based on unrealistic assumptions. An unexpectedly steep jump in the interest rate can quickly create a negative cash flow.

Hard-money loans: Private investors

When *easy* money is unavailable (money from financial institutions), you can always turn to *hard-money lenders* — private investors who offer loans that typically charge several points upfront, use higher-than-average interest rates, and require payment in full after only a few years.

Why would any investor in her right mind even consider a hard-money loan? Because you gotta have cash to do a deal, and sometimes hard money is the only money you can get your hands on. For more about financing your real estate investments with hard money, turn to Chapter 11.

Taking Advantage of Government-Secured Loans

You may be able to hit up your rich Uncle Sam for a loan to finance your real estate investments (refer to Chapter 4 for more on how government loans work). Although the government rarely loans money directly, especially to investors, it often secures loans so lending institutions can make the money available without exposing themselves to huge risks. (If a borrower defaults on a government-secured loan, the government pays the difference and sells the home to recoup at least part of its loss.)

Although many government loans are available only to finance the purchase of *owner-occupied* properties (properties that the borrower/homeowner is going to live in), in some cases you can also use these programs to finance the purchase, repairs, and renovations of investment properties.

In the following sections, we describe a host of government programs that may be available to you depending on your investment strategy and the property you're planning to purchase. We also show you how to go about tapping into these government-sponsored resources.

Tapping the FHA for a loan

Although the Federal Housing Authority (FHA) works with mortgage lenders to make loans available primarily to first-time home buyers, some FHA programs are open to investors. These loans can directly benefit you by providing government-secured financing for investment properties, especially if you're investing in residential real estate and multifamily housing. The FHA is the federal government's way of promoting the American Dream of homeownership.

As an investor, these programs can also benefit you indirectly — you can often use FHA loans to assist prospective buyers in financing the purchase of an investment property you're selling. One of the biggest obstacles preventing first-time buyers from purchasing a home is their inability to qualify for a conventional mortgage. FHA loans make qualifying much easier for them.

If you're working with a well-qualified mortgage broker (see Chapter 4) who has experience working with investors, she can direct you to FHA loan programs that you may be able to qualify for as an investor. The same is true if you're working directly with a lender who handles FHA loans.

To get more information about FHA loans and other programs straight from the source, visit the FHA Web site at www.fha.gov, where you can find information about the Good Neighbor Next Door program (described in Chapter 4), special loans for financing the development of multifamily housing and medical centers, streamlined FHA mortgages, 203(k) loans, and much more.

If you decide to sell a property you own, you can often attract more buyers if you advertise that you accept FHA financing. Also offer to put prospective buyers in touch with your mortgage broker, who can help them determine whether they qualify for an FHA loan. In addition to helping the buyers, your broker can screen out any *looky-loos* (casual browsers) who may not be able to afford the property.

If you're looking to invest in residential real estate, you may be able to turn to one of the following FHA loans. Check carefully (your lender or broker can assist you) because they have strict guidelines.

FHA 203 (b) loans

FHA 203 loans are designed for first-time homebuyers and people who don't have a lot of money for a down payment. Investors can utilize these loans to help their potential buyers finance the purchase of their residential real estate, or to acquire and occupy a multifamily property. (You'd have to occupy at least one of the units in a multifamily property.) During the writing of this book, FHA 203b loans

- ✔ Are available only for owner-occupied, one- to four-family homes
- ✔ Allow borrowers to obtain a loan for up to 96.5 percent loan-to-value (LTV), meaning they can purchase a home with a down payment of as little as 3.5 percent of the property's market value
- ✔ Are *assumable* for a new purchaser, meaning the owner can get out from under the loan by arranging to have a buyer pick up the payments

FHA offers another program that you may find useful as an investor: *streamline refinancing*. This program enables you to lower your interest rate on a previous FHA loan with low or no out-of-pocket costs faster and with less documentation than most other refinance loans. For example, if you purchased a home with a $100,000 FHA loan as a home buyer a couple of years ago, moved out, and now use the home as an investment property, you may be able to refinance at a lower interest rate through this program. Even better, you can refinance all the way back up to the original loan amount (about $100,000 in this example) without obtaining a new appraisal, and roll all costs into the new loan — including any points you may pay to lower the rate.

Title 1 loans

Title I loans are available only for owner-occupied properties to enable homeowners to finance the cost of repairs and renovations up to $25,000.

Title I loans are great for investors who want to flip the property they're living in but don't have the cash on hand to bring the property up to market conditions. In a situation like this, you can use the Title I loan in either of the following ways:

- ✔ Take out the Title I loan yourself to pay for repairs and renovations before placing the property on the market.

- ✔ Place the home on the market as is (at a lower asking price) and let potential buyers know about the Title I loan they can take out to cover the cost of repairs and renovations after they take possession.

FHA 203(k) loans

FHA 203(k) loans are similar to Title I loans in that they're available only for owner-occupied properties and they allow the owner to finance the cost of repairs and renovations. The difference is that 203(k) loans allow the cost of *major* repairs to be combined with the purchase price of the property.

This program is ideal for investors who want to purchase a property, live in it while they're making repairs and renovations, and then sell it. Just make sure you don't overimprove the property and improve yourself right out of a profit. Also, your intent has to be to live in the house for at least 12 months as a primary residence.

For example, if a home is worth $100,000 now but would be worth $150,000 all fixed up, you can obtain an FHA 203(k) loan for the full $150,000 upfront, take your time completing the repairs and renovations, and then sell the property after you've lived in it for at least 12 months total.

Multifamily loans

For larger residential properties, FHA does offer a multifamily program that allows investors to purchase and rehabilitate apartment complex–type properties. You can often combine the FHA loan with other government grants or subsidies for improvements, tax credit, or rental payments such as the Section 8 program.

You can find out more about FHA programs for multifamily housing through HUD's Web site at www.hud.gov/groups/multifamily.cfm.

Viewing Veterans Affairs (VA) loans

As one of the perks for serving in the military, the U.S. Department of Veterans Affairs (VA) offers veterans zero-down financing to purchase owner-occupied one- to four-family properties. If you're a veteran, these loans are often the best deal in town. As an investor, you can often leverage the power of VA financing when you decide to sell a property — these loans give you access to another pool of potential buyers.

Although VA loans are generally available only to veterans, even investors who aren't veterans can often obtain VA financing to purchase foreclosure properties that the VA owns.

Any mortgage broker or lender who handles VA loans can assist you in determining whether you qualify for one of the programs. Your broker may also be able to work with any prospective buyers (if you decide to sell the property) to determine whether they qualify for a VA loan, which may make the property more affordable to them. For more about VA loans, visit the VA's Web site at www.va.gov and then click "Benefits, Home Loans."

Considering REO loans

Real Estate Owned (REO) property is typically property repossessed by the bank after foreclosure. The bank now has to sell the property to recoup the remaining portion of the unpaid debt. With government-secured (FHA and VA) loans, the government agency that secured the loan gets stuck with the property.

Ideally, the government or bank that owns the REO wants someone to show up with cash and buy the property, but sometimes eager cash-heavy investors are few and far between. To add a little extra motivation, the owner of the REO property may offer to finance its purchase, sometimes offering very attractive deals and perhaps even the ever-elusive no-money down deal. These deals can be ideal for an investor because you can pick up the property at a great price *and* secure attractive financing in one fell swoop.

To obtain an REO loan, first find one or more properties that you want to purchase from a bank or government agency and then contact that agency and ask whether it's willing to finance the purchase. Experienced investors who have a proven track record of getting (and keeping) bad loans off the books have a better chance of obtaining this sort of financing. After all, the government or bank doesn't want to have to foreclose on the same property again.

For more in-depth information about REOs, check out our book *Foreclosure Investing For Dummies* (Wiley).

One of the best times to pursue REO's is when the housing market is in a slump and foreclosures are on the rise, as we discuss in Chapter 17.

Tapping into state and local grants and loans

State and local governments often identify certain target areas (such as rundown downtown districts, renaissance zones, and other areas in need of a pick-me-up) for redevelopment. They then offer incentives — usually in the form of state or local grants or low-interest loans — to get investors like you involved in pitching in.

State and local grant and loan programs rarely get you *all* the money you need to purchase and rehab a property. They're intended as add-on programs, typically used in conjunction with other loans. Here we describe the most common types of state and local programs you're likely to find:

- ✔ **State housing development authorities:** Meant to encourage redevelopment in areas like Detroit or areas hit by disasters such as hurricanes, state housing development authorities often sell bonds to make money available to both homeowners and investors. They also fund special first-time home buyer programs and foreclosure rescue grant programs.

- ✔ **Renaissance zones:** Great for investors, *renaissance zones* are areas that federal, state, and/or local governments have declared tax-free (or tax-lite) to encourage development. In these zones, investors can secure loans with significantly lower monthly payments, sometimes saving hundreds or thousands of dollars per month. It's like getting an interest-free loan, which dramatically increases your cash flow.

✔ **Economic development department:** To encourage development within certain areas, many larger cities have economic development departments that provide tax breaks, investment funding, capital expansion funds, construction, or rehabilitation grants to projects within their district.

✔ **Grants and specific use loans:** States, local governments, and some nonprofit agencies often provide loans or grants for improvement projects — such as health care facilities, women's shelters, and emergency housing — designed to add value to specific areas.

If your property is located in an area flagged for development or meets the state or local program's criteria, contact the state housing development authority, the city housing agency, and any nonprofit housing agencies to find out about available funds and what you need to do to qualify.

Start researching at the top — HUD's Web site at www.hud.gov. Here you can search for information by state, find out about economic development programs and grants, type in the address of a property to determine whether it's located in an enterprise zone, and discover other community networks and programs that can assist you in rebuilding communities while earning a profit for yourself.

To find state-level programs, head to your state's housing authority Web site. To find it, use your favorite Web search tool to search for your state's name followed by "housing authority." Your county, city, or town may also have its own housing authority, so use the same strategy to search for it. The Public Housing Directors Association (PHDA) also has a directory of members, which you can access by visiting www.phada.org and clicking the "Housing Authority Websites" link.

REO financing in action

The first foreclosure I (Chip) ever purchased was a vacant two-family dwelling, which I bought for $500 down and simply had to pay the balance of the previous loan. The seller, the Bank of Florida, financed the purchase over a five-year term. No qualifying, no closing costs!

We can't guarantee that a bank or government agency will be willing to finance the purchase for you, but it's certainly worth a try. You never know if you never ask.

Many mortgage brokers who are approved by their State Housing Development Authority can also provide valuable assistance.

Digging up USDA Rural Development loans

To encourage development of rural areas the USDA offers its own financing through Business and Industry (B&I) loans, discussed in Chapter 9, and rural development (RD) loans. As an investor, you don't qualify for the RD loans designed for residential home buyers, but these loans can benefit you indirectly if you buy and sell property in rural areas. Prospective buyers who can't obtain financing elsewhere may qualify for an RD loan.

For more about USDA loan programs to encourage rural development, visit www.rurdev.usda.gov/rd/index.html.

Avoiding the Prepayment Penalty Trap

When a bank loans you money for 30 years, it's counting on the fact that you're going to be paying interest to them for a long time. They have invested a certain amount of time and energy in originating that loan and need time to be able to make a profit off their investment (just like you do). The bank also doesn't want you refinancing with another bank a year or two down the road and cutting them out of the deal.

To discourage you from refinancing, and to help keep their initial costs low, the bank may try to slip a *prepayment penalty clause* into your mortgage. With this clause, if you refinance and try to pay off the loan early, you have to pay a stiff penalty — sometimes thousands of dollars.

When shopping for mortgages, be sure to ask whether the mortgage loan has any prepayment penalties and then read the mortgage carefully before signing it. Prepayment penalties typically apply for up to the first three years of the loan but can extend to longer periods on larger investment properties. If you have to refinance later, you don't want a prepayment penalty getting in the way.

Chapter 6

Bargain Hunting for Low-Cost Loans

. . . .

In This Chapter

▶ Grasping interest rates concepts and calculations

▶ Understanding the term *term*

▶ Exploring closing costs and how they affect your wallet

▶ Figuring the bottom line — the total cost of a loan

. . . .

*W*hether you're borrowing money to buy a place to live in or invest in, you're not just buying real estate — you're also buying money to finance the purchase. You're a consumer buying a product — in this case, a loan program — and you need to compare costs and benefits just as you do when you make any major purchasing decision.

Your goal is to find a loan that costs you the least amount of money over the life of the loan and requires monthly payments that you can afford and that ensure positive cash flows (as discussed in Chapter 5). The monthly payment part is fairly easy to figure out — lenders have to tell you what your monthly payments are going to be upfront. Determining how much it will cost you over the life of the loan, however, is a little trickier.

In this chapter, we show you how to shop for loans to find the one that costs the least and is best suited to your investment goals.

Understanding How This Interest Thing Works

Banks and other lenders primarily earn their money by charging *interest* on loans — a certain percentage of the *principal* owed on the loan (*principal* is the amount you owe on the loan). Well, that's certainly easy enough to understand, especially if you've purchased any big ticket item like a car or a house on credit.

In practice, however, interest can get pretty complicated. Lenders may choose to collect interest upfront in points, calculate your rate as simple interest, amortize the loan, or even play a game of "moving target" by adjusting the interest rate over the life of the loan. In the following sections, we sort out the complexities that surround interest rates and explain the essential jargon you're likely to encounter in plain English.

Keeping simple with simple interest

Simple interest is simple because you can usually calculate the amount of interest you need to pay in your head or with a very basic calculator. The formula goes like this:

Principal × Interest Rate = Annual Interest

You can then calculate your monthly interest by dividing by 12:

Annual Interest ÷ 12 Months Per Year = Monthly Interest

For example, say you borrow $100,000 at 8 percent interest:

$100,000 × .08 = $8,000 interest per year

$8,000 ÷ 12 = $666.67 interest per month

Because the formulas calculate only the interest owed on the loan, simple interest is perfect for interest-only loans. (Check out Chapter 5 for the ins and outs of interest-only loans.) Unless you're dealing with interest-only loans or smaller loans, such as home equity loans or lines of credit, you're unlikely to encounter simple interest. Most loans use more complicated methods to calculate interest.

Grasping the concept of amortization

If you ever looked at an amortization table or tried to set up your own spreadsheet to calculate amortization, you probably ended up bleary-eyed from trying to figure out how anyone could possibly have devised such a convoluted system for calculating house payments. *Amortization* is a method for calculating the retirement of debt that applies significantly higher portions of early payments toward interest and significantly higher portions of later payments to pay down the principal.

The mathematicians who devised this system had a method to their madness. They were attempting to create a system to provide for constant loan payments over a fixed period. The system also had to account for interest on the loan and the fact that each payment reduces the principal owed on the loan, which ultimately results in extinguishing the loan. In other words, they set some lofty goals.

Explaining how amortization works in theory is way too complicated, so consider the following example: Say you owe $100,000 at 8 percent interest over a 30-year term. The following steps show you how to calculate amortization and determine the amount of interest due for each payment:

1. **Determine the total monthly payment due.**

   This step is the most mathematically complicated. To figure your payment, plug the numbers into the following formula:

   $$A = \frac{i \times P \times (1+i)^n}{(1+i)^n - 1}$$

   A is the total monthly payment, i is the periodic interest rate, P is the principal, and n is the number of *periods* (payments over the life of the loan). The *periodic interest rate* is the annual interest rate divided by 12 months. The *number of periods* is the number of years times 12 months.

   Using this formula, your monthly payment on a $100,000 at 8 percent interest over a 30-year term comes to $733.76. Yep, this is why everyone uses a loan calculator or a spreadsheet instead of doing the math by hand, but we think you should know where the numbers are coming from.

2. **Calculate how much of the payment is interest by using the same formula you use to calculate simple interest.**

   Your payment consists of interest plus a reduction in the loan balance (principal). Here's that formula:

   Principal × Interest Rate ÷ 12 = Monthly Interest

   So, in this example, your interest on your first payment is $666.67: $100,000 × .08 ÷ 12 = $666.67

3. **Subtract your interest payment from your total payment to figure out how much principal you pay off.**

   Your first monthly payment of $733.76 breaks down like this:

   Total payment of $733.76 – $666.67 in interest = $67.09 of principal.

4. **For the next payment, subtract the amount you paid toward the principal from the total.**

   $100,000 – $67.09 = $99,932.91, so this figure is the number you use when you figure your next payment.

5. **Repeat Steps 1 through 4 for each subsequent payment.**

   Based on the calculation in Step 4, the interest portion of your second payment is $666.22:

   $99,932.91 × .08 ÷ 12 = $666.22

   With this payment, $67.54 goes toward principal, and with each subsequent payment you end up paying more toward the principal and less toward interest. This pattern continues until the entire balance is paid off in 360 months (30 years).

If you have Microsoft Excel, select File⇨New and check the templates on your computer to determine whether your version of Excel comes with an amortization schedule. If it does, you can click it and click OK to create a new loan amortization schedule. Just plug in the loan amount, term, and interest rate, and Excel does the rest. If your version of Excel has no amortization template, you can download a free one and other real estate finance–related templates from Microsoft's Office Web site. Go to office.microsoft.com, click the Templates tab, click in the search box, type "amortization," and press Enter. You have several results to choose from.

Telling the difference between the interest rate and APR

Most people know that the interest rate and the annual percentage rate (APR) differ, but few people understand how they differ. The *interest rate* reflects the simple cost of the money you're borrowing. The *APR* is designed to reflect the total cost of the loan, including any loan origination fees and prepaid costs. As a result, the APR is higher than the simple interest rate.

Why use an APR? Congress designed the system back in 1974 as a way to enable consumers to more easily compare the actual costs associated with the loans. It sort of functions as a consumer protection tool, helping borrowers compare apples to apples in the world of personal finance.

For example, say you came into my (Chip's) office and I quoted you a 30-year mortgage loan for $200,000 at 6.50 percent. You talk to another loan officer who offers you the same deal at 6.25 percent. On the surface, you think this is a no-brainer — paying one-quarter percentage point less is going to save you money over the life of the loan. However, what if I'm charging zero points (*points* are pre-paid interest; see "Paying interest upfront with points" later in this chapter), and this other guy is charging three points (in this case, $6,000)? Now it's not such a no-brainer.

Which deal is better? All other factors (loan origination fees and any other costs) being equal, mine is, and you can quickly see by looking at the APR:

> ✔ APR on 30-year fixed mortgage $200,000 at 6.50 percent with zero points: 6.5 percent.

> ✔ APR on a 30-year fixed mortgage $200,000 at 6.25 percent with three points: 6.626 percent.

What makes my deal even more attractive is that if you were to pay off the loan in less than 30 years (highly common, especially for investors), you'd save the $6,000 you would have paid in points to the other guy.

You can find several APR calculators on the Web by searching for, you guessed it, "APR calculator." One of our favorites is at `mortgages.interest.com/content/calculators/aprcalc.asp`.

Exploring how adjustable rate mortgages work

Adjustable rate mortgages (ARMs) are mortgage loans with interest rates that can fluctuate (rise or fall). During the mortgage meltdown, many unsuspecting homeowners got burned by ARMs they probably never should have been placed into. Although this has given ARMs a bad name, they're actually very useful, particularly for investors, as long as you use them strategically.

Not all ARMs are created equal, though. Several factors influence the best-case and worst-case scenarios of how low or high the interest rate can go, including the initial interest rate, the *adjustment period* (how often adjustments can be made), the *index* (the base interest rate you pay), the *margin* (the lender's markup on the index), and the *cap* (the highest rate the lender can charge). We explain these factors in greater detail in Chapter 5.

For example, say you take out an ARM to purchase a property that you're almost certain you can renovate and sell within a year. Taking out an ARM with a rate that stands to rise at the end of one or two years could be a reasonable gamble. And if you can get the ARM for a lower interest rate than the going rate for fixed-rate mortgages, the ARM can actually save you quite a bit of money.

Of course, taking out an ARM always carries some risk. Being "almost certain" you can sell the property within the year for more than you have in it is no guarantee. Whenever you invest in anything, you need to assess the risk/benefit ratio for yourself and determine just how much risk you're willing and able to take on.

Paying interest upfront with points

Plenty of lenders, particularly hard-money lenders, charge interest upfront in the form of points. (Hard-money lenders are private lenders; check out Chapter 11 for more on using these types of lenders.) So what are points? One *point* is equivalent to 1 percent of the total loan amount, so for every $100,000 you borrow, a point costs you $1,000. A point on a $200,000 loan costs $2,000.

So why do lenders use points? Lenders typically charge points for one of the following reasons:

✔ **To lower the interest rate:** When you choose to pay interest upfront, the lender may reduce your interest rate, so you pay less interest with each payment.

✔ **To get the money upfront:** If you pay back the loan quickly, the lender earns enough for taking the time to process your loan.

When you pay interest upfront to lower the interest rate, you may not see a net savings for several years. You can calculate the break-even point to determine whether you'll actually save money by paying upfront for a lower interest rate. The *break-even point* is the payment period at which you've saved enough money with the lower interest rate to pay the cost of the points:

1. **Start with the cost of the points.**

   Two points on a $100,000 loan cost $2,000.

2. **Determine your monthly savings per payment as a result of the lower interest rate.**

   To do this, simply subtract the monthly payment at the lower interest rate from the monthly payment at the higher rate. In this example, assume you're saving $50 per month.

3. **Divide the cost of the points by the monthly savings.**

   In this example, you divide $2,000 by $50, which equals 40. Your break-even point is at 40 months. If you plan on keeping the property for more than 40 months, you'll save money paying points. If not, it costs you more to pay points.

Of course, it gets more complicated when you take taxes into consideration, but this gives you a general idea of how points work.

Another reason you may want to pay points is so you can qualify for a larger loan, because the points you pay lower your monthly payment. Does paying points make sense? That depends. Crunch the numbers yourself. For example, a $100,000 loan at 7 percent interest over 30 years with zero points requires a monthly payment of $665.30. The same loan at 6 percent with 2 points would cost an extra $2,000 upfront but lower the payment to $599.55 — a monthly savings of $65.75. At that rate, breaking even on the upfront cost would take just under 31 months, but the investor would likely be able to claim a tax deduction for the costs, depending on his tax situation. In this case, paying points is an okay deal.

Although some people say they never pay points, and others recommend doing everything you can to lower the interest rate, points really have no *never* or *always.* Sometimes you have to pay points to gain access to the cash you need to do the deal, as we explain in Chapter 5.

Considering the Mortgage Term

When investing in residential real estate and looking for a low-cost loan, you need to take a close look at the mortgage term. A lender often quotes the mortgage *term* in years; for example, you may have a 15- or 30-year mortgage. However, for payment purposes you calculate the term on a monthly basis — 12 payment periods per year over 30 years equals a total of 360 months or payment periods. A 15-year mortgage has 180 payment periods.

Understanding the term is important because it ultimately affects how much money you end up paying for the loan over the life of the loan. For your average homeowner, a shorter term can pay dividends. Pay off a $200,000 loan in 15 years rather than 30, and you save a whopping $155,437.

However, as an investor, you have a different perspective. Investors like longer terms because they increase a property's cash flow, giving them more cash to do more deals. For example, payments on that 15-year mortgage would cost in excess of $467 more per month. That would significantly reduce monthly profit on any rental property and give you much less money to work with on other deals. ***Remember:*** As an investor, the longer the term, the better.

Accounting for Closing Costs

Every major newspaper has a financial section where banks, brokers, and other lending companies post their interest rates and often the points (prepaid interest) they're currently charging. Although this financial information gives you a general comparison of the going rates, it really doesn't help investors or home buyers comparison shop. These figures usually don't mention other costs associated with the loan, such as the loan origination fee, discount points, processing fees, paperwork fees, and junk fees. (For more about junk fees, see "Forking over other fees" later in this chapter.)

When comparison shopping for loans, you need to take these fees into account. In the following sections, we explain the most common closing costs you're likely to see.

Getting socked with origination fees

The *loan origination fee* is what the lender or broker charges you as a service fee for processing your loan. They're usually calculated the same way as points are — as a percentage of the total loan amount and charged as a cost to the borrower. For example, a 1 percent loan origination fee is 1 percent of the total loan amount, or $1,000 for every $100,000 you borrow.

Although most lenders charge a maximum of 1 percent, the loan origination fee is always negotiable. Sometimes, all you need to do is ask the loan officer to reduce the fee. In other cases, you may need to mention that Julie Swanson on the other side of town is charging less. For more tips on negotiating, check out *Negotiating For Dummies* by Michael C. Donaldson and David Frohnmayer (Wiley).

Although you may not consider the loan origination fee part of the loan, you should always include it in your calculations of the total cost of the loan. This strategy enables you to more effectively comparison-shop for the best deal.

Forking over other fees

Points and loan origination fees are only a couple of the legitimate expenses you can expect to see on a Good Faith Estimate (GFE) or HUD-1 (see the next section). Other legitimate fees include the following:

- ✔ Appraisal fee
- ✔ Closing or escrow fee

- Credit report fee
- Flood certification fee
- Lender fee (negotiable)
- Recording fees
- Reserves for paying taxes or insurance
- State tax/stamps
- Title insurance
- Underwriting fee (negotiable)

Some lenders include a *processing fee,* which is fairly standard but usually negotiable. (This fee covers the time and effort invested in handling the paperwork, along with any copy or printing costs.) You can usually figure out whether any of these fees is exorbitant by comparing a few Good Faith Estimates from other lenders.

Although we like to think of brokers and bankers as being trustworthy professionals, some are less forthright than others and are infamous for padding their closing fees with what the industry calls *junk fees.* One time I (Chip) was surprised to find an "e-mail fee" of $35 tacked onto my closing statement. Upon inquiry, I was told that this amount was what the title company charged to e-mail the documents over to the lender. How ridiculous! I was able to get it removed in about 45 seconds. Here are some other more common junk fees to watch out for:

- Administration fee
- Affiliate consulting fee
- Amortization fee
- Application fee
- Bank inspection fee
- Document preparation fee
- Document review fee
- Express mail fee

- Funding fee
- Lender's attorney fee
- Lender's inspection fee
- Messenger fee
- Notary fee
- Photograph fee
- Settlement fee
- Signup fee
- Translation fee

Junk fees can also be inflated costs of standard fees. If the going rate for overnight fees is $75, for example, and one lender tries to charge you $150, ask why.

Are Good Faith Estimates standardized?

When you start shopping for loans, you're likely to see all sorts of Good Faith Estimates, each of which categorizes its expenses differently and assigns each expense a different name. All these differences can make it difficult, if not impossible, to compare estimated closing costs.

Fortunately, the federal government is stepping up to deal with this issue. On November 12, 2008, HUD announced several new mortgage rules to help consumers shop for lower-cost home loans. One of the new rules requires that starting on January 1, 2010, lenders use a standardized GFE. The new three-page GFE benefits borrowers in two ways:

✔ When all lenders start using the form, the standardized model enables borrowers to compare costs line by line without having to decipher different names for the same charges.

✔ The new GFE contains line-item references to the same amounts on the HUD-1, making it easier to spot any changes between the estimated charges on the GFE and the actual charges on the HUD-1 at closing.

Examining the Good Faith Estimate

By law, your broker or lender is required to provide you with a detailed breakdown of all the costs associated with the loan (residential, not commercial loans). Lenders typically provide a Good Faith Estimate prior to processing your residential loan application and then a HUD-1 statement at closing detailing the actual final costs. (The *Good Faith Estimate* is a list of projected costs to the borrower, while the *HUD-1* breaks down all the actual costs that the seller and buyer are responsible for paying at closing.)

If the lender doesn't provide a Good Faith Estimate upfront, ask for one and make sure it's legible and understandable. Some lenders like to use fine print and shading to conceal what they're really charging and then give you a copy of the copy of the copy of the faxed original to make it completely unreadable.

Costs, particularly the loan origination fee and points, shouldn't change dramatically from what's on the Good Faith Estimate to what you see on the HUD-1 at closing. If you notice any change, bring it up at the closing table and don't sign the papers until any issues are resolved to your satisfaction and in writing. See Chapter 7 for more about covering your back at closing.

Calculating a Loan's Total Cost

Your bank or mortgage broker is likely to lay out a virtual buffet of loan types for you to choose from: fixed-interest, adjustable rate mortgage (ARM), interest-only, and others. We describe the pros and cons of these loan types in Chapter 5. If you're still unclear about the benefits and drawbacks of a particular loan program, ask the bank representative or your mortgage broker lots of questions.

Don't get too caught up in the various loan types. For people buying houses they plan to reside in for 30 years, loan type is a big factor. For real estate investors, particularly those who plan to sell the property or refinance the loan within a couple of years, the cost of the loan over the life of the loan becomes more important. To compare loans and find the best bargains, take the following steps:

1. **Start with the amount the bank charges you upfront in loan origination fees, points, and other fees.**

   When performing these calculations, include all points, but realize that not all points are created equal. Lenders can charge *discount points*, defined by some states as the legal cost associated with reducing the interest rate for a borrower. Lenders can also charge points as a fee (for example, *origination points*) that don't reduce the borrower's interest rate.

2. **Multiply the monthly payment times the number of months you plan to pay on the loan.**

3. **Add the two amounts to determine your total payment.**

4. **Total the amount of each payment that goes toward paying the principal of the loan.**

   Your lender can tell you how much of each payment goes toward principal.

5. **Subtract the total you determined in Step 4 from the total in Step 3.**

   The result is the total amount you can expect to pay for the loan over the life of the loan.

To save yourself some time performing these calculations, check out the mortgage payment calculator on our Mortgage Myths Web site at (www.themortgagemyths.com).

Say that you're considering two loans, each for $100,000. You plan on using the loan to buy and renovate a home over two years and then sell it and pay off the remaining principal on the loan. You have a choice between a 30-year, fixed-rate mortgage at 6 percent or a 30-year, interest-only loan at 5 percent. Look at the 6-percent, fixed-rate mortgage first:

Loan origination fee and discount points:	$1,000.00
Monthly payment of $599.55 × 24 months:	$14,389.20
Total payments (fees plus monthly payments):	$15,389.20
Total paid toward principal:	$2,531.75
Total cost of loan (payments minus principal paid):	$12,857.45

Here are the numbers for the 30-year, interest-only loan at 5 percent:

Loan origination fee and discount points:	$1,000.00
Monthly payment of $416.67 × 24 months:	$10,000.08
Total payments:	$11,000.08
Total paid toward principal:	$0.00
Total cost of loan:	$11,000.08

As you can see, even though you're not paying down the principal on the interest-only loan, over the life of the loan, you pay about $1,700 less. In addition, the interest-only loan has much lower monthly payments, freeing up cash to use for renovations and other investments.

As a general rule for *quick flips* (buying and selling a property in less than a year's time), opt for loans with low (or no) closing costs, low (or no) discount points, and low interest rates. Avoid any loans that have early-payment penalties.

Don't forget to account for cash flow and tax benefits that may be available. A lender may charge you $3,000 in points, but if you can write off a portion of that mortgage interest on your taxes, it may end up costing you less than $3,000. Also, always remember that having access to financing is often more important than the cost of that financing. Crunch the numbers to get the lowest-cost loan available, but don't beat yourself up if you have to pay more than average — as long as you can walk away with a decent profit and a positive cash flow.

One more, very important word of caution: Always factor in a margin of error to account for the unexpected.

Chapter 7

Navigating the Loan Application and Processing

. . . .

In This Chapter

▶ Filling out a loan application

▶ Tracking your paperwork through the approval process

▶ Gathering 'round the closing table

▶ Getting a loan to finance investment-based residential property

. . . .

*A*ssuming you own the home you live in, you've already filled out at least one loan application and have been through one closing. Whether you did everything correctly is another question, but at least you have a general sense of how the process works.

As the buyer of a residential property and the borrower, you have the most papers to sign — papers dealing not only with the property you're buying but also with the loan you're taking out to finance the purchase. Faced with mountains of documents to sign, borrowers (even seasoned investors) often give the paperwork a cursory check at most before signing on the dotted line. This carelessness can be a big mistake, however, leaving you open to signing up for something you never really agreed to.

In this chapter, we review the closing process in greater detail and show you how to avoid many of the traps that ensnare even the savviest real estate investors.

Completing Your Loan Application

Filling out a loan application isn't exactly rocket science, but it does call for some careful attention to detail. The application requires specific and accurate financial details that enable your *loan originator* (broker or loan officer) and your lender to properly evaluate your current financial situation and your ability to make payments and repay the loan. In addition, the lender provides you with specific information, by way of lender disclosures, about the loan program and its costs.

In the following sections, we show you how to complete the loan application, review the various disclosures, supply the additional documentation your lender needs to process your application, and sign a release of information, so your lender can confirm the information you supply.

Walking through the parts of the loan application

In order to be able to accurately complete the loan application, you first need a good grasp on what the form comprises. Everything in your loan application package revolves around the *Uniform Residential Loan Application* — a five-page, fill-in-the-blank form that requests all sorts of information about the property you're buying and your financial situation. Although your loan originator actually prepares the form for you, go through the process yourself first so that you can gather the necessary information ahead of time and see for yourself what the lender looks at to determine whether you qualify for the loan.

The Uniform Residential Loan Application is commonly referred to as the *FNMA (Fannie Mae) 1003 application* or simply the *Ten-Oh-Three*. To download the form, visit www.efanniemae.com/sf/ formsdocs/forms/1003.jsp and click the link for the desired version — the blank form or an interactive version you can type your own entries into.

The form consists of ten sections:

- ✔ **I. Type of Mortgage and Terms of Loan:** Basic information about the loan, including the type (FHA, VA, Conventional, Rural), total loan amount, interest rate, *term* (number of months), and amortization type. Your loan originator can supply this information. Refer to Chapter 6 for details about amortization.

- ✔ **II. Property Information and Purpose of Loan:** Description of the property (including its location) and how you plan to use it: as a primary residence, secondary residence, or investment property. This section also covers whether the loan is for new construction or refinance, how the title will be held, and the source of the down payment and any closing costs.

- ✔ **III. Borrower Information:** General information about you, including your name, address, previous address, Social

Security Number, marital status, number of children (if any), and so on.

✔ **IV. Employment Information:** Information about your and any coborrower's employment, including names and addresses of the most recent three employers, dates of employment, and monthly gross income. The lender wants to know the past two to five years' history.

✔ **V. Monthly Income and Combined Housing Expense Information:** Information about monthly income including base pay, bonuses, overtime, commissions, dividends and interest, and rental income, along with housing expenses that include any monthly rent, existing home loan payment (principal and interest), property taxes, mortgage insurance, homeowners' association fees, and so forth.

✔ **VI. Assets and Liabilities:** The value of what you own *(assets)* and how much you owe *(liabilities)*. Assets include balances in checking and savings accounts, stocks and bonds, the current cash value of any life insurance policies, vested interest in retirement funds, the value of any real estate you own, and so on. Liabilities include any current loans you have, credit card debt, alimony or child support payments, and job-related expenses (including child care).

✔ **VII. Details of Transaction:** Overview of the financial aspects of this particular loan, itemizing the costs and sources of financing. Costs include the purchase price, cost of alterations and improvements, cost of land (if purchased separately), *refinance costs* (debts to be paid off through the refinance), closing costs, cost of mortgage insurance, and so on. Sources of financing include the loan itself, closing costs paid for by the seller (if any), cash from the borrower, and other sources. You may need to consult your loan officer and others involved in the transaction to gather all the information you need.

✔ **VIII. Declarations:** Yes/no questions for you and your coborrower (if applicable) to determine whether past or present situations may affect your ability to make payments and pay the loan. Questions include whether you have any outstanding judgments, whether you've declared bankruptcy or suffered foreclosure, whether you're obligated to pay child support or alimony, and so on.

✔ **IX. Acknowledgement and Agreement:** Here is where you sign, acknowledging that the information in this loan application is correct to the best of your knowledge and that you and any coborrower are knowingly entering into this agreement with the lender.

✔ **X. Information for Government Monitoring Purposes:** Information that enables the government to track statistics on mortgages and homeownership relating to race and ethnicity. The information also enables the government to enforce any antidiscrimination rules and regulations.

As an investor, you know that the more prepared you are, the more quickly you get things done. The same is true with financing. By having all the necessary information at your fingertips, you can work with your lender (or loan officer) to complete your loan application in a matter of minutes.

Although you may be tempted to fudge the facts on the Uniform Residential Loan Application, don't do it (or allow anyone else to do it for you). Lying on a loan application is all too common, but it's also a felony. The rules are ultimately meant to protect you. If your net assets are too small to qualify for the loan, for example, then having your application rejected protects you from a potential financial nightmare. See lenders as your partners, not your enemies. For more about dodging the real estate and mortgage fraud bullet, turn to Chapter 2 for more info.

Reviewing the lender's disclosures

In the Declarations section of the 1003 (see the previous section), you and any coborrower must answer several disclosure questions as a way of "coming clean" about your current financial situation. Your lender also must commit to a certain level of transparency regarding its practices and the loan you're applying for. For example, by law, a lender can't play some cruel game of bait-and-switch on you by dangling an attractive set of numbers during the application process and then sticking you with a real stinker of a loan at closing.

Be sure to examine the lender's disclosures carefully before signing on the dotted line, as explained in the following sections. At the closing, make sure the lender adheres to whatever those disclosures stipulate. (For more about closing, skip ahead to the section entitled "Navigating the Closing.")

Program disclosures

Regardless of the loan program, be sure you fully understand the *program disclosures* (the terms of the loan agreement) before you sign anything. If you don't understand how a particular type of loan works, keep asking your mortgage expert questions until you fully understand what you're getting yourself into.

For example, some loan programs are straightforward. If you're taking out a 30-year mortgage at 7.5 percent interest, the lender has very little to disclose about the program itself. On the other hand, more-complicated loan programs may require that the lender provide an additional disclosure. With adjustable rate mortgage (ARM) programs, for example, the lender must notify you of the index it uses, the margin associated with the loan, and how and when the lender calculates changes to your interest rate. For more about ARMs, including the roles that the index and margin play, check out Chapter 5.

The disclosure may also contain a hypothetical example showing a brief history of changes and how your rate may have changed under that program if you had a loan with those terms. (For more about ARMs, including the roles that the index and margin play, head to Chapter 5.)

Good Faith Estimate

For all loan types, your lender is required by law to provide you with a ballpark figure of all the costs associated with this loan in the form of a *Good Faith Estimate* (or GFE, in industry lingo). The GFE provides a complete breakdown of all the costs associated with the loan you're applying for, including the loan origination fee, appraisal fee, and underwriting fee. Only by comparing GFEs can you get a good feel of what's normal and what's excessive in the market. Although the lender must supply the GFE to you within three days of receiving your application, most lenders offer the GFE prior to the application.

Ask for the GFE in advance, so you don't waste time applying for a loan you have no intention of following through on. In fact, obtain a GFE from at least three lenders so you can compare the programs and their costs. Watch for *junk fees* (unfair charges), as discussed in Chapter 6. If any of the costs on the GFE look out of the ordinary, ask about it.

Truth In Lending statement

The *Truth-In-Lending disclosure* (TIL) gives you a reflection of the true cost of the loan, including the interest rate and fees. In short, the TIL makes it easier for you to comparison-shop for loans.

One of the key items on the TIL is the *annual percentage rate (APR),* as discussed in Chapter 6. The APR shows you how much interest you're really paying on a loan if you include the upfront costs in your calculations. For example, say you're comparing the following two loans:

- ✔ $100,000 30-year fixed rate loan at 7 percent interest with finance costs of $5,000

- ✔ $100,000 30-year fixed rate loan at 8 percent interest with finance costs of $4,000

With numbers like these tossed about, comparison-shopping becomes almost impossible. At first glance, the second loan may seem like the better deal, costing $1,000 less upfront, but if you look at the APR, you get a different picture:

- ✔ The first loan has an APR of 7.52 percent and costs you $251,485 over the life of the loan.

- ✔ The second loan has an APR of 8.44 percent and costs you $274,723 over the life of the loan, or $23,238 more than loan one.

The TIL also discloses any late-payment fees associated with the loan, whether the loan has any early-payment penalties, and the proposed payment schedule. If the loan is an ARM loan, it may illustrate what will happen to the payments as the rate starts to change.

The TIL is a great tool for taking a quick look at which loan among several is the best deal, but it doesn't provide enough information to evaluate specific costs associated with a particular loan. Use it in tandem with the GFE.

Real Estate Settlement Procedures Act (RESPA)

RESPA standardizes closings for residential real estate transactions in order to clamp down on any funny business that may occur at closing. According to the act, all closings must use a HUD-1 form to disclose the costs of the loan and show where all the disbursed funds are going.

Take a copy of your GFE to the closing to compare the fees disclosed on it with the fees actually being charged according to the HUD-1. This practice is one of the best ways to catch any discrepancies between what your loan originator told you and what it's actually charging you.

RESPA also controls certain actions of settlement providers such as the closing agent, and service providers (including the title insurance provider, credit company, and appraiser) to prevent them from working together against the best interests of the consumer (as in the case of price-gouging or kickbacks). Section 8 of RESPA has two important components:

- ✔ The first part prevents a lender from overcharging for settlement services and keeping the difference. For example, if the appraisal costs $400, the lender can't charge you $600 and pocket the extra $200.

- ✔ The second part prevents lenders and service providers from accepting or offering kickbacks for referral business — for example, a lender can't refer a specific appraiser and then accept part of the appraiser's fee as a reward.

RESPA's provisions cover all aspects of services, companies, and individuals, including title companies, attorneys, and real estate agents.

HOEPA — Section 32

The Home Ownership and Equity Protection Act (HOEPA) is an amendment to the *Truth In Lending Act* (TILA) to protect homeowners from paying excessive fees and interest. HOEPA is part of TILA but stands alone in its application; Congress passed these two separate acts:

- ✔ TILA covers all residential loan transactions (one- to four-family units), whether they're owner-occupied or investment properties. It doesn't apply to commercial loan transactions.

- ✔ HOEPA, also referred to as "Section 32" or "high-rate, high-fee loan disclosures," applies to residential owner-occupied dwellings for purchases and refinances. It includes one- to four-family owner-occupied properties (which could be a multiunit investment property in which one unit is occupied by the investor). It also applies to anyone you sell the property to. HOEPA doesn't apply to pure investment properties or commercial loan transactions, but you should always be aware of it so you know what's considered fair in terms of fees.

Under this regulation, lenders must warn borrowers if APRs exceed 10 percent of the comparable Treasury yield (which means Treasury securities having a similar period of maturity, such as 30 years), or if the deal's total points and fees exceed 8 percent of the loan amount.

Most lenders don't offer loans that fall under Section 32, including to investors, so this regulation usually isn't an issue. Just be aware of these restrictions and limitations to make sure you're working with a lender who plays by the rules.

Supplying the requested documentation

In order to review your loan application, your lender needs some supporting documentation that verifies the information you supplied. Gather the following documents:

- ✔ Federal tax returns (with all attachments and schedules) for the past two years

- ✔ W-2s from the past two years

- ✔ 30-days' worth of paycheck stubs

> ✔ List of real estate owned, complete with income and expenses
>
> ✔ Any and all supporting documentation for assets and liabilities listed on the Uniform Residential Loan Application (bank statements, credit card statements, divorce decree, retirement earnings statements, and so on)

Make a copy of each document in the list and place them neatly in a folder labeled with your name and contact information. You can then hand the entire package (the copies, not the originals) over to your loan originator at your next meeting.

Signing a release of information

Providing your loan originator with a loan application package is like submitting a resume for a job — it paints a picture of you on paper, but it may not be an accurate portrait. To make sure the information is factual, your loan originator needs to verify it in the real world, usually by checking independent sources such as employers, banks, and even providers of government benefits.

Most lenders require that you sign a *borrow authorization form,* which gives them permission to check your credit and independently verify any information you provide for this transaction.

Before you sign the release, read it carefully to make sure it covers only this transaction. You don't want to give anyone carte blanche to poke around in your financial affairs whenever they want.

Additionally you may be asked to sign an IRS Form 4506 or 8821 for verifying tax return information. These forms are standard, but make sure you don't sign blank ones — make the lender fill out the years covered, or else it can go get your tax returns from six years ago.

Following the Loan Processing Trail

After you supply your prospective lender with a completed loan application and supporting documentation, all you can really do is wait. During this time, you may be wondering what the lender is doing, whether you need to be doing something, and how this whole loan application process is going to unfold.

To prevent anxiety from overtaking you, the following sections lead you through the course of a processing and keep you posted on the possible outcomes.

Getting up to speed on the underwriting process

You may be under the illusion that right now an accountant is combing through your loan application and supporting documents for proof that you're worthy of a loan. The fact is that nowadays computers actually do the initial screening. The information you provide is entered into an *automated underwriting* (AU) system, which performs a preliminary evaluation and spits out the conditions and documentation requirements of the loan.

The AU system can't deny your loan application. It can only place your application in one of the following three categories:

- ✔ **Accept/Eligible:** This category is the best; it means that you're approved for the loan, subject to certain conditions. Those conditions show up on the *findings* report and must be part of the file for final approval. The loan officer or processor obtains the necessary documents as requested and then submits the complete file to the underwriter to review for accuracy. The file is already approved at this point, so they're only looking to make sure you've submitted and signed each of the required supporting documents and disclosures.

- ✔ **Accept/Ineligible:** This category indicates that the loan is approved but is ineligible for purchase in the *conforming market* (Fannie Mae or Freddie Mac). For example, it may be a *jumbo* loan, where the loan amount is outside the upper limit of what Fannie and Freddie can purchase. Many investors still use AU systems and approve/buy these loans anyway.

- ✔ **Refer:** This category is also typically known as a *dead deal*. An underwriter still has to review the file before it can be denied, but loan files that fall in this category don't come with the same lender guarantees against loan losses, so the lender has no incentive to take on the additional risk of approval. Unless the loan can be repackaged and resubmitted to obtain a different AU result, the deal is likely DOA.

Don't let a dead deal get you down. Even if you can't obtain a loan from traditional sources, you can usually find other means of financing your investments, as we explain in Part IV.

Obtaining an appraisal or AVM

One of the first things any lender wants to know is whether the property you're buying is worth the money you're borrowing to pay for it. Actually, it wants to make sure the property is worth more than the money you're borrowing so that if anything prevents you from paying back the loan, the lender has something of sufficient value to sell and recoup its investment.

To assess the value of a property, the lender orders an appraisal, an *Automated Valuation Model* (AVM) report, or both and usually charges you for it as a part of the cost of processing your loan. This appraisal isn't something you order — the lender wants to be in charge of picking an objective appraiser.

Expect to pay the full price for an appraisal, even if the property was recently appraised. Old appraisals can't be recertified no matter how recent they may be.

Appraisers generally take one of the following three approaches when performing an appraisal:

- ✔ **Sales comparison:** This most-common form of appraisal for residential properties compares the property to similar, recently sold properties in the same vicinity. The appraiser can then adjust her estimate by accounting for differences between the comparable homes and depreciation.

- ✔ **Income approach:** This method is used for income-producing properties, such as rental units. The appraiser compares similar properties in the same market to determine how much income the appraised property is likely to generate.

- ✔ **Cost approach:** This method is commonly used to establish the value of a unique property or properties in areas where few comparisons are available. The appraiser determines the value of the land and *improvements* (the building on the land) and then subtracts for depreciation.

An appraisal that uses the income approach is likely to cost a little more than a market-comparison appraisal, but not a whole lot more. If the lender tries to charge you hundreds of dollars more than you'd be paying for a standard appraisal (for a typical owner-occupied residential dwelling), find out why.

Having the property inspected

Whenever you make an offer on a property, make the offer contingent upon the property passing inspection, and then have the home professionally inspected. (This action is more for your protection than the lender's. Lenders usually don't require an inspection, even on government-secured loans.) This contingency ensures that you don't get stuck holding the bag on any of the following big-ticket items:

- ✔ Damaged foundation or other structural anomalies

- ✔ Electrical wiring problems

- ✔ Broken sewer lines, poor plumbing, or aging septic systems, especially if the house has been vacant for some time

- ✔ Leaking, nonfunctioning, or nonexistent gas lines

- ✔ Poorly functioning furnace or central air conditioning units

- ✔ Leaking or ramshackle roof

- ✔ Termite damage

- ✔ Health hazards such as lead-based paint, toxic mold, radon gas, asbestos, and hazardous insulation

In the following sections, we show you how to track down a professional home inspector and ensure that you obtain a thorough inspection.

Hiring a qualified home inspector

If you decide to hire an inspector, you can crack open the phone book and find listings for dozens of home inspectors in just about any area of the country. Finding a qualified home inspector, however, is a challenge. So where do you start? Ask the following individuals for referrals:

- ✔ **Your real estate agent or other real estate professionals you know:** By networking with homeowners, investors, and colleagues, real estate professionals know the best service providers in the area. Ask them for references to the best inspectors. If one inspector's name pops up on several lists, you've probably found a winner.

- ✔ **The National Association of Certified Home Inspectors (NACHI) Web site:** NACHI is a nonprofit agency that works toward educating and ensuring the quality of home inspectors. Its Web site at www.nachi.org features an online referral service that you can search to find certified home inspectors in your area. Make sure the inspector you hire is NACHI-certified — meaning the member has performed at least 250 inspections and passed two written proficiency exams.

- ✔ **Friends, family members, and colleagues:** Gather referrals from people you know and trust. Using an inspector who's done a satisfactory job for someone you know usually delivers better results than choosing someone blindly.

- ✔ **Your town's building inspection department:** Most towns have building inspectors who examine buildings as they're being constructed or renovated to ensure that they adhere to the local building codes. In some cases, you can hire the town's building inspectors to perform your inspection for you. They tend to be more thorough, and they're well versed on local building codes. The inspectors often show up as a team that typically includes a plumber, an electrician, a heating and air conditioning specialist, a builder, and someone who specializes in zoning. You get a thorough inspection and a complete write-up for about the same price as you'd pay a private inspector.

- ✔ **Better Business Bureau (BBB):** Although the BBB has a policy of not recommending certain businesses, it does offer a tool that enables you to search for BBB-certified businesses in your area. Start your search at `welcome.bbb.org`, where you can enter your ZIP code to skip to the Web site for the nearest BBB. You can then click the Find an Accredited BBB Business to start your search.

When you have a few leads, contact your candidates and ask them the following questions:

- ✔ **Are you certified, licensed, and insured?** Certification and licensing ensure that the inspector has the basic qualifications for the job. Insurance covers any serious defects he may overlook.

- ✔ **How long have you been a home inspector?** Length of service is often, but not always, a good indication of experience and expertise. Someone who's been in the business for 10 years probably has more experience than a person who's just getting started.

- ✔ **How many homes have you inspected?** "One or two" isn't the answer you're looking for. A busy home inspector is usually busy because she's good.

- ✔ **What did you do before becoming a home inspector?** Someone who's a retired carpenter or home builder is probably a better candidate than, say, a burned-out English teacher.

- ✔ **Do you have references I can call?** If the inspector has a good track record, people don't hesitate to provide positive references.

- ✔ **Do you recommend remedies or simply identify problems?** Look for an inspector who's had experience in construction. Someone who not only points out problems but also recommends repairs and renovations is a good choice.

> ✔ **How much do you charge?** Most inspectors charge a flat fee of a few hundred bucks — more or less depending on the size of the home and the complexity of the inspection. As you interview candidates, you can get a pretty good idea of the going rate for a typical home inspection in your area.

After you gather answers and information from all your candidates, make a decision. Sit down with your list and identify the inspector who has the best experience and credentials of the bunch but doesn't charge an exorbitant fee.

Attending the inspection

Although attendance isn't mandatory, you should show up for the inspection prepared to take notes. Your notes should include the following:

> ✔ **Possible structural defects:** The inspector will point out cracked foundation walls, weak roof trusses, or shifting footings or joists. These problems can be extremely costly and can kill a deal quickly.

> ✔ **List of functional defects:** Examples include a furnace that no longer functions or is leaking carbon monoxide, or a toilet that doesn't flush. These are critical repairs that have the most impact on your ability to resell the property or lease it out.

> ✔ **List of potential environmental problems:** An example includes insulation that contains asbestos or ground on the lot that's been contaminated by a local industrial plant. These can be costly to fix.

> ✔ **List of cosmetic defects:** These include divots or dents in the walls, peeling paint, and other defects that just look bad. They're less-serious stuff.

> ✔ **Anything else the inspector points out:** These may range from minor issues, such as a leaky faucet, to more major issues, such as a stained ceiling that may be a sign of something more serious, but the inspector can't gain access to the area above the ceiling to check it out.

If you're note-taking challenged, consider carrying a digital recorder with you during the inspection. Just don't forget to turn it on.

Requesting repairs

With your list of property defects in hand, highlight the ones you expect the seller to repair and then have your agent present the list to the seller or seller's agent. The seller agrees to make all repairs, refuses to make all repairs, or agrees to make only some of the repairs. It's up to you to decide whether you want to move forward with the deal.

For any repairs you're willing to take on and other renovations to improve the property, obtain estimates from independent contractors to determine approximate costs. Get three bids from licensed professionals, including the time estimated to complete the work, as well as the lead time needed to schedule the work.

Don't get your inspector involved in providing estimates or doing any repairs or renovations to a property. This creates a conflict of interest, which is prohibited on government-insured loans.

For additional details on how to determine whether a property is likely to be a profitable investment, check out Ralph and Joe's *Flipping Houses For Dummies* (Wiley) and *Real Estate Investing For Dummies,* 2nd edition, by Eric Tyson and Robert S. Griswold (Wiley).

When you're estimating the costs of repairs and renovations, keep in mind that as soon as you take possession of the property (at closing), you're responsible for the holding costs on the property when repairs are being done. (*Holding costs* are the expenses you incur when the property is just sitting there — they include the monthly mortgage payments, insurance, property taxes, and utilities.) By planning your repairs and renovations prior to closing and lining up contractors to begin work as soon as possible after closing, you can slash your holding costs.

Testing the water

You may not need to test the water as a condition for obtaining loan approval, but if the system is served by a well, get the water tested for your own protection. Your county health department or an independent lab can perform the required tests, but you need to collect the water:

1. **Get a clean bottle from the lab or your county health department.**

2. **Go to the water faucet farthest from the well source.**

3. **Let the water run for at least five minutes.**

4. **Fill the bottle and label it as instructed.**

5. **Have the sample tested right away.**

   The lab usually returns the results within a couple of days and lets you know the chemical makeup, including minerals and any detectable E. coli in the water.

If the property is serviced by a community well, request maintenance records.

I, Chip, usually steer clear of properties serviced by community wells. I also avoid properties on which the well is located in a crawl space or basement. These pose financing risks, and any eventual buyer will be limited in financing options.

Having the septic system inspected

If the property relies on a septic system, have a qualified septic contractor inspect the field, saturation levels, and estimated remaining life of the system. These systems can be very costly to replace.

Also, research the pumping records with the owner and the county (usually the county health department), and check with the county on the age of the system and its maintenance history. The county should have records of when the system was installed and a pump card that shows when it was last pumped out.

If the system is more than 10 years old, we highly recommend that you have a qualified professional perform a *perk test*. This test makes sure the septic field is draining properly and isn't saturated (a situation that indicates a short remaining life).

Obtaining a survey

Your lender will request a survey on the property, regardless of the size of the parcel, even if it's a *platted lot* (a lot with boundaries shown on a map). To insure the transaction, the title company requires a survey or certification of an existing survey. Surveys come in two types:

- ✔ **Boundary survey:** This type illustrates where the property lines are and is usually sufficient for a platted lot, because the parcel's boundaries have already been recorded.

- ✔ **Stake survey:** With this type the surveyor actually goes out and places or finds metal boundary stakes to certify the actual boundary lines of the parcel. The stake survey is slightly more expensive, but it's the better choice for waterfront property, irregular parcels, and properties with a *metes-and-bounds description* (commonly found in a deed).

Walk the property with the owner to be sure you know where the boundary lines are, and ask questions about any easements or encroachments that may exist. If the owner/seller has a copy of the previous survey, obtain a copy so the surveyor can recertify it instead of performing a new survey — you may save a few bucks.

Navigating the Closing

Although the closing (or settlement) is the final step in the real estate transaction, it can feel a little anticlimactic. You and the other participants in the transaction have completed your work. Now you're simply meeting to sign off on the deal you've all agreed to and shuffle the money around to the appropriate recipients.

Even though the process may seem like an afterthought on a long journey, you really need to stay on your toes to avoid any last-minute mishaps. In the following sections, we show you how to ensure that the closing proceeds smoothly without any glitches that can negatively affect your bottom line.

Keeping your attorney in the loop

A good real estate attorney can keep you from spending thousands of dollars later to clean up a mess that you can easily avoid now. Get your attorney involved sooner rather than later in the following ways:

- ✔ **Make sure your attorney reviews the purchase agreement before you make an offer.** Consider working with your attorney to develop a boilerplate purchase agreement you can use for all of your transactions, so your attorney doesn't have to review it every time.

- ✔ **Have your attorney present during any sensitive or unusual negotiations.** If you're not completely comfortable with something the seller or seller's representative is saying, consult your attorney before giving a final response. Backing away from something you agreed to, even verbally, can make your attorney's job more difficult later.

- ✔ **Ask your attorney to review the closing papers prior to the closing date.** Have the company handling the closing supply you with copies at least three days in advance.

 Get your attorney involved early. She probably won't be able to help you after the closing; even if she can, it'll cost you a whole lot more than if you had corrected the errors *before* you signed the papers.

Dealing with the preliminaries

Closings usually proceed smoothly as long as you have all the parts in place prior to closing. In the following sections, we show you how to prepare for your next closing.

Hiring a title company

Closing is pretty easy, at least from your perspective. In most cases, your agent or the seller's agent selects a title company, and the title company does the rest — gathering all the essential paperwork, making sure everyone shows up to the closing on time, and then routing the closing documents around the table to make sure everything gets signed.

The title company also provides title insurance — your only protection from future claims against the property, including old co-owners, *lien holders* (other parties that claim rights to the property), *backside deals* (private negotiated or unrecorded agreements) with neighbors, and a whole host of other potential problems. Approximately a month after closing, the title company sends you a complete policy. Store it in a safe place — in addition to providing you with a record that you have title insurance, the policy can earn you credit toward the next policy when you sell or refinance the property.

Never ever purchase a property without title insurance. Without title insurance, you can lose your entire investment overnight. One way this can and has happened is when a scam artist sells a property he doesn't own. The con artist waits until the owners are on an extended vacation and uses a phony deed to transfer the property into his own name. He then lists and sells the property and takes off with the cash. If you happen to have bought the place, and you don't have title insurance, when the rightful owners return from vacation, you lose the property, but you still owe on that loan you took out to buy it.

Under RESPA (Section 9), you as purchaser have the exclusive right to select the title insurance provider. We encourage you to go with one of the national agencies or one of their agents — someone with a solid reputation in the marketplace. In addition, larger companies have several offices, making dealings more convenient when closing time arrives.

Request an *insured closing letter*, indicating that the title company is insured for handling the transaction. This document provides you with the assurance that if the closing company mishandles anything, you don't get stuck with a bill for its mistake.

The title company disburses funds on investment properties immediately upon the close of the transaction. Request a copy of each disbursement check for your records.

Reviewing the documents in advance

You have the right to review any closing documents at least 24 hours prior to closing (preferably three days before closing, so your attorney has time to review them, too). As soon as you've chosen a title company, contact the company and let your representative know that you want a copy of the closing packet as soon as possible so you have time to review the paperwork.

Check the mortgage, deed, note, HUD-1 closing statement, and all other documents for spelling or calculation errors, and make sure the figures on the HUD-1 match up with those on the Good Faith Estimate. If anything looks odd, call the title company and have your issues addressed *before* closing.

Insuring the property

Several days prior to closing, meet with your insurance provider and review coverage options for the property you're about to purchase. Let your agent know the closing date so he can prepare a policy for you in advance of the closing.

Make sure you obtain a *policy* and not just an *insurance binder* (a promise to insure) — some lenders don't accept binders.

Signing the documents

Be prepared to sign a lot of documents during closing (and no, you can't use a rubber stamp!) You have to provide a picture ID (such as a driver's license). The closing agent witnesses and notarizes your signature many times during the closing.

Request a complete copy set of all *signed* documents (not just blank ones) and keep them in a safe place just in case you need them in the future. In the court of real estate law, only signed documents count, so be sure you get a copy of the signed documents showing what you and the seller agreed to.

Knowing your right of rescission . . . or lack thereof

The *right of rescission* is a federal law that gives you three days to change your mind on financial deals. It protects consumers from high-pressure sales tactics. Commonly called the "cooling-off law," it also allows you to back out of refinance deals on owner-occupied residences.

As an investor, don't count on the right of rescission to protect you. It doesn't apply to the purchase agreement — after you sign the agreement, your offer is binding. In addition, the right applies only to owner-occupied residences, not investment properties.

Dealing with surprises

The key to dealing effectively with surprises at closing is to not have any surprises. In the following sections, you discover some prevention maneuvers that ensure a smooth closing.

Rate changes

Your interest-rate lock agreement is only as good as the loan officer who gave it to you. You have nothing in writing to say that the person actually locked in the rate with an investor or that the terms of your application didn't change just enough to allow (or require) the loan officer to place it with a different lender-investor or a completely different loan program.

At least two days prior to closing, confirm your interest rate and program with the loan officer. If you had been floating the interest rate, he will require you to lock it in at least three days prior to close so that he can prepare the documents. If it's not what you agreed upon, hold out until you're satisfied with the rate and terms. You won't be able to change them after the closing.

Term changes

Confirm the terms of your loan (including index, margin, and start rate for an ARM loan) prior to the closing. Your loan terms should remain fixed unless something major occurred between the time of your application and the closing, but ask anyway. You don't want any surprises.

Dodging disaster

How would you like to purchase a property and have it burn down the next day without having insurance to cover it? I, Chip, almost had that happen to me. However, the property actually burned down a day *before* closing. Fortunately, the previous owners hadn't cancelled their policy prior to close, or it would have been a real mess. We had to wait for the property to be rebuilt before we could close on the transaction — a delay of five months!

The moral of this story: Obtain an insurance policy before closing. Don't leave the property uninsured for even one minute — too many things can happen.

If rates improved since you obtained loan approval, or the property numbers no longer meet your expectations, you may consider changing loan programs in order to maximize your cash flow. Just remember that any changes you make now cancel out the rate and terms you locked in. Even a slight change can jeopardize your lock, giving the lender an opportunity to charge extra fees and interest, so be careful.

Other unexpected events

Once in awhile, other events throw a wrench into the proceedings — and they're completely beyond your control. The seller may have a change of heart, the title company may require additional documentation to insure the title transfer, you may have to get lien waivers, and so on. Take it all in stride — and prepare for a delay. We've had lots of closings slightly postponed while someone fixed a glitch, so keep your schedule (and that of your contractors) a little loose.

You're dealing with professionals, and they're programmed to get any problems resolved as quickly as possible. If anything sounds too strange or flat-out made up, simply ask your attorney to call the title company or closing agent. That usually gets the process back on track pretty quickly!

Financing Other Types of Residential Properties

Most of the information in this chapter relates to financing the purchase of primary residences. Variations arise, however, when you're financing the purchase of other types of properties, including vacation and investment properties and vacant land. The following sections introduce the variables you can expect and show you how to deal with them.

Digging up money for vacation properties

If you're in the market for a vacation property or second home, expect the financing requirements to be a lot tighter, the interest rate and costs to be higher, and the down-payment requirements to be greater, with many lenders requiring at least 20 to 25 percent down.

Due to the higher costs, you may want to consider purchasing a *fractional ownership,* in which you share the property with several parties. This can be a great way to invest in higher-end properties located in expensive markets. You can usually find a loan officer who specializes in these types of loans.

Banks and other more traditional lenders rarely handle loans for fractional ownerships, so you have to go through a specialized group of finance companies. Shop around carefully for one that specializes in this type of financing, and make sure that you have a solid agreement with the other parties involved. Make absolutely sure that your real estate attorney reviews all the paperwork and that you fully understand what you're getting yourself into.

A management company often makes all the arrangements, but make sure you understand your obligations as an owner and how the parties plan to share the income and expenses of the rentals or the burden of expenses when the rentals are vacant? For more information, check out *Second Homes For Dummies* by Bridget McCrea and Stephen Spignesi (Wiley).

Financing investment properties

Lenders approach the financing of *residential investment properties* (dwellings you rent out) more carefully than they do financing the purchase of primary residences. As a result, you need to adjust your expectations and approach to financing these properties in a different way as well. We cover the main differences that come with these properties in the following sections.

Options for financing residential investment properties are somewhat limited. Expect interest rates, costs, and the down-payment requirements to all be higher. Often, lenders require a minimum of 25 percent down.

Shop around for a lender that offers several options for investment properties, and be careful of extra fees. You should have to pay only an additional 1.5 to 2 points above a normal owner-occupied transaction. Check out Chapter 4 to find out how to shop around for lenders.

Before approving a loan for any income-producing property, your lender wants to know whether it promises a positive cash flow. Of course, you want to know this, too, so before you even submit an offer, perform a complete cash flow analysis of the property, as explained in Chapter 3. Do the math before you do the deal, and if the return on your investment is less than you'd earn by investing the money in a CD, we recommend sticking your money in a CD instead.

Purchasing vacant land

You may be considering buying some vacant land, but before you purchase any land, remember this point: Only purchase land if you intend to use it for a specific purpose — not as strictly an investment in and of itself.

The saying goes that land is such a great investment because "they're not making any more of it." Truth be told, land is rarely such a grand investment for two good reasons:

✔ **It's tough to finance.** Even if you find a lender willing to finance the purchase, they usually require a high loan-to-value, (LTV, as discussed in Chapter 3), which means you're locking up a lot of your investment capital in a down payment. (Most land sales involve owner financing over a period of time, with flexible terms and conditions.)

✔ **It has a long holding period.** Land isn't a liquid asset. You usually have to hold onto it for quite a long time before you realize your gains. Again, your investment capital is locked up in something that's not producing any cash flow.

Two exceptions do exist to our recommendation: Land is a good investment when

✔ You know that the land is very likely to be rezoned, causing its value to increase significantly

✔ You intend to put it to personal use in construction, parking, lease, and so on.

Part III

Financing the Purchase of Commercial Properties

The 5th Wave   By Rich Tennant

"According to my numbers, we'll get soaked buying the laundromat and screwed on the hardware store, but the terms on the medical arts building look pretty benign."

In this part . . .

When you're in the market for commercial real estate investment properties, your search for financing is likely to take some unexpected turns. From the very beginning, you need to figure out the type of property you're interested in, because your choice ultimately influences the types of financing available.

This part gives you a clearer idea of not only the financing you need but also the types of commercial properties you're interested in. In this part, we introduce you to the most common commercial property types so you can choose the type best suited to your investment goals. We take you on a tour of some of the unique sources of financing available for commercial ventures. Finally, we step you through the process of applying for commercial real estate loans from application to closing.

Chapter 8

Picking the Right Commercial Property Type for You

In This Chapter

▶ Focusing your efforts on multifamily dwellings

▶ Investing in office space

▶ Examining retail rental properties

▶ Investing in motels, hotels, and B and Bs

▶ Mixing it up with multiuse properties

▶ Exploring more unique opportunities

*O*ne of the easiest ways for a novice to get started in real estate investing is through the process of *flipping* a single-family dwelling. You buy a home below market value, fix it up to market standards, and sell it at or near its true market value. (*Flipping Houses For Dummies* shows you how.) You already own a house (or you should before you start buying and selling investment properties), and you may have already sold one or two, so flipping allows you to use the knowledge you've already gained to develop new skills.

Investing in single-family dwellings, however, is only one option. Other options include multifamily dwellings, office space, strip malls, hotels, motels, gas stations, and a host of other properties that your average buy-and-sell house flipper never considers. These commercial properties are more conducive to a buy-and-hold strategy, because they offer the potential for generating a steady stream of income.

In this chapter, we address important calculations you need to make when considering investing in any commercial property, reveal the various types of commercial properties you may want to invest in, and provide you with the guidance you need to choose opportunities that are most suitable for your investment goals.

Estimating the Income Potential of a Commercial Property

Evaluating the income potential of prospective commercial properties isn't rocket science, but it does require that you perform some basic arithmetic — subtracting expenses from income to determine cash flow. By performing these calculations, you can come up with your own ballpark estimates of how potentially profitable any commercial property will be.

In the following sections, we itemize the income and expense categories so you can begin collecting the numbers you need and doing the math. (These calculations work for every type of commercial property we cover in this chapter, although the specific income and expense categories may vary.)

Calculating effective gross income (EGI)

Whatever scenario you use for your commercial rentals and whatever your sources of revenue, the formulas follow the same pattern. First, calculate your *effective gross income* (EGI) — all the revenue you can reasonably expect the property to pull in. With an estimated EGI in hand, you can then move on to other calculations that reveal the property's profit potential. To calculate the EGI, you need the following numbers:

- **Annual rental income:** Multiply the net rentable square feet by the annual lease income per square foot; for example, 3,000 net rentable square feet × $17 per square foot = $51,000 per year. Don't confuse gross square footage with net square footage — you can't charge anyone for space in a telephone room.

- **Vacancy:** Most lenders use a *vacancy factor* (to allow for the amount of time the property sits vacant) in the 5 to 7 percent range for retail properties. If you expect a higher vacancy rate for this property, use that number (but don't go lower than 5 percent).

- **Triple Net (or NNN):** Income collected from tenants to pay for taxes, insurance, and maintenance, including common area maintenance (CAM) charges for shared-use spaces, such as walkways and public restrooms. Although this is an expense to you, you also treat it as income because your tenants reimburse you. Say the tenant occupies 7 percent of the building and total expenses are $55,000. To calculate the tenant's share on a monthly basis, multiply the NNN by .07 and divide by 12 months. That would come to about $321 per month.

✔ **Other income:** This amount includes money you collect from tenants for shared secretarial services, storage facilities, shipping or loading dock usage, high-speed Internet or satellite services, conference room rental, building signage rights, and so on.

When you have these numbers, you're ready to do the math to calculate your EGI:

Annual Rental Income + NNN + Other Income = Total Income

Total Income − (Total Income × Vacancy Factor) = Effective Gross Income

For example, say you have a small office complex that's pulling in $50,000 in rental income per year. It has a cellphone tower that pulls in another $10,000 per year and a storage facility that accounts for about $5,000 in income. Plus, the tenants collectively chip in $15,000 to cover taxes, insurance, and maintenance. Rarely, if ever, is one of the offices vacant, so you estimate the vacancy factor at a low 5 percent. The calculation goes like this:

$50,000 + $10,000 + $5,000 + $15,000 = $80,000

$80,000 − ($80,000 × .05) = $76,000

Thus, your EGI for this property is $76,000.

Calculating Net Operating Income (NOI)

After you calculate your estimated EGI, you can use that number to calculate your *Net Operating Income* (NOI) — your annual income from the property prior to considering the *debt service* (the principal and interest costs on the proposed loan). Before you can proceed, you need the following numbers:

✔ **Operating expenses (OE):** Operating expenses include taxes, insurance, trash removal, maintenance, payroll, and so on.

✔ **Management expenses (ME):** Management expenses include whatever you pay yourself or others to manage the property. Remember, even if you manage the property, your time is worth money.

✔ **Tenant improvements (TI):** Calculated on a per-square-foot basis, these are costs to help renovate the space for the tenant's desired use. If the space was previously used by a dentist, for example, and now you need to convert it into a bookstore, you have some work to do. TI covers new carpeting, the relocation of walls, the proper replacement of electrical outlets and lights, and so on.

✔ **Leasing concessions (LC):** *Leasing concessions* (such as offering one month's free rent) are sometimes necessary to attract quality long-term tenants. You may also make concessions for less-desirable situations like construction periods (of common areas) and location differentials (the tenant at the end of the hallway doesn't get as good exposure as the guy in the middle of the action).

✔ **Credit losses (CL):** Unfortunately, not everyone pays their rent like they're supposed to. To account for uncollectible lease payments, budget for credit losses on a yearly basis.

When you have the required numbers, plug them into the following equation to calculate your NOI:

$$EGI - OE - ME - TI - LC - CL = NOI$$

For example, suppose a property has an EGI of $76,000, as calculated in the example in the previous section. Operating expenses come to about $20,000. You pay yourself $4,000 per year to manage the property and pay an assistant $1,500 to keep the records (for a total of $5,500 in management expenses). You're going to have to spend $7,000 in tenant improvements to transform a corner office into a small coffee shop for a vendor who's moving in. To encourage someone to move into the less-glamorous office space, you offer a lease concession of $2,500. And you estimate from the previous owner's records that your tenants are going to stiff you about 5 percent on the rent that's due. Here's how the calculation would unfold:

$76,000 - $20,000 - $5,500 - $7,000 - $2,500 - ($76,000 × .05) = $37,200

Your NOI on this property comes out to $37,200.

Estimating the property's true value

If you're wondering whether a particular retail space is worth the asking price, you can calculate that for yourself by using the NOI and *local cap rate* (market return based on risk). *Cap rate* is short for capitalization rate, which is a reflection of the rate of return that's considered reasonable for a certain type of commercial property in a given area based upon its risk.

You can get the local cap rate from a commercial appraiser. Divide the NOI by the cap rate to estimate the value of the retail center:

NOI ÷ Cap Rate = Estimated Value

If the NOI is $213,000, for example, and the local cap rate is 7 percent, your estimated value is about $3,042,900 ($213,000 ÷ .07)!

The NOI and estimated value of the property are the only two numbers that matter to the lender — and the only two numbers that should matter to you, as well.

Projecting future profits with a pro forma

Whenever you meet with prospective lenders to discuss financing for a commercial venture, the lenders often want you to fire up your crystal ball and reveal the future possibilities — especially when you have solid plans in place to build a rosy future. You can present your vision for the property's future through a *pro forma* — a document that projects the future earnings of a property after you're able to implement your plans for it. The pro forma assures the lender that you've analyzed the numbers and have realistic expectations for the property's performance.

When you first purchase a property, complete a construction project, or finish a major rehabilitation, that property may not immediately generate enough income to make it profitable. A new office building, for example, doesn't have 100-percent occupancy in the first six months! Over the course of a year or two, however, that same property may become very profitable. A pro forma shows just how profitable the property is likely to be.

To create a pro forma, start with the current numbers you calculated in the previous sections and then project the income/expenses based upon your reasonable assumptions (which you must substantiate).

For example, if you show the building with pre-leases of 50 percent initial occupancy and a projected growth of 20 percent per year, your pro forma looks like the one shown in Table 8-1.

Table 8-1	Sample Pro Forma Figures		
Year	Income (NOI)	Expenses (TOE)	DSCR
1	$42,000	$41,350	1.02
2	$58,800	$53,220	1.11
3	$75,600	$61,780	1.22

Although this example is very simplified, it shows the lender what your projected growth rate of the property is and how it will affect the loan performance. Be prepared to break out all expenses and supply real market data (including competing properties in the area) to back up your assumptions.

Most pro forma projections should extend out two to three years — five years for major new construction projects. Anything longer than that, though, is pure speculation.

Don't place blind trust in pro formas that other people present to you. Sometimes, a seller may present you with a pro forma, for example, to sell you on the potential of a property. Disreputable mortgage brokers may also exaggerate the numbers in a pro forma to convince you to move forward on a deal. Do your own projections.

Dwelling On the Thought of Multifamily Homes

People always need a place to live and don't always have the resources or desire to buy their own single-family home. As a result, multifamily property investments have always been and will always be a good long-term investment — assuming, of course, you pick winners and structure the deals to work well for you.

Before seizing these potentially lucrative opportunities, however, develop an understanding of what comprises a multifamily dwelling. Technically speaking, a *multifamily dwelling* is any piece of real estate that can legally house two or more families. But in financial circles, these properties fall into two categories:

✓ **Residential:** Two- to four-family units classify as residential properties, which qualifies them for residential financing. If you plan on living in one of the units, you can usually qualify for even more attractive loans available for owner-occupied properties.

✓ **Commercial:** The rules of the game change with any multifamily home over four units — you enter the world of commercial finance, where the lenders, terms, loan programs, qualifications, and documentation requirements are all different. (Properties with between 5 and about 20 units are considered *garden apartments*. More than 20 units constitute *large multifamily units*.)

The financing differences between these two categories are monumental, as we explain in the following sections.

Two- to four-family homes

Two- to four-family homes — called *duplexes, triplexes,* or *quads* — are *by far* the best investment opportunities in the marketplace for beginning investors. Nowadays, you can find plenty of these properties on the market due to the foreclosure crisis — just make sure to analyze the numbers carefully to account for all expenses and maintenance. (See "Crunching the numbers" later in this chapter.)

These properties are also relatively easy to finance — especially if they're owner-occupied investment properties. (If you live in one of the units, it's considered owner-occupied.)

To qualify for a loan to finance the purchase of a multifamily property, owner-occupied or not, you need strong credit and several months of reserves to cover expenses in the event that you're unable to rent out one or more units.

Securing financing for owner-occupied properties

As discussed in Chapter 4, owner-occupied properties more easily qualify for government financing, as long as you meet the following conditions:

✓ Use at least one of the units as your primary residence for the next 12 months.

✓ Make as little as a 3.5 percent down payment (FHA).

✓ Ensure that the property is *self-sufficient;* that is, the rental income must cover the monthly payments and other costs, including insurance, property taxes, landlord-paid utilities, and maintenance.

✓ Present documentation that shows you have at least three months of payment reserves.

For multifamily properties, qualifying for the loan depends much more on the revenue-generating potential of the property than your job-related income to ensure that you can afford the payments.

Even with government-secured financing, you can expect to pay more in costs and interest. The appraisal, for example, is likely to cost about twice as much — to cover the time and effort to complete an income-approach analysis on the property.

Securing financing for non-owner-occupied properties

The main difference between financing the purchase of an owner-occupied property and one that's *non-owner-occupied* (a property you don't plan to live in for at least 12 months) is the down payment. You can expect lenders to require a down payment of a whopping 25 percent, and you still need to prove that you have three months' worth of reserves to cover expenses.

The good news is that you can own the property solely as a landlord — you don't have to live in it.

Garden apartments

Properties that contain between 5 and about 20 individual units typically fall into the category of *garden apartments* — an in-between range that lenders love to finance (and in which the numbers often work very well for investors).

The only drawback here is that with garden apartments, you begin to get into the category of commercial properties, where you no longer qualify for the most attractive government-secured loans. You don't get any special breaks if you live in one of the units, either, except for the fact that you don't have to charge yourself rent. Fortunately, more lenders are willing to finance these types of properties than are willing to finance large multifamily properties.

Large multifamily properties

Large multifamily properties are, well, large. They're complicated undertakings. They can also be quite challenging and fun as long as you've mastered the art of small- and mid-sized multifamily properties first.

In terms of financing these behemoths of residential real estate, you're working smack dab in the middle of the commercial arena where everything becomes a numbers game. Plus, fewer lenders are available, and professional on-site management becomes a must. Track down a mortgage broker who specializes in financing commercial properties.

If I were young again . . .

Many of my (Chip's) first starter properties were duplexes, which provide a nice way to cover the mortgage payment and live rent free! One of my first properties was a two-family unit near the University of Michigan football stadium. We were even able to earn extra income by charging for parking on Saturdays! One game could pay for an entire month's mortgage — plus pizza and beer!

If I were to start all over again, at the age of 18, I would buy a four-family property and finance it with an FHA loan. Multifamily units are *great* opportunities for entering into the world of investment real estate without exposing yourself to a great deal of risk. You can get into the property for as little as a 3.5 percent down payment, and loan amounts can be more than $2 million. The loan amount limits do vary by county, but that's a *lot* of wiggle room to find a property!

Lenders don't want to deal with inexperienced landlords, so wade in slowly. Start with two- to four-family units and work your way up to a garden apartment complex before you attempt a large multifamily property. Otherwise, you're just wasting everyone's time. After you've gained some experience, you're ready to move up and gain some additional leverage.

When you're evaluating the profit potential of large multifamily properties, the main difference is that you have more expenses to account for, such as payroll for maintenance or office personnel, snowplowing trucks, parking lot striping, pool maintenance, and other items.

Property management is one expense that's a sure thing. Figure this expense at 5 to 7 percent of the property's gross potential income. You're better off overestimating than underestimating.

Of course, you may also have new sources of income. Coin-operated laundry, clubhouse rental, carports, and storage fees may add up to some serious cash. (Check out *Property Management For Dummies,* 2nd Edition, by Robert Griswold [Wiley] for more info about increasing your income sources.)

Lenders want to see a complete breakdown of all the sources of income and each line item expense. Work closely with a good, experienced commercial loan broker. You can expect your broker to work hard to put together a comprehensive loan package and submit it to the proper lenders who specialize in this type of financing. We guarantee it won't be your local bank.

Crunching the numbers

When you're in the market for a multifamily property (of whatever size), carefully analyze the following numbers:

- ✔ **Annual income:** Calculate what the total *annual* income would be if *all* the units were rented out for *all* 12 months. (Keeping all the units rented can be costly in both time and effort, but for the purposes of these calculations, assume that all units are rented out.)

- ✔ **Annual expenses:** Include taxes, insurance, maintenance, landscaping, management, telephone, utilities — everything except the loan payment, which comes into play later. Tally up the expenses for all units for all 12 months of the year.

- ✔ **Annual repair/replacement expense:** In rental units, you need to replace refrigerators, stoves, carpet, and other fixtures on a regular schedule. The easiest way to calculate the annual repair/replacement expense is to estimate the expense for a single unit at about $200 per year and multiply that by the number of units. For a 20-unit property, you can expect to pay about $4,000 annually in repair and replacement costs.

  For a more accurate estimate, calculate the repair and replacement costs of all fixtures in each unit. For example, the average life of a refrigerator is seven years. For a 12-unit property, that's 12 refrigerators over the course of seven years, or about 1.7 refrigerators per year. If you estimate the cost of a refrigerator at $500, that works out to $850 per year.

- ✔ **Annual mortgage payments:** Use a mortgage calculator to figure the monthly loan payment including principal and interest. Multiply the monthly loan payment by 12 to determine the annual cost of the loan.

Up to this point, you have a bunch of meaningless numbers. The following formula shows you how to use these numbers to make a well-informed purchase decision.

Say you're looking at a 12-unit property that you're pretty sure you can purchase for $785,000. You do the calculations explained earlier and come up with the following results:

- ✔ **Annual income:** $120,000

- ✔ **Annual expenses:** $23,180

- ✔ **Annual repair/replacement expense:** $2,520

- ✔ **Annual mortgage payments:** $55,296

Now you're ready to crunch the numbers. Start with the total annual income (all units together) and subtract all the expenses to determine the property's potential annual cash flow. Here's how it works in our example:

$120,000 – $23,180 – $2,520 – $55,296 = $39,004

The $39,004 represents a return of slightly less than 5 percent:

$39,004 ÷ $785,000 = 4.97 percent

If you can bump up the rent, lower expenses, or figure out other creative ways to increase the annual income by being a savvy landlord, you can improve your return on your investment.

This less-than-5-percent return represents only the minimum return you're getting. Your actual return on your investment is likely to be much greater when you take the following into account:

✔ You're not paying cash for the property. Say you put 25 percent down on the property and borrowed the rest. Your total investment isn't $785,000 but rather $196,250 (25 percent of $785,000). Divide that $39,004 by $196,250 rather than $785,000 and you quickly see that your actual annual return is a more like 20 percent!

✔ The calculations don't include appreciation. If property values increase, you stand to earn even more when you ultimately sell the property (although you can't always count on that).

Buying and Renting Out Office Space: The A-to-D Grading Scale

If midnight calls from tenants about clogged toilets aren't your cup of tea, you may want to look at investing in office properties. Although the risk is a little greater — people don't really need an office as they do a home, which could result in greater vacancies during economic slowdowns — this option offers plenty of perks. It also comes with a whole new set of income streams and expenses.

If the idea of renting office space to businesses appeals to you, start looking for opportunities. (For tips on finding great properties, check out *Commercial Real Estate Investing For Dummies* by Peter Conti and Peter Harris.)

Lenders break down office properties into different grades on an A through D basis. The nice new shiny office complex out by the new shopping mall is the star pupil, earning an A for attracting high-rent tenants and commanding higher rents per square foot. The 120-year-old building in the heart of the downtown warehouse district may be lucky to squeak by with a D both in terms of pricing and risk. Although different lenders may grade properties differently, the grading is typically pretty consistent — it's based on area, age of building, condition, and quality of tenancy (reflected in square footage income).

The higher grade the property, the easier it is to get that property financed. You have more lenders and more options to choose from. As you go down the scale, credit tightens and interest rates rise. Reserve and maintenance costs also go up. Another problem is that many older office buildings aren't up to current code requirements. If the building lacks a sprinkler system, for example, lenders don't even consider financing the purchase.

Before giving careful consideration to an office building, check with your commercial mortgage broker or real estate agent to see what the property's grade is right upfront. Generally speaking, we recommend that you invest in A and B grade properties. Some investors like the C and D properties because they're less expensive both to purchase and maintain — tenants don't expect the floors to reflect like glass. Just be aware that renting these lower-graded properties may be more challenging.

Investing in Retail Real Estate

Retail properties include strip malls, small convenience stores, single-tenant-occupied (STO) properties such as big-box stores, and even large retail malls. These units can all be great investments, particularly for those who already run a retail operation and want to offset their own operational expenses — sort of like owning a multifamily property and living in one of the units rent-free.

The calculations for evaluating these investments are the same as those you'd use to evaluate other commercial properties, but the line items for income and expenses differ, as we reveal in the following sections.

If you own a retail operation and buy a property, put the property in a separate LLC and then charge yourself rent. You can then deduct 100 percent of the rent as a business expense. (If you own the building, you have to calculate depreciation, reducing your write-offs.) Your attorney can prepare the necessary documentation and ensure that all the pieces are in order.

Collecting your cut of gross sales

Income on retail property is essentially the same as income you can expect from an office building (see "Estimating the Income Potential of a Commercial Property" earlier in this chapter), with one major difference: With retail property, you can expect an additional bonus — a percentage of gross sales.

Owners of mid-size to large retail centers commonly charge tenants a percentage of their sales as part of their leases. This practice makes sense; after all, you're boosting each merchant's sales by offering a convenient place with a high profile to attract shoppers. You're investing in additional repairs and signage and connecting merchants with other high-profile tenants. You earn a percentage of those sales.

When you're estimating the income potential of your commercial property, be sure to include commissions as part of the property's income. See "Estimating the Income Potential of a Commercial Property" near the beginning of this chapter for details. For more about charging tenants a percentage of their sales, check out *Commercial Real Estate Investing For Dummies*.

Charging for consumer traffic

As the owner of a retail center, you're at least partially responsible for attracting the consumer traffic that drives sales. Consider an airport, for example. A major airport attracts hundreds of thousands of people every day, and airport executives know that this consumer traffic is a commodity they can sell to merchants looking for store space and advertising.

Most airports have stores and restaurants. Sure, most of the merchants pay a set monthly fee as part of their rent, but the airports usually collect significantly more money by charging merchants a percentage of their gross sales.

In the same way, a small kids' clothing store is going to attract much more traffic if it's in the same strip mall that includes a major retailer. By charging a percentage of the clothing store's sales, the strip mall owner is charging the store a premium for the right to coexist with this consumer-traffic magnet.

Remember, if you have retail property in a great location, you're probably paying a premium price for it. To help offset the cost and make your property a better income generator, don't hesitate to charge your tenants a higher percentage of sales.

Comparing strip malls and convenience stores

Retail *strip malls* (sometimes known as *strip centers*) that contain between 4 and 20 individual or combined storefronts can be a great investment. Lenders love these types of properties, especially newer buildings located in high-traffic areas because they're relatively much less risky. *Convenience stores*, also referred to as *C-stores* (places where you can usually get a soda or a bag of chips at any time of the day or night) can also be good investments and attractive to lenders because they tend to stay in business longer than most other stores.

Lenders want to see the income and expense numbers (which the seller should be able to supply), as well as market data showing retail traffic patterns and area growth. Also ask for tax returns on the business so you can verify what the seller tells you. For data on traffic patterns and area growth, check with your local chamber of commerce, commercial real estate agents, visitor and convention bureaus, or economic development departments.

Be very careful about investing in a C-store that functions (or formerly functioned) as a gas station. The environmental risks are too great for most lenders, so these properties are almost impossible to finance. If you're considering such a property, check with your broker first to locate a current source of funding before you make an offer. For additional details, refer to "Gas stations" later in this chapter.

Running Your Own Hotel or Motel

If the movie *Psycho* didn't scare you clear of your dreams of becoming the owner and manager of a local hotel or motel, maybe we can do it for you. You really need to know what you're doing in this arena to be successful — it's not for the faint of heart.

If you really want to get involved in these sorts of properties, consider investing in a Real Estate Investment Trust (REIT) that specializes in hotels and motels to get your feet wet. Doing so spreads out the risk and allows you to get much-needed experience before venturing out on your own.

Still interested? Keep in mind that fewer lenders are eager to finance the purchase of hotels and motels, and those who are willing to consider it want to see stronger numbers than they'd require for multifamily, office, or retail properties. The risks are greater to the lender, so they want to see that the property has a greater profit potential. The good news is that the reward should be better for you as an investor.

In the following sections, we bring you up to speed on the basics of evaluating hotels and motels.

Distinguishing between flagged and unflagged properties

When you're in the market for a hotel or motel, keep in mind the differences between *flagged* and *unflagged* properties:

- ✔ **Flagged:** Properties associated with a national chain or franchise.
- ✔ **Unflagged:** Independently operated hotels or motels not connected with a national chain or franchise.

Lenders prefer flagged properties because they tend to carry less risk. In the following sections, we break down the differences in greater detail.

Flagged properties

Flagged properties are premium real estate for several reasons, including the following:

- ✔ They generally have higher occupancy rates.
- ✔ They offer greater support in the form of national reservation systems, online booking, payment-processing systems, group reservations, and many other benefits.
- ✔ Consumers know what to expect and, as a result, are less hesitant to book a room. (On the flip side, you may have to jump through hoops to meet the strict set of criteria set by higher-end chains.)
- ✔ You may be able to finance the purchase directly through the chain itself under certain conditions. If not, guarantees and concessions from the chain can improve your chances of obtaining attractive financing.

Amenities, age, location, proximity to other chain properties, management, and the property's physical condition all play a part in how lenders flag a property and how it performs financially.

Make sure you work with a commercial loan broker who has access to specific hotel/motel lenders.

Unflagged properties

Due to their lack of national exposure and support, unflagged properties are much more difficult to finance. Lenders take a very critical approach to the income and expense numbers, especially if you
have little or no experience in running successful hotel or motel
establishments.

The only real advantage of owning an unflagged property is that
you don't have to pay national franchising fees. Other than that,
unflagged properties offer no clear advantages.

Encountering income challenges

When dealing with hotel and motel properties, expect to face a
whole new set of income and expense categories, including the
following:

- ✔ **Convention tax or visitors fee:** Taxes may be computed differently based upon occupancy numbers. In addition, trans-
  portation such as airport shuttles, taxis, or bus service may
  affect the rates.

- ✔ **Use fees:** Resorts that use other public or private amenities
  such as lakes, health clubs, casinos, parks, or nature pre-
  serves may also be subject to use fees or membership
  requirements.

- ✔ **Costs of meeting government requirements:** Bed-and-
  breakfasts (known as B and Bs) have to be careful of zoning
  restrictions, business licenses, and health department
  requirements. Because most of these businesses are
  residential-turned-commercial properties, the property may
  be subject to additional upgrades such as Americans with
  Disabilities Act (ADA) requirements or expensive sprinkler
  system installations.

As a general rule, hotel/motel properties pose greater risk to the
lender and require a higher Debt Service Coverage Ratio, or DSCR.

DSCR is the number that lenders use to evaluate the risk versus
the rewards. To calculate the DSCR, you first need to calculate the
property's NOI, as discussed in Chapter 3. Divide the NOI by the
annual debt service on the loan (total annual payments on the
loan, including interest and principal). If, for example, a property
has an NOI of $60,000 and the total loan payments for the year are
$50,000, the DSCR is $60,000 ÷ $50,000, which equals 1.20. A DSCR
of 1.00 means that the property is breaking even. Typical DSCRs
are between 1.04 and 1.50. A hotel/motel would need to come in

about 1.30 to get approved in today's market (a slow market at the time of writing this book).

The higher the ratio, the better the deal — and the better the financing options. Ask the lender or loan officer about the DSCR requirements for the types of properties that interest you. This can keep you from wasting time on properties that don't come near to meeting the lender's DSCR requirements.

Checking Out Industrial or Warehouse Properties

At first glance, you may think that industrial or warehouse properties are the simplest investments to finance and manage, but they come with their own challenges. In the following sections, we explore the unique costs you're likely to encounter, introduce storage facility opportunities, and warn you about zoning and use issues related to these types of properties.

You can finance the purchase of industrial and warehouse properties through a variety of lenders, but as with any type of commercial property, the numbers need to work. Consult with a broker who can put you in touch with the right lenders and assist you in crunching the numbers.

For any industrial or warehouse type of facility, make sure to check with the local building department and zoning board to understand the present zoning restrictions, limitations on use, and any grandfather clauses in place under present operations. Those regulations can change with a change in ownership, and you don't want to get caught by surprise!

Calculating income and costs

With industrial and warehouse properties, you calculate rent and income on a square-foot basis, just as you do with retail space. Multiply the net rental square footage by the annual rental income per square foot to estimate your annual rental income from the property.

Expense categories are generally much different, however, and include purchase and maintenance of loading docks, forklifts, major heating and cooling systems, truck bays, and structural components.

Some industrial properties also lend themselves to special permits, wastewater discharge requirements, and neighborhood noise restrictions. Check all the regulations before proceeding with an investment of this nature.

Considering storage facilities

Those self-storage facilities that blemish the U.S. landscape rarely seem so ugly to investors because they can be great investments. They enable you to spread the risk among dozens or even hundreds of tenants and require little maintenance (and no refrigerators to replace). Income is straightforward on a per-unit, per-month basis, and expenses are limited mostly to external maintenance issues.

Check with your commercial loan broker to connect with lenders who specialize in financing the purchase of self-storage units.

Exploring Mixed-Use Properties

Mixed-use properties are those that combine any of the functions covered previously in this chapter; for example, a multifamily apartment that includes a grocery on the first floor or an office complex that has retail shopping inside.

Financing for mixed-use properties can become rather complicated. Lenders who provide financing for office buildings may lose interest if you're planning to add a restaurant, making it a riskier proposition. As the risk to the lender rises, loan costs and interest rates rise accordingly, and you need to budget for them.

When evaluating the income and expenses, break out each portion separately and then combine the totals. This practice allows you to change the lender package easily, if necessary, to illustrate different tenancy income/expense flows or restructure the transaction.

Sampling Some Special Use Properties

With all the different types of properties out there, some just don't fit into any square box like the rest. These are known as *special use properties.* Common special use properties include restaurants and bars, gas stations, and adult foster care facilities. We cover financing considerations for these beasts in the following sections.

More specialized properties in this category include churches, casinos, theme parks, golf courses, and bowling alleys, which are all too specialized for us to cover in this book. Check out *Commercial Real Estate Investing For Dummies* to get a complete picture of what properties like these really entail.

Special use properties are much more difficult to finance and require special lenders and preparation. For all practical purposes, novice investors would do best to steer clear of these properties.

Restaurants and bars

Although lenders are just as likely as anyone else to eat out or drop in at the local watering hole, they generally avoid financing restaurants and bars. Almost all these establishments fail within five years, leaving lenders to deal with the hangovers.

The exception would be for an established franchise (or flagged) property with a proven track record, or destination-type properties such as a Chuck E. Cheese or a microbrewery (and no, you can't combine those two!)

If you're committed to buying a restaurant or bar, your best bet for obtaining financing is through hard-money lenders (see Chapter 11), seller financing (also see Chapter 11), or local banks (not likely), in that order.

Look that gift horse in the mouth

I (Chip) once financed a property for an industrial manufacturing company that was given a new piece of equipment by General Motors. Nice gift — it was worth well more than $1 million. The catch was that the warehouse floor had to be rebuilt with a six-foot concrete slab! Yes, it was quite expensive.

The take-home lesson is this: Budget for your expenses upfront. If I hadn't budgeted for this expense, it would have been a hidden expense that could have really taken a chunk out of my bottom line.

Gas stations

A few lenders out there take chances on financing gas stations, but the station must be newer and have EPA-certified tanks (as opposed to the old steel tanks that may end up leaking).

Due to the possibility of past tank leakage and the environmental issues and cleanup costs associated with contaminated soil, most lenders don't consider financing these properties. Inexperienced investors should avoid these types of properties, too. Even properties now used for something else (but with a history of underground gas or oil storage tanks) pose a problem for an investor seeking financing. It's not impossible, but it's definitely a much bigger challenge.

Financing often is available through the distributor (such as Shell or Sunoco). Options are much better if the station is combined with a convenience store or fast-food operation.

Adult foster care

With the graying of America, demand has increased for adult foster care, but these properties can be difficult to finance and come with their own set of legal and practical challenges. Some national lenders may be willing to do the deals, but do your homework to protect your interests and those of the lender. Check zoning requirements, ADA and licensing requirements, and state health records for histories of violations, sanctions, or limited use restrictions.

Group homes and primary child-care facilities are treated the same way, and the same lenders are the primary source of financing for these properties. A residential home in which the homeowner runs a small part-time day care facility wouldn't be subject to these guidelines; instead, it would be eligible for standard residential financing (as long as the day care constituted less than 25 percent of the total use).

Chapter 9

Exploring Sources of Financing for Commercial Properties

*W*hen financing commercial property you can't always find money in the usual places. In some cases, for example, you may be able to obtain loans for commercial properties that are secured by the Small Business Administration (SBA). You can't get that money when you're buying houses! In other cases, you may be able to combine a few sources to get a project off the ground — perhaps purchasing the property with a commercial loan and then fixing it up with a rehabilitation loan.

If you want to purchase a commercial property, you need a firm grasp on the financing options available to you. In this chapter, we lead you on a quest for cash to finance your acquisition and development of commercial properties. When you're aware of all the different programs available, you can then begin to mix and match to come up with your own creative financing plans.

Sizing Up Various Commercial Loan Programs

When you're searching for a commercial loan, the resources aren't nearly as useful as when you're buying a home to live in. Sure, you can (and should) trek down to your local bank to see what it has to offer or dial up the lender that currently services the mortgage on your two-family unit for a quick source of financing. They may be able to assist you, but in all likelihood, commercial lending isn't their specialty, and it's likely to end up costing you more — both in money and hassles — than other alternatives.

You may be better off dealing with lenders who specialize in financing commercial real estate deals. In addition to having a clearer understanding of your goals, these lenders know what's available and reasonable in the current market. When choosing a commercial loan program, you have three options: middle market, hard money, and conduit loans. The following sections describe these three options.

Exploring the middle market (local and national banks)

Local and regional banks comprise the *middle market* — lenders who deal in loan amounts from $50,000 to $2 million. Although your bank may not be the best place to score a commercial loan (depending on market conditions), it's one of the best places to begin your search. Local and regional banks love to find quality projects in their areas because they can evaluate and monitor the risk and performance much more easily.

Pros

Financing your commercial venture through a local bank offers several distinct advantages:

- ✔ You have many lenders to choose from.
- ✔ A bank may be willing to consider unique or complex deals.
- ✔ A bank is more likely than a conduit lender to accept lower loan amounts — typically starting as low as $50,000.
- ✔ You may be able to work with your bank to combine other types of financing, such as loans that use inventory or operating capital as collateral. (See "Considering other potential sources of capital" later in this chapter for details.)

Cons

Because banks tend to be more averse to risk than other types of lenders, financing through a bank has several potential drawbacks:

- ✔ Interest rates and terms are higher.

- ✔ A bank is likely to require that you move all your accounts (personal savings account, business accounts, and so on) to its institution.

- ✔ A bank may not be willing to approve large loans.

- ✔ Banks can change the type of properties they're willing to finance on very short notice.

Pitching your deal to the bank

Taking out a commercial loan through a bank requires that you proceed through entirely different channels than you're accustomed to. Start with the bank's manager, who can refer you to one of the bank's commercial loan officers.

Most commercial loan officers are paid on commission — which works to your advantage. They get paid only if and when you get the loan, so they're motivated to make it work. Spend some time getting to know the loan officer. Ask for his input on how to structure the deal. Ask for a commercial loan package, or at least how he wants the information presented.

The only thing that matters in getting the deal done is the numbers. Yes, you need to demonstrate that you're a strong borrower with good credit, cash in the bank, and a solid investment background, but in the end, these qualities only reinforce the decision. Eighty to 90 percent of the decision hinges on the property's numbers. Be prepared with an income statement for the property, rent rolls, balance sheets, tax returns, bank statements, personal financials, and a resume — the loan officer wants to see that you have the skills and experience to handle the transaction.

Hitting up the private sector: Hard-money lenders

Thanks to the mortgage meltdown that started in 2008, hard money may be the only money you can get your mitts on for some deals. Hard-money lenders are private individuals, finance groups, and small- to mid-size specialty finance companies that concentrate on lending money to real estate investors.

Going the hard-money route has its advantages and disadvantages. Check out Chapter 11 for the complete lowdown on hard money.

Financing Main Street property with Wall Street money

Using commercial mortgage backed securities (CMBS for short), *conduit lenders* provide financing through Wall Street investment firms to commercial real estate investors. The lenders allot the funds in huge pools based on the type of investment property — retail, office, multifamily housing, and so on — and they rate the securities based on their risk and performance.

Conduit lenders typically deal only with high-quality borrowers and properties — and in larger loan amounts. These loans are most suitable (and only available) for large multifamily projects (200+ units), shopping centers, large office complexes, and similar types of properties. You must have a good track record for making payments and a proven ability to make profitable commercial investments.

Pros

Financing commercial real estate ventures through conduit loans offers several advantages:

- ✔ Financing is readily available.

- ✔ Interest rates and terms are more attractive than with other forms of financing.

- ✔ Financing terms and property requirements are more standardized and predictable.

- ✔ You have numerous lenders to choose from.

Cons

Conduit loans aren't always a viable (or the most attractive) form of financing for commercial ventures. Here are some of the reasons:

- ✔ Minimum loan amounts are typically $2.5 million or more.

- ✔ To qualify, you must have very strong credit and show that the property has a solid cash flow potential.

- ✔ Property standards are very specific with regard to higher quality, income performance, and newer construction standards, which can exclude many properties from consideration.

- ✔ If you sell or refinance the property before the term is up, you may face stiff prepayment penalties.

- ✔ Older properties or ones located in more run-down or neglected areas of town typically aren't eligible.

With the collapse of several large Wall Street investment firms in 2008 (including Bear Stearns, Lehman Brothers, and others), conduit options are becoming scarce and very picky.

Tracking down conduit lenders

Finding large conduit lenders can be tricky. They work only through commercial mortgage lenders and brokers, so the best place to start is with an experienced commercial broker.

Get some referrals from your state mortgage association or ask experienced real estate developers in your area. Another option is to do a little research down at your county recorder's office. Look up and contact the lender of record for a large complex. In most cases, the lender won't work with you directly but can refer you to one of its local or regional lending reps.

Prepping for your first meeting

When dealing with conduit lenders, you're playing in the major leagues and dealing with big money, so be prepared. A good loan rep can help you put together an Executive Loan Summary (ELS) that lays out the entire proposal. Concentrate on the numbers. Make sure you know them inside and out, and have all the data to back up why this property makes financial sense. You need to sell it to the rep before it goes to the underwriter.

Pursuing Government Loans

Only one person in this country has an endless supply of money. No, it's not Bill Gates or even Warren Buffet. It's your rich Uncle Sam, who has his own printing press specifically designed to churn out those greenbacks. When credit is tight, Uncle Sam actively tries to stimulate the economy by making money available to investors and developers just like you.

Several agencies help Uncle Sam make money more available, including the Federal Housing Authority (FHA) and the Small Business Administration (SBA). In the following sections, we explore these options and other related opportunities.

Financing housing and medical facilities through FHA loans

When most people hear about FHA financing, they assume it's related to government-secured loans for buying single-family homes like we discuss in Chapter 5. However, FHA also insures financing for the purchase or development of multifamily homes (at least 100 units) and medical facilities.

To pursue this source of financing, track down a commercial FHA lender (not a residential lender). FHA-approved commercial lenders are scarce, but you can locate them by talking to a local commercial loan officer or searching online for "HUD multifamily financing."

 Only a handful of commercial lenders are FHA approved. Make sure you check them out thoroughly online and through HUD by calling the HUD regional office listed on the Web site (www.hud. gov). Ask how long the lender has been approved and whether it has any sanctions against it. (From HUD's home page, navigate to the Multifamily Industry page to access information specifically for commercial topics. For descriptions of multifamily housing programs, go directly to www.hud.gov/offices/hsg/mfh/progdesc/progdesc.cfm.)

 After you've found an FHA-approved commercial lender, present the property you're planning to purchase and ask for a quote. If the property qualifies, you may also be eligible for Section 8 housing payment guarantees. With these guarantees in place, the government makes up the difference if you lease to low-income renters and they can't pay the rent.

Tapping into economic development funds and grants

Many states and large cities provide financing for real estate properties as part of an economic development fund or grant. Usually restricted to downtown development areas or *revitalization districts,* these loans can come with low interest rates, low costs, and some nice perks, such as tax abatements or investment incentives. Transforming abandoned warehouses into fashionable loft apartments or rehabbing run-down brownstone apartments are perfect candidates for these types of financing programs.

 If you're looking at commercial property located in a revitalization district, contact the state housing authority and the city or county economic development office to find out how to tap into these financing sources.

Securing a loan through the SBA

SBA-insured loans are a great way to finance the purchase of a building that houses business owners and can even be used to finance start-up capital and inventory. Many self-owned restaurants, bars, grocery stores, and other businesses are financed through SBA programs 7(a) and 504, as discussed in the following sections.

The SBA requires a personal guarantee from every borrower, doesn't offer 100 percent financing, and provides outright grants only to nonprofit organizations. We can't really recommend one program over the other, because they both have pros and cons and are used for quite different situations (as discussed in the following sections). The best way to evaluate the two options is to obtain quotes from lenders that compare the numbers side by side specifically related to your property and financing needs.

For more detailed information on obtaining one of these loans, go to www.sba.gov or check out the online presentation of the program at www.sba.gov/services/financialassistance/index.html. Most SBA loans are provided through local and regional banks, so start there.

SBA's 7(a) loan program

The 7(a) is the most common SBA-insured loan available. You can use it for an existing or new business, and it can include acquisition of land, buildings, machinery, furniture, supplies, inventory, working capital, or even buying the business itself. Following are the rules governing eligibility:

- ✔ Limited to businesses with fewer than 100 employees (500 for manufacturing companies).

- ✔ Can't have more than $21 million in annual sales ($17.5 million for construction companies).

- ✔ Term can be up to 25 years (10 years for working capital).

- ✔ Rates are market rate — usually adjustable tied to the *prime rate* (the rate that banks charge one another).

- ✔ Guaranteed amount to the bank or lender is typically 75 percent and limited to $1.5 million per business.

SBA's 504 loan program

The 504 program is an economic development program designed to stimulate the economy and create new jobs. Here are the eligibility rules:

- ✔ Minimum 10 percent contribution required by Certified Development Company (CDC) or from the borrower.

- ✔ Must create or retain 1 job per $35,000 of SBA support.

✔ Business plan must demonstrate that the loan will support local economic growth through new jobs, manufacturing, or a type of business that will attract other industry.

✔ Ideal candidates for these types of loans include companies involved in high-tech development, green-energy research and development, or experimental medical technologies.

✔ Similar to the 7(a) program, the interest rate and term is close to other market rates and programs, and is tied to an index such as the prime interest rate. Other local or state grant programs may also be available for part of the financing to reflect a lower blended interest rate.

Harvesting investment capital through the USDA

The U.S. Department of Agriculture (USDA) does a lot more than inspect chickens and cows and make sure your milk gets pasteurized. It also works hard to encourage investment in agriculture and related activities. As such, it often finances a variety of projects — from warehouses to high-tech research facilities — through its Business and Industry Guaranteed Loan (B&I loan). The B&I loan is designed for real estate, equipment, working capital, and refinancing non-farm operations.

The one major requirement for a B&I loan is that the property has to be located in a rural area (or city with fewer than 50,000 people). Other conditions include the following:

✔ Loan amounts are between $1 million and $10 million.

✔ Loans require a guarantee program similar to the SBA's. (See "Securing a loan through the SBA" earlier in this chapter.)

✔ Loans are offered at market rates and terms.

Unlike FHA and SBA loans, these loans actually go directly through the USDA. It may refer you to one of its bank partners, but it can and does handle most loans directly. Contact a regional district office to obtain a loan package and detailed requirements. One problem with these loans is that the USDA has only so much funding available and can actually *run out* of funds until the government's new fiscal year provides a fresh appropriation.

The USDA offers several other grant programs and minority business finance programs. For more information, visit www.rurdev. usda.gov/rbs/busp/b&i_gar.htm.

What exactly does FHA do?

As part of the U.S. Department of Housing and Urban Development, the FHA has been lending money to finance both large and small housing projects since the 1930s. Its primary goal is to assist in making affordable housing available for U.S. citizens, which also helps stimulate the economy.

Technically speaking, the FHA doesn't really lend money. It insures loans from banks and other qualified lending institutions. This insurance is great for lenders, because it enables them to lend money with confidence, knowing that if the borrower defaults on the loan, the FHA will step in and cover any loss. It's great for borrowers, too, because it gives them access to lower-cost loans at greater LTVs than banks would normally consider. (Check out Chapter 3 for more on LTV.)

It's a true win-win!

Getting a hold of a CDBG

Community development block grants (CDBGs) are available to investors for acquiring and rehabilitating commercial properties in run-down areas.

To qualify for a CDBG, you need to write a grant proposal, which can be complicated. Every grant has unique requirements in respect to forms, time frame, type of properties, program guidelines, and approval. Network with other real estate investors to find someone who's participated in a recently approved grant and ask for his or her assistance. You may need to hire someone who really knows the system. (For more about writing grants, check out *Grant Writing For Dummies,* 3rd Edition, by Beverly A. Browning [Wiley].)

In addition, the Community Reinvestment Act (CRA), established in 1977, requires lenders to invest locally. For these types of projects, your property must be associated with a nonprofit organization or be serving an underserved segment of the local market. Inner-city, community-group, and nonprofit projects are perfect fits.

Every bank has to provide a certain amount of CRA funding each year, depending on its size and lending area. The loans are usually tied to specific types of properties or groups, including minorities, community groups, Habitat for Humanity, and so on. The bank usually wants some good PR out of it (although it rarely says so).

Deconstructing Construction Loans

Prior to mid-2008, new construction was big business, and construction loans were readily available. The market meltdown changed all that. Now when you apply for a construction loan, all the lenders see is risk with a capital *R*. (A *construction loan* is one that's used to finance the development of new homes or buildings. The big difference between construction loans and other real estate loans is that you don't get the money all at once. Instead, the bank doles out the cash when each phase of the project is completed and passes inspection.)

Due to recent credit changes, construction loans are harder to come by for commercial projects. Technically, these loans are still available, but you'd better have a strong package to get the funding.

 Before you even think about sitting down with prospective lenders, put together a *pro forma* — a document/report that projects the income and expenses for at least a three-year period after completion (refer to Chapter 8). You should also have a contingency plan in place if the numbers don't hit expectations.

Here's some of what you can expect when pursuing a construction loan:

- ✔ Short term loans — typically only up to three years
- ✔ Financing only on strong projects with proven income streams
- ✔ Lower LTVs with strong borrower credit requirements and personal guarantees

 In a soft (slumping) market, you need to show that whatever you're planning to build is almost guaranteed to generate a positive cash flow. Be prepared to provide complete blueprints and construction specifications, a completion timeline, and occupancy projections, as well as pre-lease agreements. Some lenders require that a building be more than 75 percent pre-leased before construction can begin.

Financing Fixes with Rehabilitation Loans

Securing financing for a fixer-upper is often easier than convincing a lender to bankroll an entirely new building — as long as the numbers come out right. *Rehabilitation loans* involve properties that will maintain at least 25 percent of the existing structure. The projects can involve a total do-over (essentially gutting the property) or just a quick fix-up job.

Middle-market local and regional banks are the best bet for rehab loans. Call and talk to one of the bank's commercial loan reps to see whether it does rehab loans and what its specific LTV and pro forma requirements are. Many banks shy away from these loans during market slowdowns unless they're presented with a very strong deal.

After you've scoped out some lenders who do rehabilitation loans, you need to crunch the numbers to prove that your project is a money-maker. Draw up a comprehensive plan that includes a breakdown of all improvements and materials, blueprints, and specifications. Include a pro forma, as discussed in the previous section, showing the return on the investment. If you can't show a positive cash flow without fudging the numbers, don't do the deal.

Don't over-improve yourself out of a profit. Spending $550,000 on a building where the leases are fixed for the next three years makes no sense. Be sure you can recover your investment in a reasonable amount of time.

Exploring Other Creative Financing Options

Taking out a loan is the most obvious way to finance your commercial real estate venture, but it's certainly not the only way. Other individuals and organizations have money to lend or invest. If you can't find the money through traditional sources, consider the more creative financing options covered in the following sections.

Borrowing from pension programs and life insurance companies

Pension programs and life insurance companies have large pools of cash available for investing. Much of this cash is invested in stocks and bonds, but many fund managers actively look for real estate investments to provide better returns than they can get in the traditional markets:

> ✔ **Pension programs** generally prefer conservative, short-term loans on stable commercial properties such as multifamily units, retail properties, and resort hotels. The loan amounts tend to be larger, but they can be flexible on terms and rates.

> ✔ **Life insurance companies** also look for more stable deals, but they can provide a viable alternative to borrowing from conduit lenders.

You won't be able to track down these opportunities by yourself — you have to work through a commercial lender or broker, just as if you were pursuing a conduit loan. See "Financing Main Street property with Wall Street money" earlier in this chapter for details.

Enlisting the services of venture capitalists

Some people have more money than they know what to do with: the *venture capitalists* (VCs) — individuals and companies who are constantly on the lookout for new businesses and innovative technologies to invest in. Assuming a business or new technology is promising enough, VCs are willing to finance everything, including real estate acquisition, redevelopment, and all the costs of starting and running the business, especially if it involves high-tech, bio-tech, medical technology, or other innovative operations.

Financing through VCs has advantages and disadvantages just like any type of financing. The big plus is that they can write big checks. The major drawback is that you lose a lot of control over your business and its operations. If you're running a high-tech business and want to purchase real estate as part of the business, however, this may be the solution for you.

VC firms specialize in niche markets, so talk to business brokers who specialize in selling businesses within that niche. In other words, if you're looking for VCs for a theme restaurant, talk to a broker who sells theme restaurants or franchises. She can put you in touch with venture capitalists, but she may charge a finder's fee.

Grab a copy of *Entrepreneur Magazine* and flip to the back to find listings for VC firms. Other publications and newsletters for business owners and entrepreneurs often contain similar listings. Start locally and then go online to research the VCs you turn up through your local search in depth. After you've found a few promising candidates, interview them and check references on recent projects they've done to determine their *pull-through rate* (what they actually produce versus what they promise).

Many venture capital firms are equally interested in the overall concept of the business plan and real estate development as much as the financial picture. They can be much more flexible on the returns, especially if the short-term numbers aren't extremely strong but the long-term potential looks great. Make sure your pro forma is very conservative and extends out at least five years.

Sharing the costs and the equity

Some lenders are willing to loan investors money only if they can get a little piece of the action — equity in a property. For larger real estate transactions or very unique situations that involve several investors, you may want to explore the possibility of some equity-sharing arrangement by way of an equity loan.

With an *equity loan,* you actually become partners with the bank or investor. They provide the financing in exchange for equity in the building or a portion of the cash flow or the actual business. This arrangement presents obvious drawbacks in terms of control and decision-making with regards to the property and its use, but it also requires you to be more accountable to the transaction.

Consider equity-sharing only as a last resort, unless you're looking for partners who can offer you more than money. If you pitch your plan to the last lender on your list and get a lukewarm "no," this usually means that the lender likes the deal, but it's just bigger than his budget or appetite. Ask whether he'd be more interested if his risk and exposure were reduced by bringing in another partner or lender or giving him a piece of the project. In most cases, the answer is still "no," but you never know until you ask.

If you do decide to move forward on such an arrangement, consult a qualified accountant and an attorney to write up a limited agreement. We recommend limiting your partner's share to no more than 49 percent of the outstanding equity. Also include a maximum five-year buyout provision with a first-right-of-refusal so you can protect any growth in the equity. See Chapter 13 for more on partnerships and partnership agreements.

Participating in participation loans

With a *participation loan,* several lenders chip in to share the costs, risks, and potential profits with one another and the borrower/investor. Participation loans are common in large commercial transactions that involve community development projects, such as a hotel attached to a new city convention center.

On these types of loans, several banks or financial institutions provide a portion of the financing, each taking a piece of the pie. For example, if no single lender is willing or able to finance the $20 million for the deal, they may split it up, with Bank A financing

$10 million, Bank B $6 million, and Bank C $2 million, with the balance coming from the borrower. In this case, Bank A is the primary lender, including the primary authority in decision making.

Don't try to arrange these deals yourself. Enlist the assistance of a qualified mortgage brokerage or banking firm to bring all the parties together, coordinate efforts, and manage all the in-fighting that's likely to occur as the lenders jockey for position.

Taking on a partner

For smaller, simpler commercial real estate acquisitions, you may want to consider taking on a partner — one who has access to solid financial resources or the credit needed to qualify for financing.

If you decide to take on a partner, just make sure that all the expectations and responsibilities are clearly laid out — in writing. For more about partnering, check out Chapter 13.

Considering other potential sources of capital

Thanks to the mortgage meltdown and subsequent economic challenges that began in 2008, you may have to dig deeper to find financing for your commercial ventures. As you dig, here are a few other options to consider:

- ✔ **Franchise financing:** Many commercial properties used in conjunction with a franchise operation are eligible for direct financing with the parent company. Hotels such as Sheraton or Holiday Inn, restaurants such as KFC or Applebee's, or even a Baskin-Robbins ice-cream shop can find some cheap money through its franchise operation.

- ✔ **Inventory loans:** If you have a business with a large amount of inventory, you may be able to use that inventory as collateral to finance the purchase of the property or at least part of it.

- ✔ **Accounts receivable:** If you're acquiring a property that services a large vendor such as the U.S. government or United Airlines, you may be able to use the value of future contracts as collateral for part of the down payment or financing. Some large companies even provide financing to suppliers for their production facilities.

Chapter 10

Securing a Loan to Finance Your Commercial Venture

● ●

In This Chapter

▶ Making sense of the broker agreement

▶ Tallying the broker fees and other costs

▶ Covering your back with unbiased reports

▶ Surviving the closing

● ●

*W*hen you're borrowing money to buy a home to live in, the lender wants to know that you're earning enough money to make the monthly mortgage payments. The focus is on you and your finances — how much money you earn, how much cash you have socked away in the bank, and your track record for paying your bills on time.

When you're buying commercial property, the focus shifts. The lender is less concerned about you and your earning potential and more concerned about the property's earning potential. Because of this difference and others, financing a commercial venture is quite different from financing the purchase of a residential property.

In this chapter, we lead you through the application and processing of your commercial loan, so you know what to expect and can avoid the most common pitfalls.

Deciphering the Broker-Borrower Agreement

Although you can often deal directly with lenders to finance residential deals, you usually have to work through a broker or loan officer on commercial deals. The broker or loan officer acts as the middleman who puts you in touch with the lender and advises you on which loan programs are best for you and your investment goals. (See Chapter 4 for more about brokers and loan officers.)

With commercial properties, the broker is likely to require that you sign a broker-borrower agreement. A good commercial loan broker is going to do a great deal of work on your behalf to search for, evaluate, and secure financing for your transaction. He wants to make sure that you're going to go through with the deal, so he can get paid. A well-written agreement also protects your rights.

Although no standard format governs such agreements, all of them spell out the terms of the agreement, including the following:

- ✔ **Term of the engagement:** The agreement should spell out how long you're retaining the broker to represent you. Limit the term to a period of four to six months. If they haven't found any investors for you by then, it's time to move on.

- ✔ **Exclusivity clause:** A commercial broker may ask for *exclusive rights* to represent you, meaning you can't retain any other commercial lenders or brokers during that period. Before you sign the agreement, make sure you're comfortable with your selection. If your only broker drops the ball, you may be out of the game for several months. Try to avoid contracts with an exclusivity clause, or at least get a clause that lasts no longer than 90 to 120 days. For particularly large or difficult transactions, you may have to provide a six-month window.

- ✔ **Loan acceptance terms:** Specify the loan terms you're willing to accept; for example, you may want to specify a loan that offers 80 percent loan-to-value (LTV) on a 25-year amortization at 7 percent or better. Don't set the bar so high, however, that your loan officer can't possibly negotiate a deal.

Be careful what you ask for. If your broker finds a loan that meets the terms you specified, you may be obligated to pay your broker regardless of whether the deal closes.

- ✔ **Non-circumvention clause:** This part of the agreement prohibits you from cutting your broker out of the deal and dealing directly with the lender. This clause is no biggie because circumventing your broker is bad business anyway.

- ✔ **Compensation:** Any broker agreement spells out how much you're paying the broker. The fee is completely negotiable, but expect it to run one to two *points* (1 or 2 percent) of the deal. You generally pay a larger percentage for smaller loans and a smaller percentage for larger loans. Negotiate with the broker until you're comfortable with the fee.

- ✔ **Retainer fee:** Except for very small commercial transactions, most brokers ask for a *retainer,* which covers his upfront expenses and ties you to the contract. (An agreement isn't very binding if it has no cash tied to it.) In most cases, you shouldn't have to pay more than $2,000 — less for smaller deals and more for larger ones. My (Chip's) standard retainer is $2,000, but I've collected as much as $10,000 upfront on a $28 million deal.

Make sure any retainer fee is applied toward the overall compensation. Also ask whether the fee is refundable (usually not) and under what circumstances.

✔ **Communication:** Some agreements spell out specifically how often you agree to communicate with one another. You should expect updates from the broker about once a week. The broker may in turn require that you provide certain documentation within seven days to put together a loan proposal, for example. This is a reasonable request; you can't really expect the broker to draw up a proposal together without it. On the flip side, the broker should agree to communicate with you on a regular basis and update you on the status of any loan offers or commitments.

✔ **Cancellation clause:** The *cancellation clause* stipulates the conditions under which you or the broker can cancel the agreement. Make sure the agreement has a clause that enables you to cancel the agreement if the broker doesn't deliver satisfactory results in a certain amount of time. For example, if the broker fails to deliver any financing prospects to you over the course of a couple of months, you should probably be looking for the exits. Whatever the clause stipulates, make sure you understand and agree to it. If a dispute arises, you can renegotiate parts of the contract, but this is where a shorter-term agreement can work in your favor; you can simply let it expire.

Commercial lenders and brokers generally operate with less government oversight. As a result, agreements aren't required for commercial loan transactions, nor do you see the same disclosures as in residential transactions. Lenders aren't required to produce a Good Faith Estimate (GFE) or Truth In Lending statement. Good loan brokers, however, want to secure a written agreement with you to make sure neither of you is wasting the other's time.

Don't sign any legally binding agreement without having your attorney review it first, answer any questions you have about it, and advise you on the risks and benefits of signing.

Accounting for Upfront Fees

Unfortunately, that retainer you paid the broker in the previous section covers the broker's upfront fees, but it does nothing to cover *your* upfront fees. Here are the most common fees and costs you can expect to encounter when you're purchasing a commercial property:

- ✔ **Appraisal fee:** Lenders always order an appraisal and make you pay for it. Although the appraisal isn't done until the lender approves your loan request, you may have to pay for it upfront. Depending on the size and nature of the commercial property, the appraisal may cost anywhere from $1,500 to $5,000. For larger, more complex transactions, of course, the total may be much higher. Ask your loan officer for an estimate upfront.

- ✔ **Environmental fee:** Depending on the type of property, what it is (and was) used for, or even the surrounding neighbors, you may need to have the soil tested for contaminants. For example, if you're buying property near a defunct industrial plant or a building that once housed a dry cleaner, the soil may have toxins. Find out from your loan broker whether these tests are going to be necessary and obtain an estimate of the cost.

- ✔ **Structural inspection:** The lender may require certain types of inspections and engineering reports, which can get very expensive — especially for manufacturing facilities. Ask about the lender's requirements and obtain an estimate for your area.

- ✔ **Commitment fee or loan guarantee fee:** When the lender issues a loan commitment or preliminary proposal approval, it's going to want you to make a commitment as well. This request is only fair — the lender is about to spend a lot of effort evaluating the loan package, underwriting the file, reserving the funds, and so on, so it needs some assurance that you're not going to get cold feet. The lender is likely to require that you sign a commitment letter and submit a fee as specified in the letter. You pay this standard, nonrefundable fee to the lender upon acceptance of the commitment — it doesn't go to the broker, nor is it part of the loan amount. The fee should not exceed one to two percent of the loan amount, or a few thousand dollars for most transactions.

Before you sign off on the deal (by submitting the commitment letter), realize that you still have some room to negotiate. In most cases, the broker expects you to come back with a counteroffer on the commitment fee or the loan terms offered. Don't be too pushy here, though; you don't want to sink the deal and have to start all over from scratch. After you have a lender who's committed, you're 75 percent of the way there.

Obtaining Third-Party Reports

After you obtain a commitment with the lender or investor, you've pretty much entered the final stretch and can be fairly confident that your deal is going to cross the finish line, but you're not done yet. You still need to gather some additional information about the property to protect both yourself and the investor from taking ownership of a money pit.

Fortunately, other companies and individuals are well qualified to gather the necessary information for you and deliver *third-party reports*. These reports include

- ✔ An appraisal
- ✔ A survey
- ✔ The property's title and title history
- ✔ An engineering report
- ✔ An environmental inspection

In the following sections, we describe these third-party reports in detail and point out common red flags to watch for.

Verifying a property's market value with an appraisal

When financing a commercial property, the lender or investor orders a commercial appraisal to answer two important questions: First, is the property worth the price? Second, can the property generate more than enough revenue to cover the loan payments?

Although the lender orders the appraisal, you pay for it. After it's complete, get a copy for your records, and read it over carefully to make sure that you're not making a mistake in moving forward on the deal. Make sure the appraisal shows that the property's value is in line with similar properties and that it has the potential to generate the income you expect to earn from it. Your financial backers should sound the sirens if the appraisal shows the deal is a dud, but your neck is on the chopping block, so perform your own due diligence as well. The appraisal should simply support the calculations you've already done.

Commercial and residential appraisers differ significantly in terms of training, experience, and process. A commercial appraisal offers a comprehensive review of the property, all systems and construction, and similar types of commercial properties within a certain geographical area. It also includes something that residential appraisals don't — economic feasibility information. In other words, does the area really need another retail strip center, or how does this existing center perform compared to other retail strip centers in neighboring communities?

In case you're wondering about having the property inspected, the appraisal usually serves this purpose, too. On larger commercial deals, however, the lender's representative inspects the property as part of the approval process . . . and, of course, charges you for that inspection. You can expect the lender to disclose the cost of any required inspection upfront.

Plotting the perimeter with a survey

Toward the tail end of the loan process, the lender is going to order a survey, which you usually pay for as part of your closing costs. The *survey* shows the property's boundaries — its perimeter. In addition to showing you how much land you own, the survey provides some assurance that all improvements are located within the legal boundaries and, more importantly, whether any of your neighbors' buildings encroach on your land.

The lender and title company will alert you to any discrepancies or *encroachments* (where somebody else's improvements sit on your land). Discuss any issues with your broker or loan officer. Serious problems have to be solved prior to closing.

Ask for a copy of the survey prior to the closing and inspect it carefully to make sure you understand and approve the boundary lines. At closing, the title company or closing agent requires that you sign the survey certifying that you (the borrower) have seen it and received a copy.

You'll be asked to sign a copy certifying that you know what you are buying and what the lender is placing a lien on. If the survey shows any encumbrances, the lender won't close it until they're cleared up with a recordable easement or agreement with the other property owner(s). Many times you have "community driveways" that service several businesses, and a separate joint operating agreement may be in place to maintain that service drive. The lender will want to see a copy of that too.

Inspecting the title

Early in the process, the loan broker or lender orders a *title commitment*. This commitment provides a legal description of the property, lists any liens against the property, and stipulates any terms or conditions associated with the commercial real estate located there.

So, why should you care? This document is important because any or all of this information can ultimately come back to haunt you. If, for example, other parties have a lien against the property, you may be responsible for paying that lien if you take possession of the property. In addition, certain restrictions may limit improvements to the property or how you can use the property to generate revenue.

Ask for a copy of the title commitment as early on as possible and review it carefully. If any deed restrictions, operational limitations, or municipality conditions have been placed on the property, you need to know about them prior to signing on the dotted line. Some limitations can completely undermine your plans for the property.

Obtaining an engineering report

Engineering reports focus on the structural integrity of a building and its proposed use. They may include stress load tests or even earthquake tests for buildings in active fault zones. For one transaction, I (Chip) had to obtain an engineering report on a concrete slab. The slab was eight feet thick and was supporting a massive steel stamping machine in automotive production. That report alone cost several thousand dollars.

Before you get too deep into a deal, find out which engineering reports are going to be necessary and then obtain cost estimates on having them done. Lenders may require several of these reports for a single property depending on its location and proposed use. You can expect requests for more-detailed reports if you're purchasing taller buildings or manufacturing facilities.

Get a copy of all reports and review them completely. These reports may indicate a need for significant (and expensive) structural repairs that you need to make before you can use the property for the desired purpose.

Getting a clean bill of environmental health

Gas stations, dry cleaners, and car washes are notorious for leeching toxins into the ground on which they're situated, so if you're buying a piece of property that has (or had) one of these pollution-producers sitting on it, make sure you have it inspected (or at least purchase environmental insurance to protect your investment). The last thing you want to inherit is a former brownfield site! (See the nearby sidebar "What or where is Brownfield?" for more information.)

Most commercial transactions simply require *environmental insurance coverage* similar to title insurance that protects the lender against any past contaminations. Larger commercial properties may have to provide a *Phase I environmental report,* which is a surface level evaluation of the soil. This report costs anywhere from a couple of hundred bucks to a couple of thousand.

If the Phase I report shows any contaminants, a Phase II is necessary — which costs even more. We can't give you a ballpark estimate on the cost because it varies depending on the nature of the contaminants and the size of the parcel subject to the study.

If you have reason to suspect problems with the history of the site, you can do a little of your own research on the government Web site at www.epa.gov.

Navigating the Closing

After the lender receives and approves all the third-party reports, it sends you a final commitment letter signaling the beginning of the end. This notification gives you and the lender the green light to proceed to the closing table — the final chapter of the process (or at least the final section in this chapter).

Protecting yourself with title insurance

Every property has a title showing all the parties that have a legal claim to the property. The list of parties obviously includes the current owners, but it can also include lenders from whom the owners borrowed money, the government (which may lay claim to the property for any unpaid taxes), and utility companies (which may lay claim to the property for any unpaid utility bills).

Before you close on a real estate transaction, make sure you get *title insurance* — protection against any financial loss resulting from an overlooked valid legal claim to the property. Title insurance is even more important when you're closing on a commercial transaction because you usually have a lot more money on the line.

Prior to making an offer on the property, you should have received a copy of the title commitment and taken care of any issues regarding unresolved property liens. Just prior to closing, however, ask your title company for an updated title commitment. Check for any new liens or changes based on the title underwriter's most recent research. Be especially careful about tax liens and utility liens because they transfer with ownership.

Make sure your closing addresses all liens listed on the title. If, for example, the title shows that a mortgage lender still holds a lien against the property, make sure the closing is set up in such a way that the balance of that loan is going to be paid from the proceeds of the sale. Go over the list of lien holders with your attorney and title company to be sure that everyone who's supposed to get paid at closing does.

Have your attorney review the title documentation in addition to the Warranty Deed prepared by the seller or the title escrow agent. Compare the legal descriptions line by line and word for word, point out any discrepancies (none of which is too small to correct), and have all issues resolved *before* closing.

Insuring your property

Prior to the closing, meet with your insurance agent to discuss the nature of the property and its insurance requirements. Your lender requires that you have at least enough insurance to cover the amount of the new loan, but you need even more than that.

Make sure you have enough insurance to cover the replacement cost of the building(s), including operational systems such as elevators, HVAC units, pools, laundry facilities, appliances, machinery, and so on. Also be sure to order enough liability insurance to cover you in the event of personal injury claims and other lawsuits.

What or where is Brownfield?

A *brownfield site* isn't a specific place. It's a term used to designate an abandoned commercial or industrial facility situated on contaminated land or land generally believed to be contaminated with pollution or hazardous wastes. In many cases, the owners face a situation in which it would cost them more to clean up the property than they would earn from the sale of the restored site, so they choose to leave it as is.

People who buy brownfield sites (knowingly or unknowingly) also get stuck with the cleanup bill. This situation is certainly okay as long as you know what you're getting into and figure the cleanup costs into your budget. If you don't make the necessary budget accommodations, however, you may end up with a useless piece of property or expenses that completely wipe out your profit.

Have the policy ready to go prior to closing, and make sure it takes effect on before the closing date and time. Most commercial policies have an effective time, and you want that time to be the minute the closing takes place or before.

Attending to existing tenant rights

If you're buying a rental property that already has tenants in it, those tenants can make or break your ability to profit from the property. Prior to closing, you want to take inventory of your tenants, check on their status (especially in terms of paying their rent), and connect with them to ensure a smooth transition from one landlord to the next. Here's a checklist to help ensure a smooth transition:

- ✔ **At or just prior to the closing, ask the seller to execute a certification of tenancy.** This information is your assurance that you know of all tenants and the conditions of their tenancy.

- ✔ **For larger commercial properties, obtain an estoppel certificate from every tenant confirming their position with the current owner.** (Your attorney can supply you with copies of the certificate.) This certificate confirms all lease terms and conditions (including monthly payment and security deposit) and the date on which they made their last payment. Using the estoppel certificate, you can identify tenants who are behind on their rents and identify any early payments and security deposits that the previous owner is holding, so you can be sure that the money is transferred to you at closing.

- ✔ **Review all the rent rolls and have the seller certify them at closing.** Retain an original copy of the signed rent roll in case you need it later if discrepancies arise.

- ✔ **Account for all security deposits that the seller still holds, and make sure that the closing statement credits you for them.** If they're all held in an escrow account, make sure that they're transferred to you exclusively.

One of the first things you need to do as the new owner is communicate with your tenants and set the tone for your relationship. If the property is a large commercial multifamily housing complex, you may need to do it through a newsletter. For smaller properties, do it in person. Send a letter of introduction, and schedule an appointment with each tenant. Don't just show up on their doorstep.

With permission from the seller, I (Chip) usually try to meet each of the tenants face to face prior to the closing. This process helps me get a better feel for the property and what I need to do to address any tenant concerns right away. It also helps prevent tenant uneasiness that naturally arises when a new owner's in town — although the prospect of a new owner may be cause for celebration!

Part IV
Sampling More Creative Financing Strategies

"Let's see if we can determine your capacity for assuming risk. Now, how familiar are you with snake handling?"

In this part . . .

When most people hear the phrase *real estate financing,* they think "banks" and "mortgage brokers," but you — the savvy investor — can get your mitts on some investment capital in other ways, and in this part, we show you how.

These options aren't for everybody, but when you're in the market for investment properties and can't get your hands on conventional financing, these unconventional sources can really come in handy. In this part, you discover the pros and cons of what we call *hard money* — typically high-cost loans from private lenders. "High cost?" Why would you want a high-cost loan? We explain the (pleasantly) surprising reasons this may be a good option. We also show you how to finance through the seller by purchasing properties on contract, how to partner with an investor who's cash heavy, and how to track down no-money-down deals.

Chapter 11

Financing in a Pinch with Hard Money and Other Tough Options

- -

In This Chapter

▶ Deciding whether hard money is the option for you

▶ Minimizing the high cost of hard-money loans

▶ Discovering sources of hard money (including friends and relatives)

▶ Covering additional expenses with a line of credit

▶ Racking up charges on your credit card as a last resort

- -

*Y*ou just discovered the deal of a lifetime, but your bank won't loan you the money, you can't find a willing partner, and the owner refuses to finance the purchase. What do you do? You can give up and wait for another golden opportunity to come your way, but you don't want the promise of profit to slip through your fingers over something as mundane as money.

Another option is to obtain a loan from a private lender — a *hard-money* lender. Hard money is called *hard* because it's generally harder to pay back. Loans are short-term, and the lenders tend to charge a high interest rate plus *points* (a percentage of the loan amount) upfront. For the savvy real estate investor, though, access to cash is often more important than the cost, so when credit is tight, hard money may be the only option.

We begin this chapter by weighing the pros and cons of hard money to determine whether it's an option you want to pursue. We offer a few suggestions on how to keep the costs down and show you how to locate hard-money lenders in your market. We also show you how to tap into other sources of hard cash by borrowing from relatives, taking out a line of credit against the investment property to cover repair and renovation expenses, and using your credit cards as a last resort.

Although we recommend the hard-money option for situations in which a bank may turn you down for a loan, keep in mind that banks may turn you down for good reason — perhaps the investment is far too risky for them. When banks turn you down, take a closer look at the numbers. Sometimes, a lost investment opportunity may be the best thing that never happened to you.

Weighing the Pros and Cons of Hard Money

Before you decide to travel the hard-money route, consider the following potential benefits and drawbacks so you know what you're getting yourself into.

Perusing the pros

Hard money is a high-interest, short-term loan that offers four big benefits:

- **Easy access to cash:** You can get your hands on cash you may not be able to get through a conventional lender.

- **Reduced personal risk:** You don't have to borrow against your own home and place it at risk because hard-money lenders often accept the future value of a property as *collateral,* something of value they can take from you and sell if you happen to default on the loan.

  You can use your own house, possessions, and retirement savings as collateral, but doing so places your current possessions at risk and can get you into loads of trouble with your significant other. A safer way to borrow money is through a hard-money lender who's willing to accept just the investment property as collateral.

  Don't give lenders an ownership position by naming them on the deed, unless you truly want them as a partner. Give them only a lien holder position in the mortgage document.

- **Flexibility in financing repairs and renovations:** You can often set up a separate escrow account with a hard-money lender to pay for repairs and renovations.

- **No extra paperwork:** You can get your hands on it fast — without having to fill out a lot of extra formal paperwork.

Hard money by any other name

Although we like the term *hard money,* others may use other terminology to refer to this type of financing. Some of these terms apply to other types of financing, as well, which can get a bit confusing, but don't be surprised if your lender uses one of the following terms to refer to the hard-money option:

✔ **Bridge loan:** Because the loan functions as a short-term bridge between not owning the property and refinancing it later with a long-term loan.

✔ **Equity loan:** Because you're borrowing against the equity of the property you're purchasing rather than using your job and income as a way of securing the loan. (Don't confuse this with a standard home equity loan, in which you use financing to pull equity out of a property you own. In this case, you're essentially pulling equity out of a home you don't own so you can afford to buy it.)

✔ **Portfolio loan:** Because the lender holds the mortgage instead of selling it on Wall Street.

✔ **Rehab loan:** Because you're using the loan to purchase and renovate a distressed property to make it profitable, and the property doesn't qualify for a regular loan due to its condition.

✔ **Private financing:** Because individuals, rather than institutions, typically make the loans available.

 Hard-money lenders are often more willing to negotiate with investors, especially if you have a solid track record of profitable investments and paying back loans. Remember, these folks earn money from the risks you take on and the efforts you invest. As long as you're successful, you can find people willing to invest in you.

Considering the cons

Now for the bad news. Hard money is called *hard* for several reasons. Before choosing the hard-money option, be aware of the following key areas of hard-money loans:

✔ **Points or discount points:** You can expect to pay anywhere from two to six points or more for the loan upfront. See "Calculating points" later in this chapter for details.

✔ **Interest rates:** Hard-money lenders often charge nearly double the interest rates of conventional loans. If the going interest rate for conventional loans is 6.5 percent, for example, a hard-money lender may charge 10 to 15 percent. Because hard-

money loans are typically short term, however, you'll probably refinance or sell the property long before you rack up a lot
of interest. See "Adding up the interest" later in this chapter
for details.

✔ **Loan-to-value (LTV):** Hard-money lenders typically approve you
for a loan of only 65 to 75 percent of the property's value, not
the typical 85 to 90 percent you can expect from conventional
lenders. However, if you're buying distressed property for well
below what the value of the property will be after it's repaired,
this drawback really shouldn't matter. For example, if you're
buying a property for 20 to 30 percent below what it will be
worth after you fix it up, your hard-money loan should be able
to cover the full purchase price you're paying. Still, you may
need additional funds to cover holding and renovation costs.

When buying into a declining market, LTV becomes even more
critical because your loan amount stays the same while housing values are declining. If the value of the house dips below
what you owe on it, you place yourself in a situation of owing
more on a property than what you can sell it for.

✔ **Amortization:** Hard-money lenders often want to *amortize* the
loan over 5 to 15 years rather than the standard 30 years, which
ends up increasing your monthly payments because you're
paying down the principal on the loan faster. To lower the
monthly payments, amortize over 30 years or negotiate for
interest-only payments. You want to have enough free-flowing
cash to finance renovations and cover your holding costs.
(See Chapter 6 for more about amortization.)

✔ **Balloon payment:** Hard-money loans typically have balloon
payments or *cash calls* after so many months, so you may be
required to pay off the loan in full in a matter of 6 to 36 months.
This isn't a problem as long as you have a solid plan in place
and sufficient funds on hand for when the balloon payment is
due. If you don't, you may end up losing the property when you
can't make the payments.

✔ **Prepayment penalties:** Avoid any loans that stipulate a prepayment penalty — extra money you have to pay if you
choose to pay off the loan early — that remains in effect for
more than the first couple years. We've seen investors lose
thousands of dollars when they sold a house because they
agreed to pay a 2 to 3 percent prepayment penalty.

✔ **Closing costs:** As with any lender, you have to close on a loan
from a hard-money lender. Figure in the cost of the title insurance, closing fee, credit report, and appraisal survey. Be particularly careful of any discount points or loan origination fees —
these are areas where the lender and mortgage broker can really
jack up the cost of the loan, so ask questions in advance.
Refer to Chapter 6 for more about closing costs and fees.

> ✓ **Cross collateralization:** If you're investing in two or more prop-
> erties, the hard-money lender may want to *cross-collateralize*
> the properties. If you sell one property for a $10,000 profit, for
> example, the lender may want to use the profit to pay down the
> loan on the other property. This route isn't terrible — it may
> even benefit you by reducing your interest on the second
> loan — but it's something you should be aware of. Cross collat-
> eralization simply secures the lender's position.

Some hard-money lenders offer something called a *bullet loan*, in
which you make no monthly payments. Interest accrues and is
rolled back into the loan's principal, which increases the total
amount required to pay off the loan and can significantly increase
the total amount of interest you end up paying. A bullet loan frees
up your cash flow so you have more money on hand for renovations and other investment properties. However, it can also significantly increase your risks, especially if the market heads south
when you're scheduled to pay back the loan.

Managing the Expense of a Hard-Money Loan

Hard-money loans are notorious for costing a lot of money, but just
how much money is a lot? And can you do anything to limit the
expense? In the following sections, we answer these questions by
showing you how to calculate interest over the life of the loan, subtract the amount you save in taxes, and practice two strategies for
slashing the amount you pay in interest.

Calculating points

A *point* is 1 percent of the loan amount, so if you're paying six
points on a $200,000 loan, you're paying $12,000 upfront to get your
mitts on the money. To calculate the total amount of money you're
paying in points, multiply the total loan amount by the total
number of points by 1 percent or .01:

Loan Amount × Number of Points × .01 = $ Total Points

Some hard-money lenders may agree to refund a point or two if
you pay back the loan on time. If the lender is socking you with a
huge amount of interest in points, consider asking for a refund if
you can pay back the loan on time or early. The sooner the
investor can put that money back in play, the sooner she can collect points from the next borrower.

Adding up the interest

Calculating the total interest you can expect to pay over the life of a loan is no different for hard-money loans than it is for conventional loans. To do so, just follow these steps:

1. **Multiply the monthly payment by the number of months you expect to be paying on the loan.**

2. **Add any balloon payments (or cash calls) you're required to make.**

3. **Subtract the total amount you borrowed.**

   The *remainder* is the interest you stand to pay through your regular payments.

4. **Add the total amount you paid upfront in points.**

   These can be *discount points* (interest paid upfront) or *loan origination points* (fees). Technically, anything calculated as a percentage of the loan is deductible as far as the IRS is concerned. From a legal and regulatory perspective, origination points and discount points differ even though they function the same.

The resulting number is the total interest paid over the life of the loan.

Interest is only one expense you incur as the price of doing business with a lender. The lender or broker who's handling the transaction may charge additional fees. When comparison-shopping for loans, even hard-money loans, don't forget to account for these expenses. For details, refer to Chapter 6.

Subtracting the tax savings

When you're calculating the cost of money into your equations, think of your expenses as tax deductions. Keep in mind that you pay taxes only on your profits, so all expenses you incur — including the interest you pay on loans — reduce your profits whether you sell the property or rent it out.

This silver lining doesn't mean you should rejoice in having to pay a huge amount in interest and points, but it can alleviate some of the psychological pain you may feel. If, for example, you sell the house and have to pay 30 percent in short-term capital gains tax, the government is essentially covering 30 percent of the interest you paid on your loan.

Paying back the loan sooner to save money

Although hard-money loans have a reputation for costing the most money, you can contain the costs by paying back the loan sooner rather than later. The following sections describe two ways to achieve this goal.

If you already paid most of your interest upfront in points, paying back the loan in a hurry may not benefit you a great deal. Cash is still king! If paying the loan back early means you don't have the cash to pursue other deals, take your time.

Refinancing in a hurry

Conventional lenders tend to play it safe. As a result, they steer clear of deals that they see as speculative. If you're buying a run-down property in the hopes of renovating it and selling it for a profit, they're likely to deem the project as too risky. To move forward, you have to work through a hard-money lender or find financing elsewhere.

After you renovate the property, however, or after it's generating some rental income, the risks are likely to be minimal. At this point, conventional lenders are often more than willing to offer you financing because you're in a better position to make payments and eventually pay back the loan.

Think of hard-money loans as short-term solutions. You pay a premium for gaining access to much-needed cash in a hurry. However, after you've established the property as a profitable venture, you don't have to continue paying astronomical interest rates. By refinancing through a conventional lender, you can often reduce your monthly payment and interest and improve your cash flow. In addition, if you negotiated a refund for early payment with the hard-money lender, you can reduce your loan expenses even more.

Due to *seasoning restrictions* that most lenders have, though, plan on holding the property for a full 12 months before refinancing. (A seasoned loan is more attractive to lenders, because it shows that the borrower has made at least 12 payments on the loan and that the original lender was able to make some money for its trouble.) Conventional lenders may consider less time, but then you can obtain financing only for the original sales price plus repairs, as opposed to the actual new value, which should be greater.

Selling the property fast

Hard-money loans are often ideal for investors who *flip* properties (buy-fix-sell within a year or so). With a hard-money loan, assuming everything goes as planned, you can purchase a property, renovate it, and sell it by the time you have to pay back the loan in full.

If you're flipping properties, make sure you cover yourself by doing the following:

- ✔ **Calculate the finance charges (including points) into your expenses and always make sure you're on track to earn a profit of 20 percent or more.** This margin gives you a cushion for unexpected expenses and cases in which the property sells for less than your target price. (Overestimate expenses while underestimating the sales price for additional protection.)

- ✔ **Have enough money on hand to cover the balloon payments or cash calls.** Many investors get into trouble when they have to make a large payment while renovating the property and trying to sell it. Plan ahead, so you don't lose the property before it starts to turn profitable.

- ✔ **Give yourself enough time to sell the property.** If the renovations are probably going to take you three months and another three months to sell it, make sure you have enough funds to cover the holding costs for at least nine months — perhaps even longer in a slumping market.

- ✔ **Keep copies of all receipts, work orders, invoices and bids — even for the smallest items.** If a lender limits you to the original purchase price plus repairs, you're in a better position to establish a higher value — and thus a higher loan amount.

Hard money isn't always that hard

Hard-money lenders can be a real lifesaver when the right deal comes along. A few years ago, I (Chip) was involved in a deal that required a facility to quickly be converted in order to comply with international contract requirements. The owner would receive several million dollars within 60 days, but only if the property was converted.

A hard-money lender answered the call with $7 million in just 21 days, allowing the owner to realize a net profit of more than $13 million. The loan cost more than $500,000 to put together, at an interest rate of 12 percent, but the cost was irrelevant when my client was netting that kind of money!

Although this tale is true, the profits don't represent a typical real estate investment deal. Earning $7 million in three weeks on a single deal isn't something that most real estate investors, even the successful ones, ever experience.

Locating Local Hard-Money Lenders

Walk down Main Street in any town or city and you can find at least a few traditional lenders like banks or mortgage companies. What you don't see, however, is a hard-money lender. They're not hiding in the alleys and cellars — they just do business in less-conspicuous places. You need to know where to look (and this section tells you just that).

Asking your broker for leads

The most obvious and perhaps safest way to find hard-money lenders is to ask your broker or loan officer. Many hard-money lenders avoid the messiness of dealing directly with investors, so they hire a loan officer or broker to manage the transactions. Your broker may have several clients who are hard-money lenders.

Working through your broker adds another level of protection, ensuring you that the hard-money lender is legitimate. If you find a hard-money lender on your own, you need to rely solely on your own judgment and that of any references you can dig up to determine whether the lender is trustworthy. When you work through your broker, you have the benefit of an expert opinion on whether the lender is reputable.

In addition to asking your broker for leads, consider networking with local accountants, CPAs, financial planners, or estate attorneys. They often work with clients who are looking for good investment opportunities, and many people prefer to invest locally, where they can keep an eye on things!

Networking through local investment groups

One of the best ways to track down any real estate professional, including brokers and private lenders, is through a local *real estate investment group* — organized individuals who meet regularly to share information and advice about investing in real estate. Networking in a local real estate investment group ensures that you're dealing with people who have a proven record and an established reputation.

If you're not a member of a local real estate investment group yet, we strongly encourage you to find a group and start attending meetings. To find a group in your area, try visiting the National Real Estate Investors Association Web site at www.national reia.com, click *Find a REIA,* and use the resulting map to track down a local group.

Another way to find local groups is to ask your real estate agent, broker, attorney, or other real estate professional. Most people who work with real estate investors know which groups are the most active and reputable.

Perusing ads in local newspapers

Hard-money lenders often place ads in the local newspapers letting people know that they loan money. The ad may include something like the following:

> Stop Foreclosure!
>
> Real Estate Loans
>
> No Credit Required
>
> Quick and Easy Financing
>
> Call 1-800-555-5555

These ads may appear to be a little suspicious, but they're the way hard-money lenders often advertise their services.

Don't hand over your personal information without performing your own due diligence. Contact the lender and ask about the area he lends in, the types of properties he specializes in, whether he's an individual or representing an investment group, and how many transactions he's done in the past year. Call the newspaper you found the ad in and ask how long the person has been an advertiser and whether the paper has received any complaints. Ask for and check at least three references. Check search engines for the lender's name and company name. Check with the Better Business Bureau and your state's attorney general to determine whether they have any complaints against the person on file.

Searching the Web

Many hard-money lenders advertise their services on the Web, although they may not advertise as "hard-money lender." Use your favorite Internet search tool (Google, Yahoo!, MSN, whatever) to search for the following:

✔ Hard-money loan

✔ Equity lender

✔ Private lender or private investor

✔ Real estate investment group

Follow your search phrase with the name of your state, county, or city to focus on local lenders who do hard-money loans. By dealing locally, you have a better chance of finding someone who has a track record of dealing with investors in your community.

Getting preapproval

Conventional wisdom has it that you should make friends *before* you need them. In the same way, line up hard-money lenders before you need them, so you can act quickly when the best opportunities come your way. The best way to do so is to obtain preapproval for a set amount of funds by going through the screening process before you have a loan application on the table. (You should already have a price range in mind for properties in the market you want to target.)

Meet with and interview a few hard-money lenders before you need a loan. As mentioned earlier in this chapter, some hard-money lenders have loan officers who handle the transactions for them. Proceed through the preapproval process as explained earlier. Then, whether you need $50,000, $250,000, $1 million, or more, you know exactly what types of renovation projects you can pursue. As soon as you identify a prospective investment property in an approved price range, you can then move on it quickly, knowing that you're already approved for the money.

Hitting Up Friends and Relatives for a Loan

Charity should begin at home. (One thing we have in common is that our grandmothers were our first and best investment partners.) If you have a rich Uncle Jeb or Auntie Emily, or friends who have a stash of cash they're eager to invest (and you don't mind calling in some favors), hit them up for the money. With family members, you may be able to get a short-term, no- or low-interest loan, assuming you're not the family pariah. Friends may charge a little more or a little less, but if they have the dough and you know what you're doing, you can establish a mutually lucrative relationship.

In the following sections, we reveal the pros and cons of financing investments through friends and relatives, offer advice on recognizing opportunities, cover the basics of drawing up agreements, and offer some words of wisdom to ensure that you don't break any securities laws when doing these deals.

Friends and family members are more likely than institutions (and hard-money lenders) to become emotional about their money.

Grasping the pros and cons

Mixing business into relationships with family and friends can be a risky proposition, particularly when your investments fall short of expectations. Handled properly with the right people, however, teaming up to invest in real estate can be one of the most rewarding activities you can ever hope to experience. Before immersing yourself in the experience, be aware of the potential benefits and pitfalls, as laid out in the following sections.

Potential benefits

Scoring investment capital through friends and family members delivers a host of potential benefits, including the following:

- ✔ Access to cash you can't get anywhere else
- ✔ More attractive interest rates and low or no closing costs (usually)
- ✔ The joys of sharing a common goal and interest in your success with those closest to you
- ✔ Flexibility in negotiating the terms of the loan
- ✔ Less pressure (sometimes) to pay the loan back precisely on the agreed upon date

Potential pitfalls

Disagreements over finances trigger a lot of divorces, which says something about mixing money and personal relationships. Before borrowing money from friends or family, consider the common challenges that often arise when you mix business with personal relationships:

- ✔ Disagreements over when the loan is to be repaid
- ✔ Disagreements over the amount to be paid back (if you agreed to pay interest)

✔ Conflicts over how the investment is being managed — which property to buy, how to renovate it, how to manage it (for a rental property), or how to sell it (and for how much)

✔ Bad feelings for a long time if an investment goes bad and you're unable to repay the loan on time or at all

For these reasons, make sure you have a written agreement that clearly spells out the terms of the loan (see the "Drawing up an agreement" section later in this chapter).

Identifying the moneybags in your circle

One of the keys to avoiding the worst possible scenarios is to borrow money only from those who can afford to lose it. If your kid brother and your sister-in-law have a little nest egg set aside for a rainy day, hitting them up for a loan may not be the best option. It may strain their relationship in addition to leaving them strapped for cash if one of them is laid off or they experience some other crisis.

Instead, scope out the rich relatives in your circle, the friends and family members who are cash heavy and are often looking for ways to invest their money that are often safer than Wall Street and promise a better return than they can get on CDs at their local bank. In addition, given the recent craziness in both the housing market and the stock market, family members may look more favorably on the option of investing through a knowledgeable family member than with someone or some company they don't know.

Drawing up an agreement

When it comes to borrowing money from family members and friends, most strife arises not out of differences of opinion but out of misunderstandings. Perhaps you and your uncle discussed the details, and you each walked away *thinking* you understood the agreement, but when it comes time to execute, you discover that you really didn't hash out the details or that one of you has forgotten a key clause you both agreed to.

For example, say you borrow money from your grandma with the intent of just borrowing the money. Your idea is that your grandma is putting up the money, but you're in charge of everything else. You head out, find a property you want to buy, and let grandma know that it's time for her to deliver the cash. You head over to grandma's, where you find her dressed to the nines and ready to look at the property she's buying.

The best way to avoid such uncomfortable scenarios is to draw up a written agreement that covers the key details. Here are some items your agreement should address:

✔ Amount of money (range) that your friend or relative is willing and able to invest.

✔ Whether the cash can be used for the purchase of the property, renovations, or both.

✔ The amount of time you have to pay back the loan.

✔ The amount of interest (if any) or the percentage of the profit (if any) your friend or family member will be entitled to.

✔ Who's in charge of making decisions on which property to buy, the purchase price, which renovations to perform, how much to pay for renovations, whether to rent or sell the property, and so on. (You should try to retain as much control as possible.)

✔ How you will proceed if the investment fails. How will the property be liquidated, and how are you going to share the loss?

✔ How and how much information you plan on sharing. Are you going to share all the financial figures with your investor(s)? Will you provide them with written reports, and if so, how often?

✔ How you will resolve any disputes. Can you name an unbiased intermediary?

Enlist the assistance of a qualified attorney in drawing up an agreement that protects everyone's interests. One form that such a "contract" can take is a pro forma agreement. You can download a boilerplate of such an agreement at www.themortgagemyths.com. Keep in mind, however, that laws vary among states, so you're best served by consulting an attorney.

So, what do you do if you live in Florida, are going into business with your grandma who lives in Arizona, and are buying property in Georgia? In most cases, the court of jurisdiction is the state in which the property is located, so make sure you have an attorney licensed to practice in that state prepare the documents for you.

Honoring securities laws

When soliciting money from private investors, be careful not to break any *securities laws* (rules and regulations that govern partial ownership in a business venture). If you're hitting up your grandma or Uncle Fred for a loan, you should be in the clear, but if you pass the hat among private investors, post an ad in the local paper or on the Internet, or try to get a group of lenders to pool their resources to finance your projects, you may have to be licensed, and the Securities and Exchange Commission (SEC) may categorize these solicitations as a *public offering* — sort of like selling stock in a corporation rather than a simple loan transaction. State regulators may also join the party, and it won't be a fun one.

If you plan on soliciting funds from multiple individuals, strangers, or the public at large, consult an attorney who's familiar with securities regulations first to make sure you handle the transactions properly.

Financing Fix-Ups with a Home Equity Loan or Line of Credit

A hard-money loan can often cover the purchase price, but it may not be sufficient to cover the costs of repairs and renovations. If the property is valued at significantly more than what you paid for it, however, you can often take out another loan to pay for repairs and renovations — a *home equity loan* or *home equity line of credit* (HELOC, or LOC for short).

In the following sections, we cover the basics of home equity loans and lines of credit, encourage you to max out your LOC, and show you how to apply for an LOC.

Although we cover both home equity loans and lines of credit, for the purposes of financing repairs and renovations, an LOC is almost always the preferred tool. With an LOC, you pay interest only on the money you actually use. With a home equity loan, you pay interest on the total amount you borrow whether you use the money or have it sitting in a bank account.

Understanding home equity loans and LOCs

A home equity loan or line of credit unlocks the equity in your home without affecting your current mortgage:

- ✔ A *home equity loan* provides you with a single chunk of money — a one-time payment to you. Lenders may choose not to charge closing costs on home equity loans. Some banks even pay for the credit report and appraisal. (When credit is tight, as it was during the writing of this book, lenders are likely to waive closing costs only for borrowers with the absolute best credit scores.)

- ✔ A *home equity line of credit* enables you to borrow only what you need and pay interest on only what you borrow, making this option attractive for financing renovations. It's sort of like the line of credit you get with a credit card, but with a lower interest rate (usually).

Home equity loans and lines of credit often come with adjustable interest rates, which carry additional risks, as we explain in Chapter 5. The good news is the interest on home equity loans and lines of credit qualifies as mortgage interest, so it's tax deductible.

Maxing out your LOC

When applying for an LOC, don't be shy about asking for the maximum amount you can borrow against the property. You pay interest only on the amount you use, so you're not penalized for maxing out your LOC.

However, just because you have $50,000 available for repairs and renovations doesn't mean you should use every penny of it. Stick to your budget so you have a better chance of hitting your profit target.

Keep in mind that your ability to "max out" your LOC can change depending on what's going on in the marketplace. When housing values are soaring, lenders are often willing to let you cash out every penny of equity in a property. Some lenders even allow you to borrow equity in excess of what the property has in it. However, when property values take a dive, lenders are often stung by these loose lending practices and may significantly restrict the amount of equity you can cash out.

Applying for an LOC

Applying for an LOC is very similar to the application process for a conventional loan, as explained in Chapter 7. You need to fill out a loan application and supply the loan officer with supporting documentation, including copies of your most recent federal income tax returns, 30 days' worth of pay stubs, and a list of assets and liabilities.

In addition, the lender typically requires an appraisal to ensure that the estimated equity in the property is accurate. With a home equity line of credit, the home's equity (market value minus what you currently owe on the property) serves as the collateral to secure the loan.

Supplementing Your Financing with Credit Cards

Many families are over their heads in high-interest credit card debt, so it may seem a little strange that we would even consider suggesting the possibility of using a credit card account to finance real estate investments. Who in their right mind would want to pay 18 percent or more in credit card interest when they could get an LOC for less than 10 percent?

We're not suggesting that you max out your credit cards to purchase property, but credit cards can give you quick access to cash for repairs, renovations, and unexpected expenses.

This section looks at advantages to using your credit cards, helps you decide which cards to use, and explains the importance of staying current with your payments.

Eyeing the pros to credit card use

Using a credit card to supplement your financing is an easy way to get your hands on cash fast. Consider some of the advantages that credit card financing offers:

- ✔ Most credit cards enable you to take cash advances, no questions asked. (Some companies send you checks to make it even easier.)
- ✔ You can usually get hold of some cash within 24 hours.

> ✔ Credit card debt is *unsecured*. In other words, you put up no collateral to secure the credit, so the credit card company can't seize your property in lieu of payment if you happen to default on the "loan."
>
> ✔ The credit card company doesn't charge closing costs. You probably have to pay a substantial amount in transaction fees and interest, but if you use the money short-term, it can be less than you'd pay a hard-money lender. Do the math.

Keep the credit card option off the table until you *really* need it in a pinch. If you play the card too early, you may not have the option when you really need it. In addition, keeping your personal finances separate from your business (investing) finances can significantly reduce your exposure to risk. We advise using a credit card only as a last resort.

Choosing a credit card with low interest and plenty of perks

Credit cards aren't all created equal. Some companies charge lower interest, others offer perks — frequent flyer miles, free groceries or merchandise, cash back on purchases, and so on. Shop around for credit cards that have the lowest interest rates and the most perks. Be sure to read the fine print so you're not just comparing *introductory rates*. The fine print tells you what the rate jumps to after the introductory period expires.

You can comparison-shop for credit cards online at www.credit cardguide.com. If you have some major renovations lined up, consider applying for a credit card at your building supply store. Many of these stores offer a discount on your entire purchase the first time you apply for and use the card. If you order $5,000 in materials and receive a 10 percent discount, that's $500 you save in renovation expenses.

Check your monthly statement to determine your credit limit and stay within that limit. Also, pay off the balance as soon as possible. We know people who charge everything on their credit card — their phone bill, electric bill, groceries, gas, auto maintenance, clothing, cable bill, and so on — and then pay the balance as soon as the bill arrives. They collect the perks (often something like 1 to 2 percent cash back on merchandise) without paying a penny in interest!

Chapter 12

Capitalizing on Seller Financing

*W*hen most people think about purchasing a home they can't afford to pay cash for, the only option they consider is borrowing the money from a bank. They automatically assume that the seller wants cash at the closing table.

Highly motivated sellers, however, may be willing and perhaps even eager to sell you the home on contract and finance the purchase themselves. Doing so enables them to profit in two ways:

✔ By selling you the property for a profit

✔ By collecting interest as a part of the financing agreement

Financing the purchase is a pretty secure investment for the seller. It allows them to place their cash in an investment vehicle that they are very familiar with — as opposed to investing it with those friendly folks on Wall Street.

In this chapter, we reveal two ways you can purchase a property on contract with seller financing: by using a land contract (or contract for deed) or a lease option (rent-to-own) agreement.

Buying Property on Contract with a Land Contract

With a *land contract* (also called a *contract for deed* or *installment sales contract*), you buy the property directly from the owner/seller, just as you always do, but you also finance the purchase through the seller. The seller becomes the bank, but instead of using a mortgage to secure the loan, you sign a land contract stipulating the terms of the transaction.

The legal language in a land contract is very similar to what you find in a mortgage, but you don't actually take title to the property. You instead have what is called *equitable interest,* which basically means that you own the property as long as you honor your part of the contract (including making payments on time). The land contract stipulates the interest rate, contract length, and the amortization method. (Refer to Chapter 6 for more on amortization.) For you, as the buyer/investor, the arrangement differs very little from what you may expect working through a bank. The seller is forgoing a lump sum payment in exchange for regular income and may qualify for some tax advantages as a result.

In the following sections, we unveil the potential benefits and drawbacks of buying properties on contract, show you how to protect yourself by inspecting the title first and avoiding the due-on-sale-clause trap, and walk you through the process of buying a property on contract.

The ups and downs of buying a property on contract

Purchasing a property and financing the purchase through the seller appeals to the entrepreneur in everyone. It cuts out the middleman (the bank) and cuts to the chase, reducing fees and hassles. It's a model of free-market, freewheeling economy at work. Buying on contract, however, is also riddled with risks. In the following sections, we explore the pros and cons of this path so you can make a well-informed decision as to whether buying on contract is right for you.

The pros of using a land contract

Purchasing properties through a land contract rather than financing the purchase through a bank offers several advantages for investors, including the following:

- The seller may provide financing when a bank won't.
- You save on closing costs.
- The seller may offer lower monthly payments than a bank would charge you.

✔ The seller may also agree to a low- or no-down-payment deal, assuming you have outstanding credit.

✔ You may not have to jump through so many hoops to prove that you're creditworthy.

✔ The seller may be more flexible if you're late with a payment or two (but don't count on it).

The cons of using a land contract

Purchasing a property on contract seems to be the ideal scenario. You purchase and finance the purchase through a single entity (the seller) and avoid all the red tape and hassles that large institutions use to trip you up. However, the land contract does come with its share of potential drawbacks, including the following:

✔ You don't have a bank covering your back. By having an attorney and title company in your corner, however, you can gain the protection you need.

✔ The seller may require a larger down payment or charge higher interest.

✔ Most contracts have a forfeiture clause stating that you give up your rights to the property if you fail to honor the contract. See "Beware of the Forfeiture Clause" later in this chapter for details.

✔ You increase your chances of becoming a victim of fraud. If, for example, you fail to record the land contract at the register of deeds, the seller (listed as the official owner) can borrow against the property and try to stick you with the debt.

✔ When the time comes to refinance or sell, you and the seller may have disagreements over the balance.

✔ If the sellers fail to pay their obligations or end up in bankruptcy court, you may end up having to defend your interests in court.

Inspecting the title

Before you even consider financing the purchase through the seller, do your homework to make sure the owner/seller is the rightful (and sole) owner of the property and has no undisclosed liens against the property. In order to do your preliminary title research, you can head down to your county's register of deeds office and ask the clerk for whatever info is recorded on a particular property's title. At the bare minimum, obtain a copy of the deed and any other recorded documents for the current and previous owner. If possible, obtain copies of all documents recorded in the past 24 months.

Inspect the title work and deed for the following crucial pieces of data:

- ✓ **Mortgagor (homeowners') names:** Note whether the mortgagor's name matches the name actually listed as the property's title holder. Differing names raise a red flag — make a note of any discrepancy.

- ✓ **Price and previous price paid for the property:** This info can help you estimate the property's current value.

- ✓ **Warranty deed names:** The names on the deed should match the homeowners' names on the title. If they don't match, the difference raises a red flag; make note of it.

- ✓ **Previous mortgagor:** Check the previous title and jot down the names on the title. Note any chinks in the *chain of title* (series of owners). For instance, say your title work shows that Johnson sold the property to Davis and then Howard sold it to Pinkerton. But whom did Davis sell the house to, and whom did Howard buy it from? This gap indicates a problem in the chain of title; consult your title company whenever you notice any irregularities in this chain.

- ✓ **Mortgages or liens:** Make sure the owner/seller owns the property outright. If you see any liens against the property, you want to make sure the seller pays off the lien holders *before* you sign the contract.

- ✓ **Property tax liens:** Check with the county tax assessor's office for recent tax bills that are due and owing, or even previous years' taxes that haven't been paid, which may have been transferred to the state. Any tax liens trump your rights!

If you notice any discrepancies in the chain of title or any other red flags, ask the register of deeds about it, consult your title company, and bring up the issue with the current owner. If the answers don't satisfy you, don't do the deal.

Although you can do this research yourself (and you really should do it yourself to learn about title research), we recommend that as a beginner you consult your title company for a second opinion and order a *title commitment* (a preliminary report). After you feel comfortable doing your own research, you can take on more of the burden.

Beware of the due on sale clause

If you have documented proof that the owner/seller owns the property free and clear, you can skip this section. If the seller has a mortgage, however, that mortgage almost certainly has a due on sale clause that may cause significant trouble if you move forward with the deal. A *due on sale clause* states that if the owners sell or transfer equitable ownership in the property, they must immediately pay off the remaining balance on the loan in full.

Here's how that little clause can affect you: Say the seller has a mortgage on the property and sells it to you. As soon as you complete the transaction, you head down to the register of deeds office to record the contract; this act protects your rights to the property by recording your name as the new owner. However, the fact that the property has changed hands is now public knowledge, and if the bank finds out, it can call in the loan. Now the seller has to come up with the money to pay the total balance remaining on that loan, which means he'll probably try to squeeze the money out of you.

Of course, you may be able to get away with not recording the contract, but this clever ruse can expose you to even greater risk:

- ✔ If the lender finds out, it can pursue legal action against you for conspiring to commit fraud. And the lender *always* finds out through the change in the insurance coverage.

- ✔ If you're dealing with an unscrupulous seller, the seller can load up the property with other liens and mortgages. Remember, until you record the contract, the seller is still the official property owner and can borrow against it.

Almost every nongovernmental mortgage contains a due on sale clause. No matter how much you want a certain property, don't ever consider trying to sneak a seller-financed deal through without notifying the bank. Otherwise, you put yourself in great financial peril.

The how-to: What you need to do

Buying a property on contract doesn't require any more effort or expertise on your part than financing through a bank. It does, however, require that you have the wisdom to have a qualified real estate attorney examine the contract before you sign it. If the seller wasn't originally planning to sell the property on contract, you may even be able to have your attorney prepare the paperwork.

If you're looking for a step-by-step guide on how to buy a property on contract, here's a general breakdown of the steps:

1. **Find a property that interests you.**

   If you use a real estate agent to help you identify potentially lucrative investment opportunities, try to choose an agent who understands these creative financing deals and can explain how they work to prospective sellers.

   If the property has been on the market for several months, the seller may be more motivated than usual to finance the purchase. Don't just look for listings that advertise seller financing — find the property first and then pitch your offer to the seller.

2. **Research the property carefully to be fairly certain that you're investing in a profitable property.**

   Check out *Real Estate Investing For Dummies,* 2nd Edition, by Eric Tyson and Robert S. Griswold (Wiley) for information on researching your market and specific properties.

3. **Pitch a reasonable offer.**

   Because you're going to be asking the seller to finance the deal, don't try to lowball the seller too much on the purchase price (but make sure you're not overpaying and can still earn the desired profit). Explain that although you can afford to make the payments, you don't meet the bank's stringent requirements and need seller financing to do the deal.

4. **Ask your agent or attorney to write up your offer.**

   Make sure the offer specifies your down payment, the interest rate you're willing to pay, and the monthly payments and any other lump-sum payments you make over the life of the loan. Here are some additional tips:

   • Offer a low down payment to maximize your cash flow.

   • Offer a higher interest rate than the seller is likely to get by keeping the money in a savings account or CD.

   • Specify the date on which you agree to pay the loan back in full — typically in three to five years. (You should have plans to sell the property or refinance with a conventional loan by then.)

5. **Hire a title company or real estate agent to manage the closing to ensure that all the *i*'s are dotted and the *t*'s are crossed and that all the paperwork is properly recorded with the register of deeds.**

Before you sign the contract, obtain a formal title insurance policy. This protects you just in case someone shows up later claiming rights to the property. *Never buy a property without buying title insurance for it.*

Protecting yourself against fraud

By carefully researching the properties that interest you (particularly the legal documents associated with them), you protect yourself not only from inadvertent errors but also from con artists who are trying to fleece you. Con artists often file false or doctored documents as part of their scams. Sometimes, they can even sell a house they don't own or sell a house several times to different buyers.

To protect yourself from falling victim to a real estate scam, take the following precautions:

- ✔ **Check the records to see whether the mortgage on the property was recently paid off.** Sellers rarely pay off mortgages right before they sell, so any document that shows the mortgage as having been recently paid off should make you more cautious.

- ✔ **Be wary of an investor pitching you an unbelievably great deal on a property.** Con artists often target novice investors in double-sales scams and often offer incredibly great deals so they can find buyers in a hurry.

- ✔ **Analyze the title commitment for suspicious transactions.** If the title shows that the property's been sold several times over a short period, for example, the property may be involved in an illegal flipping scheme. Make sure the title commitment covers the past 24-month history of the property, including mortgages.

- ✔ **Purchase title insurance as soon as possible and pay for it upfront.** Sometimes, title insurance is your only protection against fraudulent activity that's impossible to detect prior to purchasing a property.

Renting to Own with a Lease Option Agreement

A *lease option agreement* is essentially a rent-to-own deal. You agree to pay rent for a fixed period, after which you have the option (but aren't required) to buy the property. Normally the sellers charge

5 to 10 percent upfront and treat it as a down payment, deducting it from the purchase price. You pay monthly rent of about 1 percent of the purchase price.

For example, if you have a lease option agreement on a $200,000 house, you can expect to pay $10,000 to $20,000 down and $2,000 per month. A portion of the monthly payment usually goes toward the principal. At the end of the lease term, if you choose to purchase the property, you pay the remaining balance due on the purchase price you agreed to pay.

A lease option agreement can be a great financing solution, assuming you're working with trustworthy seller and you can secure the funds needed to purchase the property by the time your option to buy rolls around. If you don't have the money ready when the time comes to exercise your option, you may forfeit the deal and end up losing your down payment and any interest you paid in monthly payments (depending on how the agreement is worded).

As suggested by its name, the lease option agreement consists of two parts:

- **The lease part:** In the lease part, the seller and the buyer (you) have a landlord-tenant relationship. The seller agrees to let you live in the property for a certain period as long as you pay the rent and don't trash the joint.

- **The option part:** The option part covers the terms of the sale.

In the following sections, we highlight the important areas of each part to steer you clear of the most common pitfalls.

You may be wondering whether you should proceed with repairs and renovations prior to exercising your option to purchase. If you're certain that you're going to exercise your option, feel free to begin working on the property. The seller will like to see you improving the property, because it demonstrates your commitment to the deal. However, contracts usually require the seller to preapprove all repairs, additions, and renovations. If you're not sure you're going to exercise your option, you may want to avoid moving forward with any extensive renovations — recovering your investment later can become problematic or even impossible.

Grasping the fundamentals of a lease option agreement

A lease option agreement is a legal document. As a result, it's usually packed with legal language that you need an attorney to decipher. As an investor, however, you should understand the key points of the agreement:

- ✔ **You have the option to buy, but you don't have to do so.** If you have a lease option to buy a $200,000 home and its market value drops to $150,000 when you have the option to buy, you would probably be wise not to exercise your option (or at least renegotiate the price).

- ✔ **In addition to a down payment, the seller usually requires you to pay a fee for the option to buy.** This fee is usually non-refundable.

- ✔ **Although you can agree at signing to pay market value when your option to buy rolls around, you usually want to lock in a price from the get-go.** You especially want to lock the price if you expect property values to rise, so when you exercise your option, you're paying a lower than current market price.

- ✔ **In most cases, you lease the property for one to three years for a set rental amount.** The part of your monthly rent above the market rate is usually applied toward the purchase price, essentially paying down the principal.

- ✔ **During the lease period, the seller can't sell the property to anyone else.** As a result, you tie up the property, so nobody else has a chance to buy it.

- ✔ **In most cases, you need the seller's approval to assign the lease option to someone else.** In other words, you can't just lease the property to anyone of your choosing. The seller has a say in your selection of tenants.

- ✔ **If you don't exercise your option to buy, it expires.** At that point, the seller can sell the property to someone else, and you lose any deposit and additional rent credits you've paid.

Using the lease to earn some cash

The lease portion of the agreement stipulates the rental agreement between you and the seller. It typically covers the length of the lease, your monthly payment, the portion of the payment that goes toward the purchase price, the condition in which you must maintain the property, whether or not you can have pets, and whether you can sublease the property to other tenants. You may be able to use the lease agreement to your advantage if you're looking to make some extra cash.

Read the lease carefully to ensure that you can honor what it stipulates and that it contains no language that the seller can easily use to prove that you broke the contract. In the following sections, we point out the two key areas to focus on.

Ensuring you can sublease the property

Most people who buy homes by using lease option agreements are people who use those homes as their primary residences. During the lease period, they live in the home. As an investor, however, you probably already have a place you call home, so living in the property isn't really a choice. Leaving the property vacant really isn't a choice either, so you probably want to sublet the property until you eventually take ownership of it.

Lease options: Win-win deals

A lease option deal can be a win-win situation for both the buyer and the seller. The buyer can lock in the purchase price of a home in an area where home values are on the rise. For example, if you have a lease option to buy a $250,000 property over the course of 24 months, and the home increases in value by 10 percent over that two-year period, you have $25,000 of equity built up in the house that can help you obtain a conventional loan to purchase the property or that you can use as a down payment on the property when your option to buy the house arrives.

The seller benefits by getting tenants (potentially buyers) who treat the house with tender loving care because they're planning on eventually owning it.

The seller has less property maintenance to perform, usually collects a nonrefundable option fee upfront (with a deferred tax, meaning taxes won't be due on the option fee until the sale is finalized), has a steady cash flow from the monthly rent, and has a buyer lined up to purchase the property when the lease option term expires. In addition, instead of paying short-term capital gains on profits from the sale of the property, the seller can hold the property in excess of a year, so the profits qualify for the much lower long-term capital gains tax rate.

When examining the agreement, make sure it includes a clause stating that you have the right to sublet the property. Otherwise, you may get stuck paying holding costs for a property that's not generating any revenue for you, which is never a good situation.

When you find someone interested in renting the property, make sure the agreement you settle on with the renters fits your investment strategy. If you want to sublet the property for two years, pay the balance due on the purchase price, and sell the property, be sure the rental agreement clearly spells out when the lease ends. You also need to ensure that the other terms of your lease are incorporated into the sublease, or you risk violating the lease option agreement.

Assigning the lease to another party

Another way you can profit from the property is by selling your interest in the contract. A lease option agreement contains value that may be of interest to another party if you later decide not to exercise your option. Your lease option agreement should give you the right to assign the lease to another party, essentially allowing them to step into your position and exercise the option later.

I (Chip) once located a $300,000 property that had been on the market for quite some time. I negotiated a $3,000 lease option and then subleased it as an investment property. I negotiated a two-month delay on the initial payment and used the security deposit and first month's rent to pay for the option. I made a couple of quick fixes on the property, created a nice cash flow, and ended up selling my interest in the lease option to another investor for $7,000. So after putting in about five hours on the deal and some cosmetic touch-ups, I made a $4,000 profit in two months without taking title to the property, and using none of my own money.

Dealing with the option

The more interesting part of the lease option agreement is the option to buy — your prerogative, at the end of the lease period, to purchase the property . . . or not. When the time finally arrives, you should actually have three options:

- ✔ Exercise your option. In other words, buy the property for the agreed-upon price.

- ✔ Choose not to exercise your option, in which case the prospective seller keeps the property, whatever you paid for the option, whatever lease payments you made, and perhaps even the down payment and interest.

- ✔ Sell your option to another party.

You may actually have one more alternative — you may be able to choose not to exercise your option and then negotiate the purchase for a lower price, assuming property values have dropped or you believe that the sellers need to sell in a hurry.

In the following sections, we discuss your option options in greater detail.

Exercising your option

Assuming you signed a lease option agreement with the intention of ultimately purchasing the property and that housing values haven't dropped since you agreed to the deal, you probably want to exercise your option before it expires.

Your lease option agreement should lay out exactly what you need to do to exercise your option to buy the property. Here's a sample of how the option clause is likely to appear:

> To exercise the option to purchase, the buyer/tenant must deliver to the seller/landlord written notice of the intent to purchase. The notice must specify a valid closing date preceding the expiration date of the lease agreement or the date of the expiration of the option to purchase, whichever occurs later.

Follow the instructions to the letter. If the agreement says that you need to deliver your written notice dressed as Little Bo Peep, deliver the notice dressed accordingly. Any discrepancy can cause you to forfeit your option to purchase and result in the loss of the property and any money you've sunk into it.

Not exercising your option

You may choose not to exercise your option for any of several reasons — a downturn in the market that makes the property worth much less than you agreed to pay for it, financial woes that make you unable to afford the property, an inability to obtain the financing you need by the option deadline, and so on.

Not exercising your option is easy — you do nothing other than move out or make sure any tenants you subleased to vacate the property. You also need to make sure the property is in the condition you agreed to leave it in. Other than that, you simply walk away.

As a courtesy to the seller/landlord, provide sufficient notice that you plan on not exercising your option. Thirty days or more is best.

Selling your option

As long as the agreement doesn't contain an exclusivity clause (as discussed in the following text), you can assign the option to buy the property to another party — essentially selling your interest in the property.

A simple assignment agreement is all that's necessary, with a simultaneous notification of assignment letter to the seller. Your attorney can supply you with the agreement and letter of notification.

Typically, the lease option contract contains a *notification clause* that requires you to let the seller know your intentions at least 90 days before the option expires. No matter what you decide, you send the seller a certified letter (return receipt requested) to protect your rights.

If you decide to assign your option to buy, consult your attorney to prepare the necessary documents.

 When you purchase an option to buy a property, avoid signing a lease option agreement that contains an *exclusivity clause* like the following (unless you're absolutely certain that you're not going to want to sell your option):

> The option to purchase is exclusive and nonassignable and exists solely for the benefit of the named parties above. If the buyer/tenant attempts to assign, convey, delegate, or transfer this option to purchase without the seller/landlord's express written permission, any such attempt shall be deemed null and void.

The sellers/landlords are likely to want this language in the contract to protect themselves in the event that you try to sell the option to someone who's less likely to secure financing to execute the option. Your choice to sell the option, however, doesn't really affect the position of the sellers/landlords — it's just another way you've chosen to exercise your option.

Paying Close Attention to the Forfeiture Clause

Lease option agreements all contain a *forfeiture* or *default clause* stating exactly what happens in the event that the buyer/tenant chooses not to exercise the option or fails to comply with other terms stated in the agreement. The clause usually appears something like the following:

> If buyer/tenant defaults under this agreement, then seller/ landlord may terminate the option to purchase through written notice of the termination. If the agreement is terminated, the buyer/tenant shall lose entitlement to any refund of rent or option payment.

The forfeiture clause itself is necessary and fairly innocuous. After all, if you break the contract, you should pay some sort of penalty. What's potentially dangerous is everything else in the contract, so be sure to read the agreement thoroughly to make sure that you won't have any trouble complying.

Some con artists have used the lease option agreement as a way to scam home buyers and investors out of money. They word the agreement in a way that makes it nearly impossible for the buyer to honor it. Their goal is to collect as much money upfront and through monthly payments as possible and then repossess the property on the grounds that the buyer broke the contract.

To protect yourself, make payments through an insured third-party servicing company (commonly called an *escrow company*). Doing so makes the accounting fair and complete for both parties and helps avoid disputes when the time comes to pay off the contract or exercise the option. Many banks also provide this service.

Make sure that you make all payments by check or electronic funds transfer to avoid any question about the dates or amounts of payments, and make sure that the insurance policy names you as an "insured party" to protect your interests in case of loss.

Chapter 13

Partnering to Share the Risk and the Equity

. . . .

In This Chapter

▶ Distinguishing between partnerships and joint ventures

▶ Deciding whether to take on a partner

▶ Teaming up with the right person

▶ Drafting a partnership agreement

▶ Steering clear of common partnership woes

. . . .

To succeed as an investor, you need time, know-how, and cash or credit. If you have the time and the know-how, you can often find someone who has the cash or the credit to finance the deal and perhaps even share responsibilities and workload. Partnerships and joint ventures enable you to do just that — enlist the assistance of others to obtain financing and share costs, workload, and profits.

In this chapter, we explore the potential benefits and drawbacks of partnerships and joint ventures and then show you how to structure such deals in a way that is mutually beneficial for you and your partner.

Talent trumps money. As an investor with the skills to transform money into more money, you're at least as valuable as the person putting up the money. Don't sell yourself short — financiers need your talents at least as much as you need their money.

Differentiating between a Partnership and a Joint Venture

In your search for cash and credit, you may turn to a partnership or joint venture arrangement. These two options offer you great opportunities for raising some quick cash and credit. Before we dig deeper into the nitty-gritty of these two arrangements in this chapter, you first need to make sure you can recognize the difference between a bona fide partnership and a joint venture:

- ✔ A *partnership* is an agreement between two or more individuals to pool their skills, knowledge, experience, and resources for a common undertaking and share potential profits and losses on any and all activities they choose to engage in. For tax purposes, profits pass through the partnership to the individuals, but the partnership still has to submit a tax return.

  Partnerships are primarily useful for business ventures that involve the joint holding of assets that appreciate, such as real estate or businesses. If you want to remain the sole owner of your assets, a formal partnership isn't for you. Explore other sources for financing, such as hard money lenders, as discussed in Chapter 11.

- ✔ A *joint venture* is an agreement between two or more individuals to team up on a single enterprise, such as a particular real estate investment. With a joint venture, the IRS doesn't require that the venture file a separate tax return.

Although partnerships and joint ventures differ in legal terms and complexity, in this chapter, we treat them both under the umbrella of partnerships, because they both involve two or more parties working together on investment properties.

Whether you're involved in a partnership or a joint venture, you share liability with your partners. To provide you and your partners some protection against potential lawsuits, consider forming a limited liability company (LLC), as discussed in Chapter 2, and processing all transactions through the LLC.

Weighing the Pros and Cons of Partnerships

Partnerships, like marriages, can be good or bad, productive or destructive. A great partnership can enable you to do more and profit more than you and your partner ever could on your own. A lousy partnership, on the other hand, can drain your resources, derail your plans, and shatter whatever personal relationship you may have had with your partner.

Before you jump at the prospect of teaming up with your best friend or in-law, consider some of the pros and cons to partnerships addressed in the following sections.

Investigating potential benefits

Partnerships offer several advantages for real estate investors, including the following:

- **Additional resources:** These resources come in the form of time, money, and skills.

- **Increased networking opportunities:** Your partner can introduce you to additional business and personal contacts.

- **Shared workload and responsibilities:** Your partner can pitch in to take on some of the chores, so the two of you have more time and energy to invest in other projects. In addition, your partner may have skills and experience to take on tasks you're unqualified to perform.

- **Shared risk:** If you and your partner are sharing the profits, you should also be divvying up the risk, so you stand to lose less if a property fails to turn a profit.

- **Diverse insight and input on business decisions:** Your partner may have a unique perspective and even better insight into potentially profitable investment properties, suppliers, or past experiences.

- **Increased accountability:** Having to answer to a partner often motivates individuals to fulfill their responsibilities, follow through on promises, and avoid making impulse decisions

Considering potential drawbacks

Given the fact that partnerships often fail, they obviously have some potential drawbacks, including the following:

- **Trust issues:** Partners have been known to run off with the cash, so choose a trustworthy partner and keep an eye on the money. (You and your partners should all review the financial records on a regular basis.)

- **Disagreements about who's doing more:** One of the most common disagreements that arises in partnerships centers on who's doing more for or giving more to the partnership. If you're doing all the work and start to feel that your partner is just a bean counter, you're likely to feel some underlying resentment that will eventually find some way of expressing itself.

- **Asset sharing:** As partners, you may share ownership in properties. If you or your partner wants to liquidate a particular asset and the other person doesn't, conflicts can arise.

> ✔ **Power sharing:** If you need to call all the shots, you may have trouble with a partner who wants to share in the decision-making process.

> ✔ **Legal responsibilities:** Inside a partnership, if one of the partners makes a mistake, other partners may be held legally liable.

Asking yourself whether you really need a partner

You've reviewed the pros and cons of having a partner, and you're still not sure whether forming a partnership is the right move for you. Do you really need a partner? Here are some general guidelines to help you decide:

> ✔ If you're partnering just to get your mitts on some cash, you probably don't need a partner. As long as you found a great investment opportunity, you can probably find the financing elsewhere and keep all the profits to yourself. With a partnership, you'd probably end up paying more in profit sharing than you'd pay in interest, even if you used hard money.

> ✔ If you're partnering just to limit your exposure to risk, you're thinking about the investment all wrong. If you're already that worried about the risk, maybe you're looking at a property you shouldn't buy.

> ✔ If you're partnering because the investor has more knowledge or experience or skills than you do, you're probably making the right move. You share a cut of the profits but are likely to make wiser investment decisions and earn an education in the process.

Partnerships also make sense if you're partnering to share the workload. One partner may have more time and flexibility than the other to take phone calls, search for investment properties, and deal with contractors. Just make sure your partner has the skills as well as the time to perform these tasks.

Finding a Partner with the Right Stuff

A partnership requires outstanding communication skills to survive and thrive, so partnerships often crumble when partners disagree about the division of work and money.

Choose your partner as carefully (or perhaps even more carefully) as you would choose a spouse or significant other, and work together to communicate your visions, dreams, ideas, and any problems you may have that may negatively affect your partnership. Being open, honest, and understanding can keep your partnership on an even keel.

In the following sections, we show you how to search for partners with the right stuff, screen candidates, and make sure you both have something to gain from the relationship.

Scoping out prospective partners

Because this is a book on financing real estate investments, we assume that you have the knowledge and skills to make solid investment decisions. As such, you're in the market for the right partner who can deliver the financing, and you need to know where you can find people who fit the bill. Here's a list of places to start:

- ✓ **Family and friends:** People you already know are generally a little more trustworthy than complete strangers. The only drawback is that if the partnership suffers, your relationship with the person is also likely to take a hit, which is a very important consideration.

- ✓ **Business owners or associates:** Doctors, dentists, attorneys, and other professionals may have money that they'd prefer investing in real estate rather than the stock market, if they only knew how to go about it. In addition, these professionals rarely have the time to invest in real estate. Consider teaming up with someone you already do business with.

- ✓ **Mortgage brokers:** Your mortgage broker may be willing to partner with you, and even if she isn't, she probably knows others in the market who are eager to partner with a real estate investor. Ask your broker to put you in touch with others who may be interested in forming a partnership.

- ✓ **Real estate agents:** Real estate agents sell homes, but many also invest in real estate. After all, nobody knows the market like a qualified agent. An agent may not have the time to shop for real estate, put together deals, oversee repairs and renovations, and manage properties, so the right candidate may be willing to partner with someone who does.

- ✓ **Real estate attorneys:** In addition to knowing the market and having plenty of connections, a good real estate attorney may have money to invest in real estate. Consider asking your real estate attorney whether he'd be interested in becoming your partner.

✔ **Accountants:** By their very nature, accountants work with business owners and individuals who are looking for investments and tax deductions. Approach your accountant and ask whether she has any clients looking for income opportunities.

✔ **Real estate investment groups:** Join a local real estate investment group and network to identify potential candidates for partnerships. To find a group in your area, try visiting the National Real Estate Investors Association Web site at www.nationalreia.com, click "Find a REIA", and use the resulting map to track down a local group.

Be careful when shopping for partners through real estate investment groups. Con artists often join groups to find eager investors to scam. Remember, if a deal seems too good to be true, it probably is. Make sure the person has a long history and a strong reputation in the community.

Checking a prospective partner's qualifications

When you partner with someone, you're essentially hiring one another to do a job or provide some sort of service, such as financing. You wouldn't hire employees before checking whether they are who they say they are or can deliver what they promise, so don't partner with someone until you've checked the following:

✔ **Personal identification:** If you don't know the individual personally, make sure you have the person's name, address, and phone number. Verify that the address exists (and the person lives there) and that the phone number is accurate. Ask for a copy of his driver's license, and offer him a copy of yours.

✔ **References:** Ask the person for three personal and three business references, and then check those references.

✔ **Background:** You can order a background check on the Internet on sites such as www.ZabaSearch.com. Even if you think you know the person well, order a background check to make sure the person isn't on the FBI's Most Wanted List. Do a quick public records search at the same time to check for lawsuits.

✔ **Credit report:** Before entering into a partnership agreement, ask your future partner to provide you with a copy of her credit report. The last thing you need is to be supporting a deadbeat or someone who's on the verge of bankruptcy.

Making sure your partner has what you need and needs what you have

Investing in real estate with your favorite cousin may seem like a whole lot of fun, but you have to ask yourself whether it's a wise business decision. Sure, you two get along swell and you're so close that trust really isn't an issue, but do you have complementary skills and resources?

One of the most common mistakes people make when choosing a partner is to choose someone who's just like them. You definitely want someone you can get along with, but you also want someone with a different set of skills and resources. If you're both great at fixing up properties but neither of you is very good with crunching numbers, you may run into problems.

In the following sections, we describe the skills and resources individuals often swap when forming productive real estate investment partnerships.

Trading experience for cash or credit

Experienced real estate investment professionals often trade their skills, knowledge, and experience for cash or credit. This exchange is essentially what you're doing whenever you take out a loan to finance the purchase of an investment property. You exchange your skills and experience in exchange for the cash you need to purchase a property and profit from it, so the relationship between you and the lender is mutually beneficial.

Tripping into a partnership

Almost by accident, my (Chip's) first foreclosure property turned into a partnership deal. On a whim, I pitched an offer to the Bank of Florida on an REO property it had listed. I offered 75 percent of the listed price and asked for 100-percent seller financing (because I didn't have any money). To my surprise, the bank accepted the offer, but I faced another challenge — I still had no money to cover the cost of repairs and renovations and other expenses.

One of the real estate agents in my office had heard about my deal and offered to put up the cash I needed in exchange for a 50/50 split. I had the time and energy but no money, and he had no time but extra cash to put to work.

Six months later, we each walked away with several thousands of dollars in our pockets.

You can also trade experience for cash or credit by partnering with someone who has the cash or can qualify for loans when you can't. Perhaps the person has lots of cash or a stronger equity position to borrow against.

Trading cash or credit for experience

If you have plenty of money or a solid credit score but little experience as an investor, you may be in a better position to find a partner who's more experienced than you. You deliver the money, and the other investor provides the skills and know-how to find great deals and make them profitable for both of you.

Even if you're just the moneyman or -woman, we encourage you to acquire some basic skills and knowledge. The more you know about the real estate market in your area, the safer your investment is. Take an interest in the properties that your more knowledgeable partner is dealing in, and pick your partner's brain to find out as much as possible. If anything were to happen to your partner, would you be able to sort out where all the money and assets are? Decide who's going to keep the books, and review them together on a regular and frequent basis.

Trading cash for credit or vice versa

Most real estate deals require a combination of cash and credit. You need cash for a down payment and closing costs, and credit for the rest. In some partnerships, one partner has a stronger position in terms of cash, and the other has a better credit history. Working together, they can make deals happen that neither of them could do on their own.

Drawing Up a Partnership Agreement

Establishing a partnership requires no formal steps, but having a partnership agreement in place can be very useful in avoiding problems down the road. A *partnership agreement* lays out all the rules governing the relationship — who's in charge of what, how much money each partner is contributing, how they're going to divide the workload, and how they plan to share the profits (and losses). It also spells out how the partners divvy up the assets in the event that the parties choose to dissolve the partnership. This section gives you the lowdown on putting such an agreement in place.

Without an agreement in writing, any conflict resolution occurs not in accordance with what you and your partners agreed on but rather by the guidelines in the Uniform Partnership Act (UPA) and Revised Uniform Partnership Act (RUPA). Ask your attorney whether your state has adopted either of these acts, because it may affect the way the partnership is handled upon dissolution.

Drafting the agreement

A partnership agreement is only as good as the details it contains. Simply by going through the process of writing up an agreement and discussing its terms, you and your partner can clarify your roles, responsibilities, and division of profits and losses.

Your partnership agreement should cover the following:

- ✔ **Nature and purpose:** State the type of business, the purpose of your relationship, and the exact roles that each of you will play in the partnership.

- ✔ **Capital contributions:** State how much startup capital each partner is contributing to the business and how each will be reimbursed after the business becomes profitable. If more capital is necessary later, what percentage of the needed capital is each partner responsible for contributing? What happens if that partner can't contribute his or her portion?

- ✔ **Profit and loss sharing:** Specify how the partners will share any profits or losses, including how the accounting will be done and how profits and losses will be reported to all partners. Consult an accountant who's experienced in working with real estate investors, and review the records with all partners periodically.

- ✔ **Authority:** How much authority does each partner have in making decisions? Do you each have equal say in which properties you purchase? Are each of you planning to be involved in the overall strategy — buy and sell or buy and rent? Spell out exactly which of you is the final decision-maker. What happens in the event of a tie?

- ✔ **Signature authority:** Who has the authority to sign checks, documents, and agreements? Are two or more signatures required, or does one person hold sole authority?

Even if you have an agreement with the bank that two signatures (yours and your partner's) are required on all checks, don't expect the bank to enforce the rule. The bank may only be responsible for any losses due to fraudulent activities that have occurred in the past 30 days. Carefully review your finances monthly to look for any payments that seem out of the ordinary.

✔ **Addition of new partners:** If you add new partners later, how will the profits be divided? Make sure you address this subject well in advance of taking on any new partners.

✔ **Partner problems:** What happens if one partner becomes incapacitated? How are you protected in the event of a divorce or bankruptcy by a partner?

✔ **Dissolution of the partnership:** This provision is one of the most important areas of any partnership agreement. If the partnership dissolves for whatever reason, this arrangement provides you and your partners with an exit strategy. Your partnership agreement should cover the following:

- **Death of a partner:** If a partner dies, how will that partner's share of the assets be distributed? Will they be given to the deceased's family or distributed among other partners?

- **Buyout:** Under what conditions can partners buy out the interest of another partner — death, divorce, bankruptcy, illegal activity? Specify the circumstances and how the buyout amount is to be calculated.

- **Division of property:** Describe exactly how you plan on dividing the shared assets. Do you plan to assign certain properties to each partner or liquidate the properties and divide the cash?

- **Ongoing transactions:** If a partner who is leaving has outstanding transactions, what percentage of the profits, if any, are the other partners entitled to?

Your partnership agreement should also indicate whether this is a general or limited partnership. In a *general partnership,* all partners share in the management and liability of the team. *Limited partners* have little or no say in the management of the team and can limit their personal exposure to liability. Defining what being in a limited partnership means can be confusing and complex, so consult your attorney.

Drawing up a partnership agreement can be a very complex operation, so consult an attorney with experience in this area. When drawing up and signing a partnership agreement, you and your partner each should bring your own attorney. In addition to protecting each partner's interests, this arrangement gives each partner the confidence that the process is being handled properly and equitably.

Complying with the tax code

One advantage of a partnership is that for tax purposes, the IRS doesn't recognize the partnership as a separate entity; thus, the profits and losses flow through to the individual partners, and the entity itself doesn't have to pay taxes.

Even so, the IRS still requires that the partnership file a separate tax return showing its profits (or losses). As long as you keep detailed financial records for each property, completing a return for the partnership isn't exactly rocket science, but you should still consult with a tax specialist who's experienced in working with real estate investors. In addition to filling out all the paperwork for you, a tax specialist can offer tax-savings tips that can more than cover the cost of hiring a specialist.

Avoiding Common Pitfalls

Partnerships dissolve for the same reasons that relationships commonly fall apart — lack of communication. To avoid most of the pitfalls of partnerships, meet with your partners regularly — at least once per week — to keep everyone in the loop. Be prepared to meet even more often when challenges arise or new opportunities present themselves. At these meetings, be sure you

- ✔ Review the current status of each project and timelines for completion.
- ✔ Review the income/expense statements since the last meeting to make sure your current projects are on solid financial footing.
- ✔ Discuss new developments or changes on projects.

The meeting should be a place for conversation and constructive discussion. Every partner should have a voice, but refrain from negative comments or arguments. A problem isn't something to argue over — it's a challenge that you must work together to overcome.

When an investment becomes particularly challenging, one partner is likely to feel more responsible for the problems than the other and may be inclined to hide the problems from the partner. If you begin to feel this way about a particular investment, it's the first sign of trouble. Instead of hiding the problem, share it with your partner, who may have a creative solution. One of the main benefits of having a partner is for the person's support when times are tough. Don't cut your partner out of the picture at a time when you really need him.

Partnership gone to pot

Mary and her brother decided to form a partnership. She was sharp and had excellent insight into the local real estate market, which enabled her to spot great opportunities and transform them into pure gold. They both had a fairly strong work ethic and were good with their hands, so they could work together on repairs and renovations.

Unfortunately, Mary's brother turned into somewhat of a slacker. They acquired a run-down rental property with a lot of potential, but Mary found herself getting stuck with all the work. After investing a great deal of time and effort over the course of several weeks fixing up the property, she began to resent her "partnership" with her brother.

When Mary finally found a buyer for the property, she no longer felt that the 50/50 split they had agreed upon was fair. A dispute ensued, and he refused to sign off on the title, causing the deal to fall apart. When they finally came to an agreement, the buyer was long gone, and they had to accept $12,000 less the next time around.

They haven't spoken since.

Although we can offer no surefire way to avoid situations such as this one, clearer communication early on could have saved this partnership. If Mary and her brother had agreed in advance on details regarding workload and tasks each of them would be responsible for, her brother may have realized early on that this partnership was something he was ill-prepared to do, or perhaps he would have felt more compelled to pitch in his 50 percent if it were in writing.

Chapter 14

Profiting from No-Money-Down and Other Creative Deals

*H*ow can you purchase real estate when you're flat broke? The good news is that other investors have done it. Despite the credit crunch that started in 2008, strategies are available to secure financing even when you have little or no money for a down payment. You just need to think more creatively and work with financial professionals who can think outside the cubicle. This chapter reveals some effective strategies and shows you how to employ them.

As you're reading this chapter, you may get the feeling that you're watching one of those get-rich-quick TV infomercials about making millions in real estate. Are no-money-down deals really possible? Is making millions in real estate really that easy? Yes and no. No-money-down deals are possible, but we're not promoting easy, no-risk riches in real estate. The arrangements we describe in this chapter do carry some risk and require some effort to pull together. In addition, you still have to find properties with plenty of profit potential and transform those diamonds in the rough into real gems.

Financing Your Down Payment with a Second Mortgage

Although we talk about various financing options as though they exist in a vacuum, investors commonly use two or more financing programs to fund a single project. An investor may, for example, take out a first mortgage to cover 80 to 90 percent of the purchase price, a second mortgage to cover the down payment, and a construction loan to cover the cost of repairs and renovations.

One of the most common ways to mix and match loan programs is through an 80-20 loan, commonly called a *piggy-back loan*, as discussed in the following sections.

Taking out an 80-20 loan

When you don't have enough money to buy a property, you borrow the necessary dough. If you don't have money for the down payment, borrow that, too. Although tough to find, you can go with an 80-20 loan. The only catch is that you have to disclose the details to the lenders, so they're fully aware of what you're doing.

An *80-20 loan* is actually two loans that cover the purchase price:

- ✔ **80:** The first mortgage covers 80 percent of the purchase price.
- ✔ **20:** A second mortgage covers a 20-percent down payment.

As you may have guessed, you can get creative with the 80-20 loan strategy. If, for example, the first mortgage holder requires only 10 percent down, you can do a 90-10 loan.

80-20 loans are often perfect for situations in which the value of the repaired property will be significantly more than the purchase price. Say you're buying a run-down property with a current market value of about $180,000 that would be worth about $250,000 if you fixed it up. You take out a first mortgage for $144,000, a second mortgage for $36,000, and secure other financing or use your own money to cover the cost of repairs and renovations (maybe $20,000).

You now have $200,000 into a property that's worth $250,000. You just created $50,000 in equity. You can now pull that equity out of the property by refinancing the second mortgage for close to the full value of the property, minus the balance on the first mortgage. If you refinanced the second mortgage for $60,000, for example (leaving the property at an 82 percent LTV), you could pay off the

$36,000 plus the $20,000 in repairs and renovations, walk away with $4,000, and still have $46,000 worth of equity in the property.

Ever since the mortgage meltdown of 2008, lenders have shied away from these piggy-back loans. Although these loans may be harder to find in a slumping market, however, they're always available. You may just have to look a little harder to find them.

Disclosing your second mortgage

When you take out a second mortgage to cover the down payment, you compromise your ability to make your payments when times are tough, and you weaken the lender's position. You now have none of your own money tied up in the property, so you can afford to be less committed to it. Also, if the lender has to foreclose, it has to deal not only with you but also with the holder of the second mortgage.

Lenders generally require a 10 to 20 percent down payment on a property to ensure repayment of the loan. The down payment gives you a vested interest in the property and offers some assurance to the lender that the property is worth more than you owe on it. If you encounter cash flow problems and have trouble making the payments, you may be able to borrow against that down payment (the equity you have in the property) to buy yourself some time. If you default on the loan and the lender has to sell the property, that down payment can help it recoup any loss.

Because 80-20 loans increase the first mortgage holder's risk, the law requires that you disclose the second mortgage and your plans to use it to cover the down payment. When you fill out the loan application, be sure to enter any information about "subordinate financing" in the space provided. Otherwise, you're committing a form of fraud known as a *silent second* (see the nearby sidebar).

Wholesaling for Fun and Profit

If you've watched episodes of any house-flipping show or read any of the dozen or so books on the art of flipping houses (including Ralph and Joe's *Flipping Houses For Dummies*), you know the basics. You buy a house below market value, fix it up, and sell it. Do it right and you earn a decent profit — 20 percent or better.

Some investors don't like the whole fix-it-up part of the process, so they skip that part. They buy a property below market value, mark up the price, and place it back on the market. Others don't even like to touch the property, so they skip another step — they act as bird dogs for other real estate investors, simply scoping out the best properties and charging a finder's fee. It's pure middleman stuff.

Wholesaling allows you to buy and sell a property quickly without ever actually taking possession of the property and without paying any financing costs. In the following sections, we show you a couple of ways to execute these transactions properly.

Buying and selling options

One of the safest ways (legally and financially) to control properties is to purchase an option or right to sell the property. By purchasing an option, you're not tying yourself to a purchase agreement, which legally binds you to following through with the purchase if you can't find someone to buy the property.

With an *option agreement,* you have the right, not the obligation, to purchase the property by a specified date. If you choose not to exercise your option or the option expires, you lose only the money used to purchase the option. In the following sections, we give you the lowdown on wholesaling by buying and selling options.

Buying options

Buying an option simply requires that you and the property owner sign a contract and that you pay the owner the agreed-upon amount for the option to purchase the property. Your attorney can draw up an option agreement for you or provide you with a boilerplate you can modify for different situations.

How much you pay for an option varies depending on the property's value, current market conditions, and the direction you and the owner think the market is going. In most cases, you can expect to pay anywhere from 1 to 5 percent of the property's true market value. Of course, the less you pay, the less pressure you're under to eventually buy the property.

An option agreement may also include language that makes you responsible for other expenses related to the property. The owner, for example, may require that you pay property taxes and insurance for the duration of the option. Such requests aren't unusual or unreasonable; you must gauge for yourself whether the terms work for you. Just make sure that you can *assign the option* (transfer it to another person).

Selling future cash-flow or equity positions

When you own an option, you control the property and can tap into all the benefits that come with that control. In exchange for upfront cash, you can offer a partner or investor an option on future _cash flow_ from the property or an eventual _equity position_ if certain conditions are met:

- ✔ **Cash flow:** If you're investing in a rental property, you can offer your partner or investor a certain percentage of the monthly profits for a given period of time or until you eventually sell the property.

The secret life of a silent second

To get around the down-payment requirement, some real estate insiders encourage home buyers to bend the rules by using a _silent second mortgage_ (or _silent second_ for short). A silent second is a mortgage loan from another lender or the seller that covers the down payment but isn't disclosed to the first mortgage lender. The silent second essentially fools the lender into thinking that you're a more qualified borrower than you really are.

Many people try to justify this strategy by saying, "Nothing is silent about this mortgage. I know about it, and the person lending me the money for the silent second knows about it. The bank lending me the money for the first mortgage is getting its required 10-percent down payment, so why should it care?" Well, the bank cares because several problems accompany silent second scenarios:

- ✔ By using a silent second, you're borrowing 100 percent of the home's value. If property values dip or you fail to maintain the property, it can quickly become worth less than you owe on it. If you default on the loan, the lenders won't be able to sell the property for enough to cover the balance due.

- ✔ A silent second falsely qualifies you for perks (such as a lower interest rate and not having to pay mortgage insurance) that you don't really qualify for.

- ✔ Silent seconds mislead the lender into approving a loan application it may have rejected had you provided accurate financial information.

Whenever you apply for a loan, you must sign a _Uniform Residential Loan Application,_ often referred to as a _1003 (ten-oh-three),_ stating that the information you provided on the loan application is accurate and complete. Omitting a "minor" detail, such as a silent second, makes you guilty of committing mortgage fraud — a felony. No matter how harmless it may seem, no matter how many other people are doing it, it's still fraud, so don't do it.

What if your relatives loan you the money? If they _loan_ you the money, you still fall in the silent second scenario. Now, if they _give_ you the money, you're safe and have committed no crime.

Remember, whenever you fail to disclose information to the lender that may compromise your ability to obtain loan approval, whatever the reason, it results in deceiving the lender and failing to honor the letter and the spirit of the law. Using a silent second is a crime.

✔ **Equity position:** If you're planning on fixing up and selling the property, you can offer your partner or investor a certain percentage of any profit you earn when you sell the property.

When scoping out prospective partners or investors, ask about their investment goals. Are they looking for a steady cash flow or to score a quick profit, or are they open to either strategy? By finding out about their goals, you can more easily determine whether you're the right fit and what sort of terms to offer them. If the proposed cash flow makes sense, you can even split the equity or cash flow into portions, selling off percentages of each to different investors. Typically this strategy only makes sense in larger commercial properties. Refer to Chapter 13 for more on utilizing partnerships.

Negotiating tenant sale options

When you control a property with a lease option agreement, as explained in Chapter 12, you can negotiate your own lease option with another tenant. In tougher markets with tighter credit, leasing a property may be easier than selling or flipping it.

In these circumstances, you can negotiate an attractive lease option for your tenant on top of your option, providing for some additional cash flow in the *spread* (difference between the two lease amounts). This is a great arrangement if you're dealing with a real *dontwanner* (as in "the owner don't want her") or a long-distance seller who has no use for the property (such as an estate situation).

Make sure your tenant's option to buy expires several months before yours, so if your tenant decides not to exercise her option, you have *plenty* of time to make other arrangements, such as obtaining the financing you need to exercise your option.

Assigning a purchase agreement

A somewhat riskier way to practice wholesaling is to tie up the property with a purchase agreement, find a buyer for the property who's willing to pay more than you agreed to pay for it, and then assign your purchase agreement to the buyer. In the following sections, we show you how it's done.

Securing the right to buy and sell the property

The first step in wholesaling is to get the property owner/seller to agree to sell you the property with the option to sell it to someone else. You pitch your offer the same way you would if you were actually buying the property for yourself — you present a purchase agreement. (Your real estate agent or attorney can assist you in wording it properly for your jurisdiction. For specifics on negotiating a purchase agreement, check out *Real Estate Investing For Dummies,* by Eric Tyson and Robert S. Griswold [Wiley].) The purchase agreement should include the following adjustments:

- ✔ **Instead of listing yourself as the buyer, you list yourself as "and/or assignees."** This wording means that either you or someone else can buy the property.

- ✔ **Set a closing date at least 60 days from the time the agreement is fully executed.** The more time you have to sell the property, the better.

- ✔ **Make the purchase agreement conditional upon the property passing inspection.** You don't want to get stuck with a lemon.

- ✔ **Disclose the fact that you're purchasing the property as an investor and not to reside in yourself.** Otherwise, you may expose yourself to legal issues — such as claims that you're illegally flipping the property to inflate its value.

Selling your interest

After you secure controlling interest in the property, you essentially become the seller's real estate agent. Your job is to find a buyer. You can accomplish this goal in all sorts of ways — advertising the property in the local papers, listing it online, networking with other investors, or selling it to a friend or relative.

Advertise the property for more than you agreed to pay the seller but less than the property's true market value. Otherwise, you may get stuck holding the property beyond the time you've given yourself to sell it in the purchase agreement.

As soon as you find a buyer, attach an addendum to the contract essentially stating that you're assigning the contract to the buyer for a certain amount of money. The seller, you, and the buyer must sign the addendum. After you do, you can contact the escrow company to process the transaction and schedule the closing.

Any gain you realize on the sale of your option becomes a short-term gain, qualifying as taxable income. If you do several of these, you may be considered a dealer and may need to secure a real estate license. Check with your accountant and the state licensing board.

If you can't find a buyer in time, in accordance with the contract, you lose your deposit (at the very least). You also lose *a lot* of credibility and can be sued for *specific performance* and be forced by the seller, through the courts, to purchase the property. Securing an option is a much safer route to take. See "Buying and Selling Options" earlier in this chapter for details.

Selling the Tax Benefits

When April 15 rolls around, every homeowner remembers one of the primary benefits of owning real estate in America — tax deductions. Thanks to the huge amount of interest homeowners typically pay on their mortgage, they can often itemize their deductions to claim a bigger tax write-off than they'd get from a standard deduction.

Although investors don't always get the same tax breaks as homeowners, you can deduct expenses against any income you receive from renting or selling properties to help reduce your taxes. Real estate investors are well aware of these tax breaks, but some fail to realize that they may be able to earn a profit by *selling* their tax savings to others.

This strategy may sound a little strange at first, but realize that every property has expenses, and every expense represents a potential deduction. Deductions are there for the taking, and the IRS really doesn't care who takes credit for them as long as only one party uses each deduction.

Investors receiving or due to receive significant capital gains from their investments may be looking for ways to offset those gains with capital losses. As such, they may be looking for short-term deductions or losses as a trade-off for long term equity or cash flow. If you don't need the deductions, consider selling them to someone who does.

Consult a tax advisor or accountant for advice on handling such transactions appropriately. You don't want to get yourself in a situation in which you and other investors are mistakenly claiming the same expenses as deductions. In addition, keep in mind that when you sell a tax benefit, you're losing deductions that could benefit you when tax time rolls around. Make sure you're earning enough selling tax benefits in excess of what those benefits would save you in taxes.

Trading Spaces: 1031 Exchanges

Another idea for a no-money-down option is executing a trade. A *1031 exchange* is a strategy for deferring the payment of capital gains taxes on the profit of a sale. This exchange treats the sale of the first property and the purchase of the second as a single transaction — an exchange.

A 1031 exchange is sort of like an IRA (individual retirement account) rollover. With an IRA rollover, you can avoid paying taxes and penalties on money withdrawn from one retirement account by depositing it into another qualifying retirement account within a certain number of days. The same principle applies to 1031 exchanges. You can sell one qualifying property and buy another of equal or greater value (within a certain period) to avoid paying a capital gains tax on the profit from the sale.

Flipping contracts? Tread carefully

Some real estate investment gurus promote a strategy called *flipping contracts*, which involves a double-closing — often referred to as a *pass-through transaction*. We strongly discourage you from doing it, but we believe you should understand how this scheme works in case someone calls it something different and tries to convince you it's okay. Here's how it works:

1. You (the *contract flipper*) sign a purchase agreement with the seller obtaining the right to purchase the property by a specified date.

   You pay a deposit — typically anywhere from about 1 to 10 percent of the asking price. (You agree to buy the property for less than market value so you can sell at or slightly below market value and earn a profit.)

2. You find a buyer who signs a purchase agreement with the commitment to pay more for the property than you've agreed to pay the seller.

   The typical goal is to earn $5,000 to $10,000, but this amount can vary.

3. The seller deeds the property to you, depositing the deed with an escrow company.

4. You deed the property to the buyer, depositing the deed with the escrow company.

5. The buyer obtains financing, giving the lender instructions to pay the loan proceeds to the escrow company.

6. The escrow company performs two closings back-to-back — closing the deal between you and the buyer and between you and the seller.

   You receive your profit, the seller receives the remaining proceeds, and the escrow company records the deeds with the county's register of deeds, showing the buyer as the new legal owner of the property.

Flipping contracts may sound rosy, but we strongly discourage you from doing so for several reasons, including the following:

✔ **Flipping contracts is borderline fraud.** Traditionally, a property's market value is determined by the price a seller is willing to accept and a buyer is willing to pay (whichever is lower). By jacking up the price as a middleman, you're artificially inflating the market value.

✔ **You put your reputation on the line.** Reputable real estate investors rarely engage in this practice. We suggest only a more experienced investor do so.

> ✔ **Doing a quick flip like this makes the property ineligible for certain types of financing.** HUD has an anti-flipping provision for FHA-insured loans; it won't finance any property that has been transferred within the last 90 days, and requires two appraisals for any property that's had a transfer of ownership in 91 to 180 days (to confirm the property's true market value). A double-closing that hikes up the price of the property in a matter of seconds obviously makes it ineligible for FHA financing. This guideline has also become standard practice for most conventional lenders.

Without such an exchange, any profit from the sale is subject to capital gains tax, which can negatively affect your cash flow and purchase power. If you pay a short-term capital gains tax of 30 percent, for example, on the sale of a $300,000 property, you pay $90,000 in taxes and have only $210,000 left to make your next purchase.

Qualifying for a 1031 exchange

To fully qualify for a 1031 exchange, the two properties must meet the following conditions:

- ✔ **The two properties must be *like kind*.** This rule essentially means that they have to be investment properties both located in the United States. You can exchange a farm for an office building, but you can't exchange an office building in the U.S. for an office building in Italy or vice versa. (Like kind applies to real estate investments, not primary residences or vacation homes.)

- ✔ **The purchase price of the property you're receiving must be greater than or equal to the purchase price of the property you're giving up.** In other words, you can't exchange a more valuable property from one of lesser value and pocket all the proceeds; although you can do a partial exchange as long as you pay taxes on the net gain, as discussed later in this section.

- ✔ **All the equity in the property you're giving up must be used to acquire the replacement property.** In other words, you can't use any proceeds from the exchange for other purposes, such as fixing up the property you received in the exchange or buying yourself a new car (too bad for the auto industry).

You can qualify for partial exchanges under the rules, but whatever profits you walk away with after the exchange are subject to capital gains tax. For example, if you sell a property for $200,000 in exchange for one you purchase for $175,000, your $25,000 profit is subject to capital gains tax.

Meeting the deadlines

To qualify for a 1031 exchange, not only must the properties qualify, but you must also meet the deadlines for processing the buy and sell transactions. You can't sell a property today, buy another one six months later, and claim the exchange exemption. Your transaction must fall within the following two deadlines:

- ✔ **Identification period:** You have 45 days from the day you close on the sale of the first property to identify a replacement. You can choose more than one property (and probably should) just in case you can't close on your first choice in time.

- ✔ **Exchange period:** You have 180 days from the day you close on the sale of the first property to close on the purchase of the replacement property.

These cut-off dates are firm — you don't get an extension or grace period if the deadline falls on a Saturday, Sunday, or holiday.

You do need to disclose the exchange on your tax return. Consult your accountant to make sure you comply with the disclosure rules that govern 1031 exchanges.

Selling Other Equitable Interests

When dealing with larger commercial properties or unique real estate holdings, you can get even more creative with financing because you have more assets to offer for sale or trade. What else does the property offer? Do you have billboards you can lease out or space for a health club to divide off? Does the property have a remote corner that would be good for hunting or other recreation? You can use any or all of these options (and options like them) to finance your project.

After you control the property, you can harness the power of that property's assets to secure quick cash to fund the deal or generate cash flow. In the following sections, we offer some suggestions.

Leaseholds and other rights

Many investors have gotten rich by buying real estate and quickly leasing off their interests while retaining rights to the land itself. Using *leaseholds* or *leasehold estates,* you can sell the property rights while retaining ownership of the land. Just north of me (Chip), for example, many property owners are leasing groundwater rights to Nestle Corporation for its bottling plants. As soon as the leasehold expires, the land reverts to the original owner.

You can lease your property rights to gas and oil companies, cities and towns (for water), farmers (for harvesting corn or wheat), ranchers (for cattle grazing), logging companies, and so forth.

Timber or logging rights can bring in substantial sums to finance to acquisition or to repair and renovate a property. One investor purchased 80 acres of land and leased off the hardwood timber rights for $40,000 a year, which covered the down payment and construction costs on the home. He subsequently sold off the excess land and then sold the house for a $100,000 profit. The best part: The government financed everything.

Naming rights, air rights, and other unimaginable stuff

Many owners of investment properties are too close to their own deal to envision all the possibilities. Due to their short-sightedness, they often overlook golden opportunities and leave a lot of money on the table. When you're looking for extra sources of capital to fund a deal, replace cash you already borrowed, or generate additional revenue streams, open your mind to all the possibilities. Here are some ideas that can begin to stimulate your own creativity:

- ✔ **Lease the naming rights of the building.** Some companies are willing to pay big bucks to have a stadium named after them. Lucas Oil, for example, agreed to pay the Indianapolis Colts $120 million over 20 years for the honor of having the Colts' new stadium named after the company. Although it didn't quite cover the entire $500 million price tag, it helped ease some of the sticker shock.

- ✔ **Create leases for air rights with radio, television, or satellite services off the roof.** One of the most famous real estate deals — the creation and sale of the air rights for New York's Empire State Building — instantly doubled the building's value.

- ✔ **Allow a cellphone carrier to construct a cell tower in a remote corner of the property or on top of the roof.** These can be *very* lucrative leases. I (Chip) have a client who owns a small home on about 10 acres. Her mortgage payment is only $362, but on a high corner of her property sits a 2,500 square foot fence guarding a cell transfer tower that generates $1,467 per month for the next 10 years guaranteed!

- ✔ **Sell off mailing leases for valuable addresses.** Folks in high-rent districts like Manhattan or Beverly Hills often sell rights to their mailing addresses to small companies looking for an established or well-known address.

Part V
The Part of Tens

Looks like another new exotic investment strategy to me.

WALL ST RD

In this part . . .

Every *For Dummies* book that rolls off the presses contains a Part of Tens — two or more chapters packed with bonus tips, tricks, and other bite-sized tidbits that you can chew on whenever you have a few spare minutes and your brain has the munchies.

In this Part of Tens, we reveal the ten most common beginner blunders (and show you how to avoid them), let you in on ten questions you should always ask a lender during your first meeting, lead your through ten closing steps you should never skip, and offer strategies for holding your own in a slumping market.

Chapter 15

Ten Ways to Avoid Common Beginner Blunders

In This Chapter

▶ Overcoming any obsession over low interest rates

▶ Performing your due diligence

▶ Comparison-shopping for the best deal

▶ Staying abreast of current real estate market conditions

Many ill-informed investors become overenthusiastic about the big picture and lose sight of the critical details that can make or break a deal. They pay too much for a property, underestimate the cost of repairs and renovations, fail to inspect a property or research the title, or sign contracts they don't fully understand.

You shouldn't overanalyze to the point of paralysis, but you do need to stay on top of the details from beginning to end. In this chapter, we present ten common real estate financing blunders to help you avoid costly mistakes and maximize your profits from the very start.

Focusing on More than Just a Low Interest Rate

When shopping for attractive financing, novice investors often get so hung up on interest rates that they talk themselves out of great deals. They meet a hard-money lender who's charging six points and 10 percent interest and immediately think the person is ripping them off. Instead of thinking about how much the other person is earning, focus your thoughts on what you stand to earn.

If the numbers work, the interest rate and fees don't matter. Financing fees and interest are just another cost to include in your calculations. If you can afford the financing and still earn the desired profit, don't worry about what you're paying. Having access to the money you need to do the deal is what matters most.

Getting Preapproved

In the excitement of shopping for potentially profitable investment properties, you may be tempted to shove the question of paying for it aside. Don't do it. Before you start shopping for investment properties, meet with your loan officer or mortgage broker and get preapproval. You can then move quickly and decisively when you discover potentially profitable properties.

Although most people generally shop first and think about paying for stuff later, this strategy compromises your ability to negotiate an attractive purchase price and terms. You can certainly present a purchase agreement that includes as a condition your ability to secure financing, but if another buyer shows up with cash or preapproved financing, she has a significant advantage.

Doing Your Homework: Property Research

The real estate community has a saying: "Buyers are liars, and sellers are worse." When you're thinking about buying a property, don't take anything the seller tells you at face value. Don't rely solely on seller disclosures to identify potential problems. Do your own research:

- ✔ Obtain a title commitment (refer to Chapter 12) to make sure the person selling the property is the rightful owner and that the property is unencumbered by other *liens* (claims against the property).

- ✔ Visit the property and inspect it as closely as possible with your own two eyes. Take the following pledge: "My eyes or no buys." Never buy a property site unseen. For more about evaluating properties, check out *Foreclosure Investing For Dummies* by Ralph R. Roberts and Joe Kraynak, *Real Estate Investing For Dummies,* 2nd Edition, by Eric Tyson and Ray Brown, and *Commercial Real Estate Investing For Dummies* by Peter Conti and Peter Harris (all by Wiley).

✔ Get a comparative market analysis from your agent (see Chapter 3) to make sure the property's market value is in line with the price you're planning to offer.

✔ Pick up a copy of the city worksheet on the property by visiting your town hall (or the equivalent). The *worksheet* contains a history of the property, including any building permits and code violations.

✔ For commercial properties, get records of the property's income and expenses for the past two years. Have the seller supply you with the past couple of years' tax returns on the property. (Refer to Chapter 8.)

✔ Prior to closing, have the property inspected professionally and resolve any issues before signing the final papers. (Refer to Chapter 7 for more info.)

✔ Purchase title insurance for the property (check out Chapter 7) to protect you in the event that someone claims rights to the property after closing.

✔ Check the county tax assessor's office for tax liens or special assessments. (Head to Chapter 4 for more info.)

Making a Reasonable Down Payment

For investment properties, lenders often demand a hefty down payment for the most attractive interest rates and terms. A 20-to-25 percent down payment isn't out of the ordinary.

Keep in mind, however, that the more money you put down on a property, the less you have available for other investments. You may be better off paying a higher interest rate with a lower down payment if you can put that extra money to work in another investment property.

Instead of putting 25 percent or more down on a property, for example, try negotiating a seller-held second mortgage, or a land contract sale with a 10 percent down payment. Fix up the property, and then refinance it later with the increased equity, so you're more likely to qualify for a lower interest rate without such a hefty down payment.

Conserving cash is best — even if it means having to pay higher interest rates or increased long-term costs. It's all about cash flow!

Comparing at Least Three Good Faith Estimates

Financing real estate purchases is the equivalent of shopping for money, and to find the best deals, you need to comparison-shop. Obtain at least three *Good Faith Estimates* (a detailed breakdown of all the projected loan costs) from different lenders, and compare the following:

- ✔ Interest rate
- ✔ *Discount points* (prepaid interest)
- ✔ Closing costs and other fees
- ✔ *Annual percentage rate* (APR) or the percentage rate factoring in interest, points, and fees
- ✔ *Term* (number of months or years to pay back the loan)
- ✔ Any prepayment penalties or refinancing conditions

Although having access to cash trumps concerns over the costs of financing, you still want to get the best deal possible. For more about comparing loans, refer to Chapter 6.

Viewing at Least Ten Properties before Making an Offer

First-time investors often see a property for sale and think to them-selves, "Wow, this is a prime piece of real estate." They then pro-ceed to purchase it without spending any time evaluating the market. They have no idea what other comparable properties are selling for or what those properties have to offer. As a result, they often pay far too much.

The first property you see may be the best deal around, but you don't know that until you look around. Make a rule to view at least ten comparable properties before making an offer on one of them. Doing so forces you to slow down and make better-informed deci-sions. As you become more familiar with your market, you can begin to evaluate them much more quickly and accurately without having to follow this ten-for-one rule.

Checking Your Credit Score before Applying for a Loan

Credit is the one thing you can't buy. When you apply for a loan, the first thing the lender does is check your credit score and history. If you have a lousy credit score and a checkered financial past, the lender is going to either reject your loan application or curb the risk by requiring a larger down payment, charging higher interest and fees, and perhaps even requiring that you purchase private mortgage insurance (PMI).

To avoid wasting time (the lender's and yours) and enduring costly loans, check your credit score and history before applying for a loan. If your report contains any errors, contact the credit reporting agency and have them corrected, if possible.

If your credit score is below 680, work toward improving it. Pay your bills on time, pay down any large balances you're carrying on credit cards, and take other steps to boost your score. Chapter 3 offers some additional suggestions.

Buying with Your Brain and Not Your Heart

You may fall in love with a property, but don't follow the dictates of your heart when investing in real estate. Remember, this is business (not a hobby), and the numbers have to work. Depending on your strategy, take one of the following two courses:

- ✔ **Buy and sell:** If you're buying the property to sell it for a profit, shoot for at least a 20-percent profit and account for all of your expenses, including purchase price, repair and renovation expenses, *holding costs* (taxes, insurance, interest), marketing costs, and sales commissions.

- ✔ **Buy and hold:** If you're buying the property to rent it out, make sure it generates a *positive cash flow* — that annual income exceeds annual expenses.

Monitoring the Pulse of Current Market Conditions

Like the stock market, the real estate market has its ups and downs. Property values can rise or fall based on local economic conditions, changes in trends, and a host of other factors. Homeowners and investors witnessed just how dramatically the housing market can shift course when the bubble burst in 2008.

Knowledge is power. As an investor, keeping abreast of the fluctuations in the marketplace can pay dividends. It can prevent you from paying too much for a property, buying the wrong property at the wrong time, and perhaps even selling too early or too late. All real estate is local. Make sure you know what's going on in your own backyard.

Calculating the NOI and DSCR on Commercial Properties

With commercial properties, you focus less on the resale value of a property and more on the net revenue that property can generate for you. As a result, you're not simply looking at the market value of the property. You need to work the numbers and determine the property's NOI and DSCR:

- ✔ **Net Operating Income (NOI)** is the profit the property generates monthly or annually. To calculate the NOI, you total all the income the property brings in, and then subtract all your expenses.

- ✔ **Debt Service Coverage Ratio (DSCR)** is the number that lenders use to evaluate the risk versus the rewards. The higher the ratio, the better the deal — and the better the financing options. To calculate the DSCR, divide the NOI by the annual debt service on the loan (total annual payments on the loan, including interest and principal). A DSCR of 1.00 means that the property is breaking even. A number of 1.20 indicates that the property is generating a decent profit. Riskier properties require a higher DSCR to justify the risk.

When it comes to investing, the numbers are the only things that count! Refer to Chapter 8 for additional details about these two calculations.

Chapter 16

Ten Steps to Take before Closing

In This Chapter

▶ Examining the appraisal, title commitment, and closing documents

▶ Insuring the property

▶ Inspecting the property one last time

▶ Having your money ready to go

*T*he actual *closing* (when you receive rights to the property and pay the seller) is typically uneventful — or at least everyone involved hopes it will be. To ensure that the closing proceeds without a glitch, you need to prepare in advance. You don't want to be one of those inexperienced buyers who insist on reading every single word of every document at the closing table or shows up without the funds needed to close the deal.

In this chapter, we provide you with a checklist of ten things to do prior to closing to make sure your closing proceeds as smoothly as possible. You don't need to complete the items in the order presented here — just make sure you've attended to all the details prior to closing.

Get and Review a Copy of the Appraisal

As part of the process your lender follows in evaluating your loan application, it orders an appraisal. Obtain a copy of the appraisal and use it to double-check your calculations (to make sure the property you're about to purchase is likely to be profitable).

With the appraisal, your lender wants to ensure the following:

✔ The property value is in line with the purchase price.

✔ The property (unless it's a construction or rehabilitation loan) shows the potential to generate more than enough annual income to cover the annual loan payments.

If the appraiser seems to think that the property isn't worth the purchase price or that it won't generate sufficient income to cover the payments, the lender will probably reject your loan application. If the lender approves your loan despite flags raised by the appraiser, you should still be concerned about purchasing a questionable investment property.

So what if the numbers don't work? You have two choices:

✔ **Proceed:** If you decide to proceed with the deal, make sure the numbers on your *pro forma,* or projections, are conservative and realistic and show the lender that the property will perform — and earn a profit — within the next three years.

✔ **Recede:** If you decide to back away from the deal, you may lose your *earnest money deposit* (EMD, the money you paid the seller when you settled on a purchase agreement) and any other expenses you've already paid. If your offer wasn't conditional on a satisfactory appraisal (including value), you may also be liable for a *specific performance* suit that forces you to complete the transaction.

Review the Title Commitment and Obtain Title Insurance

Contact your title company and obtain a copy of the *title commitment* — a report issued prior to closing that shows all liens and other claims against a property. If the title commitment shows a lien against the property that the seller failed to disclose or a break in the chain of ownership (see Chapter 12), call this discrepancy to the attention of the title company and your attorney. Address any concerns you have about the title prior to closing.

A title commitment that shows a clean title is no substitute for an actual *title policy,* which insures against any losses in the event that somebody shows up later with a rightful claim against the property. A title company may miss something during its title search, so always buy a policy to protect yourself against any oversights.

Review All Closing Documents

As soon as you know who's handling the closing (usually a title company, but it can also be an attorney or escrow company), call and request a closing packet as soon as possible — at least a couple of days prior to closing so you have time to review all the documents. The closing packet should include at least the following items:

- Mortgage or land contract
- Deed
- Promissory note
- HUD-1 closing statement (see the following section for details)

Read through the documents to check for spelling or calculation errors, to ensure your name and other information pertaining to you is correct, and to verify that the numbers on the HUD-1 match up with those on the Good Faith Estimate. (See Chapter 6 for more on Good Faith Estimates.) If anything looks odd, call the title company and have your issues addressed *before* closing.

If you have an attorney (and you should), make sure your attorney also receives a copy of the closing packet prior to closing and reviews the documents.

Review a Copy of the HUD-1 Closing Statement

The *HUD-1 statement* is a universal closing statement used for all residential (and many commercial) loan transactions. For larger commercial properties, the format's the same, but it may be prepared on the attorney's or closing agent's letterhead or form.

The HUD-1 is a key document — it has all the numbers, and everyone involved in the transaction must sign off on it to enable the closing agent to move forward with the disbursements. Although you can try to get a copy several days in advance, the reality is that numbers are still coming in at the last minute, and you may not be able to review the final revised copy until just before the closing. Ask anyway — according to RESPA, you're entitled to see a completed copy of the HUD-1 at least 24 hours in advance.

Even though you're the buyer, review *both* sides of the form. Look at every line that has a number next to it and verify that each charge or credit is listed properly. Review the seller's side to make sure that each lien payoff is listed, that taxes are computed correctly, and that the sellers are paying for the charges agreed to in the Purchase Agreement. Bring any questionable items or amounts to the attention of the closing agent as early as possible. By addressing any HUD-1 issues prior to closing, you can remove at least some of the unnecessary stress and confusion. You don't want to be discussing (or arguing over) charges at the closing.

Get an Insurance Policy

For many homeowners and investors, obtaining an insurance policy is an afterthought. Meet with your insurance agent and explain the situation. Make sure your agent knows that this is an *investment property*. You're likely to pay more for a policy on an investment property, but if you buy a standard homeowner's policy, it may not provide sufficient protection or cover any damage.

Why would you obtain insurance *before* you took ownership? We can offer you two good reasons:

- The lender requires that you have an insurance policy in place as a condition for financing the purchase. The lender wants to make sure insurance is in place to protect its investment.

- If the property burns down, blows away, or is swept up in floodwaters a minute after you sign the closing papers, you can lose your entire investment.

Insurance also comes in handy if the previous owners of a foreclosure property decide to trash the place out of spite on their way out the door.

Do a Walk-Through on the Property

You may have inspected the property to the point of overkill, but the day or morning before closing, visit the property again and do a final walk-through to make sure it's in the same condition (or better) as when you submitted your offer. Anything can happen to a property between the time you first see it and closing, so perform your due diligence and visit the property prior to closing. Inspect all four sides from the outside and walk through the interior.

Obtain Utility Final Readings and Schedule the Transfer

Earning a profit on real estate often hinges on your ability to complete repairs and renovations quickly. If you've already scheduled contractors to start work but you failed to have the water, gas, and electric turned on, you may end up paying a bunch of workers a lot of money for sitting around twiddling their thumbs. To avoid this problem, call the local utility companies (water, gas, and electric) prior to closing and obtain the final utility readings (or as close as possible). Let each utility company know that you're going to be the new owner and will be transferring the account to your name.

 Make sure the HUD-1 lists any outstanding water or sewer bills and that the seller pays them at closing. These unpaid bills become a lien on the property. Most other utility charges attach to the previous owner, not the property.

In some cases, the utility company may not allow you to transfer the account prior to closing, so you may need to transfer utilities over to your name immediately after closing. Have your agent contact the sellers and request that they bring their most recent utility bills to the closing — they contain the phone numbers and account numbers you need. If necessary, the sellers can then call, request that the utilities be transferred to you, and then hand the phone to complete the transfer.

Review Updated Tenant Rent Roll

When purchasing a rental property complete with tenants, obtain an updated tenant roll prior to closing to be sure no mass exodus of renters has occurred between the time you negotiated the purchase and the closing. The *rent roll* should include a listing of each unit, the tenant, monthly lease amount, lease term and expiration, deposit amount, and any lease concessions. As a commercial investor, keep in mind that you're purchasing not only a building but also an existing business complete with customers (the tenants). If something has driven your renters from the premises, you deserve answers.

An updated rent roll at time of closing certifies when the seller received the most recent lease payments and any deposits being transferred to you.

Make sure the seller didn't collect advance rents and fail to disclose them — that's money you'll never be able to recover later. For major tenants or large properties, we recommend that you request an *estoppel* letter from each tenant that confirms the lease term, payment amount, deposit, and date of last payment.

Have Certified Funds or Wire Transfer Ready to Go

Showing up to a closing without a certified check in hand or a wire transfer ready to go for the amount you're required to pay is like going on a hot date without your wallet. Your lender is responsible for making sure the big payment is ready to hand over to the seller, but you need to show up with your check for the down payment and closing costs. Make sure it's a certified check (from your bank) or a wire transfer.

 Bring your checkbook, too, just in case you need to pay for some unforeseen expenses that appear at closing. Don't let your lender or whoever's handling the closing charge extra fees, but know that you may have to pay for legitimate out-of-pocket expenses, such as odd-days interest recalculation, an additional overnight fee for a disbursement, or an account transfer deposit with a utility company or other service provider. For assistance in differentiating between legitimate and illegitimate fees, refer to Chapter 6.

Confirm Date, Time, and Location of Closing

A lot of time and effort — and people — have been involved in the transaction leading up to closing. With so many parties involved, closings often become major ordeals to conveniently schedule. Because you don't want to end up at the wrong place at the wrong time and have to reschedule, call the closing company or attorney in charge of the closing a few days before you think the meeting is scheduled and confirm the date, time, and location.

 If you're not absolutely sure where the closing office is, get the address and find directions online. If you have one of those GPS gadgets, all the better. Show up early — if more negotiating needs to be done, you don't want it starting without you at the table!

Chapter 17

Ten Tips for Surviving a Credit Crunch

*T*he days of easy credit (in the 1990s and first few years of the new millennium) may be gone, but savvy investors know that financing never completely dries up. You can always find lenders willing to finance promising deals, particularly for real estate investors who have a proven track record (or at least an excellent plan for turning a profit).

Although some sort of financing is always available, the landscape can change. To survive and thrive under the new conditions, you need to be able to adapt, shift your strategy, and look for money in less likely places. This chapter offers some suggestions.

Don't let a slow market get you down. When sales slump, buying opportunities soar, and this is when savvy investors build wealth.

Expand Your Search

A credit crunch doesn't mean that financing disappears — it just means that you probably need to look for it somewhere else. If you're accustomed to working through banks, you may need to explore the hard money option, as presented in Chapter 11. If that's not an option, consider seller financing, as discussed in Chapter 12.

If you tried to cut out the middleman by working directly with lenders, consider working through a broker instead. Having an expert on your side can give you more options and perhaps even save you money.

The government can step in during a credit crunch (like it did during the mortgage meltdown) to stimulate the economy. Although conventional (nongovernment) loans may be scarcer, you may discover that government loans, such as FHA loans, are more accessible.

Choose Properties More Carefully

Financing follows the laws of supply and demand. When money is tight, banks can afford to pick and choose the people they decide to loan money to. As a result, they're going to be very picky about which deals they finance and which ones they reject when they start crunching the numbers.

You need to adjust accordingly by selecting properties more carefully. Overestimate costs, underestimate profits, and make sure the worst-case scenario still leaves you with a reasonable profit or positive cash flow. When the market's in a slump, you have less room for error.

Don't gamble on declining areas or areas where unemployment is rising. Stick with "bread-and-butter" properties that are easy to fix up, maintain, and rent out. Of course, it's not wise to buy into a booming market, and we're not telling you to do that, either. Buying when the market is down can be a savvy move, but opt for more stable areas and look for early signs of recovery before you go all in.

Focus on Foreclosures

As the economy slows, foreclosure rates gradually increase, but just as the economy begins to recover, foreclosure rates tend to spike. The peak in foreclosure rates typically lags behind the slump in the economy by about a year, because foreclosures take between 7 and 12 months to process. When you're in a slow economy, big opportunities lie ahead.

When you're hunting for bargains on homes, you have to go where the best sales are happening. In a slow economy, follow the foreclosures. Foreclosures are one of the best ways to acquire properties at below-market value. For more about finding and buying foreclosure properties, check out Ralph and Joe's *Foreclosure Investing For Dummies* or Chip's *Cashing In on Pre-foreclosures and Short Sales* (both Wiley).

Look for Short-Sale Opportunities

When foreclosures soar, lenders begin looking for opportunities to minimize their losses, as well. Many lenders are even open to the possibility of a *short sale* — accepting less than full payment of the current balance on the mortgage.

Why would any lender accept less than the homeowner/borrower owes? Because if lenders don't settle for less, they stand to lose even more by ending up with a bad loan on their books and a house they have to sell in a slumping market. A short sale limits their loss. With a good credit history and track record, you can negotiate a low sales price and the financing all at the same time.

 To identify short sale opportunities, network with homeowners and real estate professionals in your area. Real estate agents, attorneys (especially foreclosure and divorce lawyers), mortgage brokers, and loan officers often know about families who are having trouble making their mortgage payments. If you can negotiate a short sale on behalf of the homeowners, you may be able to purchase the property at a bargain basement price and still have a little money left over to help the homeowners move on with their lives.

 Never deal with the lenders' regular customer service representatives. They're programmed to answer every question with a "no." Track down the loss mitigation department. They have the ability and interest in negotiating with you.

Buy REO Properties

If a bank follows through on a foreclosure, nobody buys the property at auction, and the previous owners can't redeem it (in jurisdictions that have a redemption period), the bank ends up with the property. These repo properties are commonly referred to as *real estate owned* (REO) or *bank owned* properties.

In addition to getting stuck with a loan that's not generating any income, the bank has to invest more money to fix up the place and sell it — usually at a loss.

In most cases, banks prefer to clear the bad loan off their books quickly, sell the property at a reasonable loss to an investor, and wash their hands of the deal. They may even be willing to finance the purchase for a qualified investor — turning a bad loan into a loan that generates revenue for the bank.

In situations like these, the government also experiences an increased inventory of REO properties. FHA has a lending program specifically designed to allow investors to finance REOs. For more information, go to www.hud.gov/offices/hsg/sfh/reo/mm/mminfo.cfm.

During a credit crunch, consider ramping up your efforts to connect with the REO departments at local and national banks. They may not be willing to finance your first deal, but after you prove yourself, they should be more willing to finance your next purchase.

Search for High-Equity Properties

In tough markets, creativity is king. Seek out sellers who have properties with a lot of equity. These sellers can be much more flexible in structuring a deal and financing it themselves if they don't need the cash or have a huge mortgage payment tied to the property.

The advantage for them is tapping into a higher rate of return than they can probably get from other investments (and it's secured by an asset they're familiar with — their property).

If the owner is reluctant to take back a mortgage or a land contract, offer a lease-option agreement of your own to get control of the property. Take some time to fix it up, re-lease it out, or allow the market to recover a bit and then refinance it or sell it yourself.

Shift from a Buy-Sell to a Buy-Hold Strategy

If you've been buying and selling properties (fix-and-flip), you may find that strategy isn't quite as lucrative when property values take a dive. Instead of sitting on the sidelines waiting for conditions to improve, consider shifting to a buy-and-hold strategy — buy properties and lease them out, at least until the housing market turns around.

By leasing the property, you can often ride out a slow market for a year or two and then put the house up for sale. Real estate prices tend to recover after huge slumps, at least for good-quality properties, and if you can afford to hold the property, rental income may cover your holding costs until the market recovers and you can sell the house for the price you want.

You can also structure a lease-option purchase, which provides an opportunity to lock in a buyer now even though the sale occurs later.

 Don't leap into the leasing business blindly. If you're going to shift from selling to renting, know what you're getting yourself into. Check your tenants' references and rental history, and carefully screen your tenants. For more about renting out property, check out *Property Management For Dummies,* 2nd Edition, by Robert S. Griswold (Wiley).

Team Up with Your Mortgage Broker

 When the market's soft, the economy is usually in a slump, and people generally have less money to spend on housing. By teaming up with a mortgage broker or loan originator, you can often help first-time home buyers secure the financing they need to purchase the home. You don't want to finance the purchase yourself (by offering seller financing), because that ties up your money, but you can put prospective buyers in touch with your broker, who can assist them in securing the financing they need to buy the property from you. By offering access to financing, you often gain an edge in a slow market over other sellers who don't have the vision or the close relationship with a broker to make the sale happen.

Even during a credit crunch, financing is still available at attractive terms for first-time homebuyers. Get familiar with FHA and rural development (RD) loans to get buyers in for as little as 0 percent down. Rural development loans are available through the USDA and offer 100 percent financing for development in rural areas. (See Chapter 9 for more about USDA financing.)

Offer Your Agent a Bonus

If you need to sell a property in a slow market, consider offering your agent a bonus for selling the property by a certain date. In slow markets, some investors make the mistake of trying to negotiate a *lower* commission with their agent. They reason that the agent needs the work and that the commission is another expense that eats into their profits.

This strategy often backfires, however. The agent feels insulted and unmotivated, and the house lingers on the market. The investor loses more money in holding costs than she gains by reducing the agent's commission.

To increase buyer traffic, consider *raising* the commission so you can pay more in commissions to the buyer's agent. For example, if your agent typically charges you a 6 percent commission and splits the commission 50/50 if another agent delivers the buyer, offer your agent 7 percent so she can afford to offer a bigger commission to the buyer's agent.

Don't advertise a higher sales commission on the Multiple Listing Service (MLS) or your other marketing materials, because you may turn off prospective buyers who equate their agents' enthusiasm with the fat bonus you're offering. Instead, work through your agent to communicate this boost in commission to the buyers' agents.

Partner Up and Get Creative

When a market turns south, it generally affects everyone. During a credit crunch, investors get more conservative, just like the banks. One solution is to team up with other investors and spread the risk.

Join a local real estate investors club, attend meetings, and meet some fellow investors. Find out what they're looking for and offer to partner up on a property to share the risk. Taking on two other partners diminishes your risk by 67 percent. Of course, you have to share the rewards as well, but this method is a great way to acquire several properties and minimize your exposure to a declining marketplace.

Get a written agreement between all the partners in advance — a bad market magnifies assumptions and misunderstandings if things go wrong. For more about partnering, check out Chapter 13.

Appendix

Glossary

• •

*L*enders have a language all their own. In this glossary, we present and decipher the most cryptic jargon and acronyms that lenders and their ilk are likely to toss at you.

1031: See *Tax-deferred exchange*

A-to-D grading scale: A system that lenders and real estate investors often use to rate the quality of a commercial property. The better the grade, the more easily you can secure financing.

acceleration clause: A provision in the mortgage that allows the lender to demand payment of the entire balance of a loan if the borrower fails to make payments or sells the property.

adjusted basis: Value used in calculating the taxable gain on the sale of a property. The adjusted basis is the original cost of the property plus capital improvements minus accumulated depreciation and the cost of selling it.

adjustment period: The length of time that determines how often the interest rate can change on an adjustable rate mortgage. See also *index, cap,* and *margin*

amortization: Creative process of retiring debt through predetermined periodic payments.

ADS or DS (Annual Debt Service): Total monthly payments (including interest and principal) on a mortgage loan for 12 months.

appraisal: A written estimate by a licensed appraiser of the value of a property.

APR (Annual Percentage Rate): Calculation disclosed on the Truth in Lending Act (TIL) that indicates the total cost of credit when fees are taken into account.

ARM (Adjustable Rate Mortgage): A mortgage in which the rate can change.

AU (Automated Underwriting): Computerized system used by lenders to determine a borrower's eligibility for loan programs.

AVM (Automated Valuation Model): A computerized system for determining the value of a property that sort of takes the place of an appraisal.

back-end debt ratio: Total debt payments (including house payment with homeowner's insurance and property taxes) divided by total monthly income. According to the Federal Housing Authority (FHA), your back-end debt ratio should not exceed 43 percent. See also *debt ratio* and *front-end debt ratio*

balloon payment: A typically large final payment due on a loan that covers the remaining balance. Balloon payments are required when a loan is scheduled to be paid in full before the debt can be retired through monthly payments.

basis: The starting point for calculating the gain or loss on an investment — usually the purchase price.

CAM (Common Area Maintenance) charge: Additional rent charged to tenants to cover expenses for maintaining common areas, such as a pool, workout room, or parking lot. May also be used to share the cost of property taxes and insurance.

capital gain or loss: The net profit on an investment property that's subject to tax. Capital gains can be long-term (taxed at a lower rate) or short-term.

capital improvement: A renovation that increases the value or useful life of a property in excess of one year.

Cap Rate (Capitalization Rate): A reflection of the rate of return that's considered reasonable for a certain type of commercial property in a given area based upon its risk.

cap: The maximum interest rate allowed for an ARM loan.

cash flow: The net operating income (NOI) of a property minus its debt service. See also *NOI* and *ADS or DS*

closing: A meeting among all parties in a sale to sign documents, disburse funds, and transfer the ownership of real estate.

closing costs: Costs incurred by a borrower, or paid on his behalf, to close on a real estate transaction. Closing costs are listed on the GFE and the HUD-1.

CL (Credit Losses): Unpaid rent or other losses from a tenant.

CLTV (combined loan-to-value): The total LTV with all mortgages included. See also *LTV (loan-to-value)*

commercial property: Property used for business as opposed to living quarters. Technically, however, the term also covers residential real estate having five units or more. See also *residential property*

comps or comparables: Properties that are similar to the property in question and can be used to estimate its value.

conforming loan: A loan that adheres to all Fannie Mae and Freddie Mac requirements. See also *subprime loan, Fannie Mae, and Freddie Mac*

contract for deed: See *land contract*

conventional loan: A loan that doesn't require underwriting or insuring by the government (such as FHA or VA underwriting).

cost approach: An appraisal method that starts with what building the same structure would cost today, depreciates that figure, and then adds in the value of the land.

cross-collateralization: Using two or more properties to secure the repayment of a loan for only one of the properties.

debt ratio: A formula that lenders often use to determine a borrower's ability to afford monthly payments on a loan. The debt ratio equals the total monthly payments divided by the total monthly income. See also *back-end debt ratio* and *front-end debt ratio*

deed of trust: A legal document that functions much like a mortgage in that it secures the repayment of a loan. In deed of trust states, a trustee holds the deed until the loan is paid back in full. If the borrower defaults on the loan, the trustee can then sell the property to help the lender recoup any loss.

depreciation: The decline in value of a property over time usually due to wear and tear.

discount rate: Interest rate that banks and other financial institutions use when lending money to one another — sometimes used as an index for ARM loan adjustments.

down payment: A portion of the purchase price for a property that the buyer pays up front.

DS (Debt Service): See *ADS or DS (Annual Debt Service)*

DSCR (Debt Service Coverage Ratio): Calculation used to determine whether a property has enough income to support the proposed debt service. NOI divided by DS equals DSCR. See also *ADS or DS (Annual Debt Service)*

due on sale clause: Wording in most mortgages that requires the borrower to pay the balance in full in the event that the property changes hands.

easement: A limited right that someone else has to use property or a portion of the property someone else owns — such as for an access road.

EGI (Effective Gross Income): Total revenue from all rent minus any estimated loss from vacancies.

EMD (Earnest Money Deposit): Funds put up by a prospective purchaser as a commitment to follow through on the purchase of a property.

encumbrance: A restriction on the use or transfer of a property — for example, a property tax lien, unpaid mortgage, or easement.

equity: The amount of money remaining if you sold the property today and paid off any loans taken out against the property.

estoppel certificate: Legal document that tenants use to acknowledge agreements or changes in the lease or the status of rent payments.

Fannie Mae: Nickname for Federal National Mortgage Association (FNMA) — a government-sponsored entity that purchases mortgages from lenders, repackages them, and sells them to Wall Street investors.

FHA (Federal Housing Administration): Part of the Department of Housing and Urban Development that insures home mortgage loans.

FICO (Fair Isaac & Company) score: A credit scoring system commonly used by lenders to determine the risk a borrower represents related to repayment.

fixed-rate loan: A loan for which the interest rate remains unchanged over the life of the loan. See also *ARM*

forfeiture clause: Legal wording commonly used in a land contract or lease option agreement that entitles the seller to repossess the property in the event that the buyer fails to comply with the terms of the agreement.

Freddie Mac: Nickname for Federal Home Loan Mortgage Corporation (FHLMC), a government-sponsored entity that purchases mortgages from lenders, repackages them, and sells them to Wall Street investors.

front-end debt ratio: House payment alone (including property taxes and insurance) divided by total monthly income. According to the FHA, your front-end debt ratio shouldn't exceed 31 percent. See also *debt ratio* and *back-end debt ratio*

GFE (Good Faith Estimate): A list of estimated costs involved in the loan transaction that the lender provides to the borrower prior to, or within three days of, application.

GRM (Gross Rent Multiplier): A property's value as expressed as a multiple of its gross rental income.

hard money: A typically short-term, high-interest loan that investors often use to score some quick cash to move forward on an investment opportunity.

HELOC (Home-Equity-Line-Of-Credit): Credit line secured by a piece of real property. With a HELOC, you pay interest on only the amount of money you actually draw against the credit line.

HUD (Department of Housing and Urban Development): Part of the federal government that oversees FHA. See also *FHA*

HUD-1: Settlement statement used at closing to disclose all costs and credits for borrowers and sellers involved in a real estate transaction.

hybrid loan: A combination of an ARM and a fixed-rate loan; for example, with a 3/1 hybrid, the interest rate remains fixed for three years and then becomes an adjustable-rate loan in which the rate can be adjusted every year. See also *ARM* and *fixed-rate loan*

income approach: A real estate appraisal method that focuses more on the revenue-generating potential of rental property than the property's value.

index: An economic indicator used to calculate interest rates on some consumer loan products, notably ARM loans. See also *adjustment period*, *cap*, and *margin*

jumbo loan: A mortgage loan for an amount that exceeds the upper limit of what Fannie Mae and Freddie Mac can purchase.

land contract: A legal instrument that enables the seller to finance the purchase of his property. The seller functions as the lender, and the contract takes the place of a mortgage or deed of trust.

LC (Leasing concessions): Perks offered to attract or keep tenants, such as one month's free rent.

leasing commissions: Expense calculation for payments to a leasing agent or company; used in calculating NOI on a commercial property.

lease option agreement: A legal instrument that enables a buyer to rent a property for a certain amount of time at the end of which she can purchase it (or not) for the price stipulated at the time of signing the agreement.

leverage: The use of borrowed money to increase purchase power.

lien: A claim against a property. A mortgage is a type of lien.

LLC (limited liability corporation): A legal structure that protects the owner's personal assets from any loss that the business incurs.

loan officer: Someone who works for a lending institution or mortgage broker to assist borrowers in selecting and applying for loans. See also *mortgage broker*

lock: An option a borrower has when applying for a loan or for a limited time after application to obtain the loan at the currently available interest rate.

long-term capital gain: The realized profit on an investment property held more than 12 months.

LTV (loan-to-value): A ratio expressing the loan amount divided by the property's current market value. For example, the LTV on an $80,000 loan to purchase a $100,000 property is 80 percent. Lenders use LTV as one way to measure risk — the lower the LTV, the less the risk.

management expenses (ME): Whatever you pay yourself or others to care for a property.

margin: An amount added to an index to calculate an adjustment for an ARM loan. The margin remains constant over the life of the loan. See also *adjustment period, index,* and *cap*

MIP (Mortgage Insurance Premium): Term used for insurance required for FHA-insured loans.

mortgage: A loan secured by real estate. States that aren't trust states use a mortgage as the legal instrument to secure a lien against the property.

mortgage broker: A licensed professional who assists borrowers in shopping for loans made available through multiple lenders.

net worth: The value of everything you own minus everything you owe.

NNN (Triple Net): Income collected from tenants to pay for taxes, insurance, and maintenance.

NOI (net operating income): The amount of money left over after all expenses are deducted from a property's gross income.

nonconforming loan: See *subprime loan*

note: Legal instrument that describes the terms of the mortgage loan.

operating expenses: Costs for maintaining a property, including taxes, insurance, maintenance, and upkeep.

OPM (other people's money): Any financing option that gives you more money than your own to fuel your investments. OPM gives you leverage to buy more and better properties and increase your potential for earning bigger profits.

origination: The act of initiating the process for securing a loan.

owner-occupied: Residential real estate in which the owner lives.

passive income: Money that flows in without your having to lift a finger. Some real estate property may generate passive income, which is taxed differently than normal income.

pass-through expenses: Costs that a landlord incurs and then charges the tenant to pay in full or a portion of in addition to paying rent.

PITI (principal + interest + taxes + insurance): Term used to describe a payment that covers the principal and interest due on a loan along with money to be placed in escrow to pay taxes and insurance.

PMI (Private Mortgage Insurance): Insurance required on high LTV conventional loans.

points: Interest paid on a loan upfront rather than monthly. One point is 1 percent of the total loan amount.

preapproval: A lender's agreement to finance the purchase of an investment property up to a certain amount, assuming the property meets certain conditions. See also *prequalification*

prequalification: A lender's assurance that a borrower would probably qualify for a particular loan. See also *preapproval*

prepaids: Costs of a transaction listed on the GFE or HUD-1 that any party pays in advance on the borrower's behalf.

prepayment penalty: A clause in some mortgage agreements that requires the borrower to pay additional money if she pays back the loan early.

pro forma: A statement projecting the future performance of an income-producing property.

promissory note: A legal document borrowers sign as their personal agreement to pay back a loan according to the terms specified in the note.

reconveyance: The transferring of the title to the previous owner. A lender usually issues a reconveyance after the borrower pays back the loan in full.

REIT (Real Estate Investment Trust): A legal/accounting tool that gives small investors a way to pool their assets and own investment real estate as a group.

REO (Real Estate Owned): Property owned by the bank. Sometimes, you can get the bank to finance the purchase of these properties.

rentable square feet: The total square feet of a property minus the square feet of areas you can't rent out, such as stairways and broom closets.

reserves: Amount of liquid assets that a borrower has left after paying all costs for the transaction. Lenders like to see that borrowers have several months of reserves to cover payments in case of emergencies.

residential property: Dwellings designed to house people rather than businesses. See also *commercial property*

resource clause: Legal language in a loan contract that stipulates what a lender can do to collect on a borrower who's in default on a loan.

RESPA (Real Estate Settlement and Procedures Act): Federal law that requires lenders to disclose settlement costs (GFE and HUD-1) as well as the procedures for consumer disclosure. See also *GFE* and *HUD-1*

seller financing: A process by which the seller of a property agrees to accept regular payments over time rather than full payment at time of sale. See also *land contract* and *lease option agreement*

short sale: A lender's agreement to accept less than the balance due on a loan as full payment. A lender may agree to a short sale if the borrower can't possibly work out a solution to make monthly payments or pay the balance in full.

short-term capital gain: The realized profit on an investment property held fewer than 12 months. See also *long-term capital gain*

silent second mortgage: A second loan taken out against a property to cover the down payment or other upfront costs on the first loan without disclosing it to the lender of the first loan. This practice is a form of mortgage fraud.

subprime loan: A loan that doesn't adhere to Fannie Mae or Freddie Mac requirements and, as a result, typically costs more in interest and upfront costs.

tax-deferred exchange: A provision of the tax code that allows investors to exchange like-kind properties instead of selling those properties and exposing the profits to capital gains taxes. Often referred to as a 1031 in reference to this section of the tax code.

teaser rate: An attractive introductory interest rate that disreputable mortgage brokers, loan offers, and lenders dangle in front of prospective borrowers to suck them into taking out a loan with an adjustable rate that's very likely to rise in the near future.

TI (Tenant Improvements): Expense calculation used for commercial investment properties when figuring the NOI — reflects concessions to tenant for upgrades and improvements upon move-in.

TIL or TILA (Truth-In-Lending Act): Federal law that requires lenders to follow certain guidelines for disclosing loan terms, including the APR. Not used on commercial properties.

title insurance: Insurance that covers the lender and/or new owner of real estate against any title defects, such as an overlooked claim against the property.

title: A legal document showing the rightful owner of the property.

VA (Department of Veteran Affairs): Insures loans made by lenders to eligible veterans.

wraparound mortgage: A secondary mortgage loan that encompasses the first, primary mortgage and is typically used to assume a mortgage while side-stepping the due on sale clause. The borrower makes payments to the secondary mortgage holder who then makes the required payments to the first, primary mortgage holder. Although wraparound mortgages are illegal in several states, you may still encounter them in commercial transactions. See also *due on sale clause*

YSP (Yield Spread Premium): An amount paid by a lender to a broker as compensation for origination and delivery services. See also *origination*

Index

• *M* •